TALKING WITH COMPUTERS

In this lively series of essays, Tom Dean explores interesting fundamental topics in computer science with the aim of showing how computers and computer programs work and how the various subfields of computer science are connected. Along the way, he conveys his fascination with computers and enthusiasm for working in a field that has changed almost every aspect of our daily lives.

The essays touch on a wide range of topics, from digital logic and machine language to artificial intelligence and searching the World Wide Web, considering such questions as

- How can a computer learn to recognize junk email?
- What happens when you click on a link in a browser?
- How can you program a robot to do two things at once?
- Are there limits on what computers can do?

The author invites readers to experiment with short programs written in several languages. Through these interactions he grounds the models and metaphors of computer science and makes the underlying computational ideas more concrete. The accompanying Web site www.cs.brown.edu/~tld/talk provides easy access to code fragments from the book, tips on finding and installing software, and links to online resources, excercises, and sample lectures.

Thomas Dean is Professor of Computer Science at Brown University. Dean is a Fellow of AAAI and a former member of the IJCAI Inc. Board of Trustees. He has served on the Executive Council of AAAI and the CRA Board of Directors. In addition, Dean has acted as program chair to a number of international conferences in Artificial Intelligence, was recipient of an NSF Presidential Young Investigator Award, and has co-authored two popular books. His research interests include automated planning, machine learning, and robotics.

TALKING WITH COMPUTERS

Explorations in the Science and Technology of Computing

THOMAS DEAN

Brown University, Providence, Rhode Island

CAMBRIDGE
UNIVERSITY PRESS

PUBLISHED BY THE PRESS SYNDICATE OF THE UNIVERSITY OF CAMBRIDGE
The Pitt Building, Trumpington Street, Cambridge, United Kingdom

CAMBRIDGE UNIVERSITY PRESS
The Edinburgh Building, Cambridge CB2 2RU, UK
40 West 20th Street, New York, NY 10011-4211, USA
477 Williamstown Road, Port Melbourne, VIC 3207, Australia
Ruiz de Alarcón 13, 28014 Madrid, Spain
Dock House, The Waterfront, Cape Town 8001, South Africa

http://www.cambridge.org

First published 2004

Printed in the United States of America

Typefaces Stone Serif 9.5/13.5 pt., Optima, and Lucida Typewriter   *System* LaTeX 2$_\varepsilon$ [TB]

A catalog record for this book is available from the British Library.

Library of Congress Cataloging in Publication Data

Dean, Thomas L., 1950–
Talking with computers : explorations in the science and technology of computing / Thomas Dean.
   p.   cm.
Includes bibliographical references and index.
ISBN 0-521-83425-2 – ISBN 0-521-54204-9 (pb.)
1. Computer Science.   2. Computer programs.   I. Title
QA76.D3333328   2004
946–dc22   2003065531

ISBN 0 521 83425 2 hardback
ISBN 0 521 54204 9 paperback

Contents

Preface   *page* ix

Acknowledgments   xiii

1   TALKING WITH COMPUTERS   1

  1.1 Computers everywhere   2
  1.2 Everyday magic   4
  1.3 Hacking in mathematics   12
  1.4 Programming in logic   13
  1.5 Scheming in Lisp   17

2   THE SHELL GAME   22

  2.1 Shell programming   24
  2.2 Shell variables   29
  2.3 Information passing   32
  2.4 Asynchronous processes   37

3   KEEPING TRACK OF YOUR STUFF   41

  3.1 Finding stuff   42
  3.2 Organizing your stuff   47
  3.3 Database management   51

4   DON'T SWEAT THE SYNTAX   57

  4.1 Specifications and implementations   58
  4.2 Syntactic variations across languages   63
  4.3 Stylistic variations across implementations   67
  4.4 Developing a facility for language   68

5   COMPUTATIONAL MUDDLES   70

   5.1   Computational models   71
   5.2   The substitution model   77
   5.3   Syntax and style revisited   81

6   GETTING ORIENTED   85

   6.1   Structuring large programs   86
   6.2   Procedures that remember   87
   6.3   Object-oriented programming   92
   6.4   Programming with constraints   95

7   THANKS FOR SHARING   103

   7.1   Code for the taking   105
   7.2   Class conscious   109
   7.3   It's just syntax   114

8   YOU'VE GOT (JUNK) EMAIL   121

   8.1   Artificial intelligence   123
   8.2   Machine learning   128
   8.3   Learning with probabilities   133
   8.4   Learning more about learning   138

9   MODERN ARCHITECTURE   140

   9.1   Logic gates   141
   9.2   The digital abstraction   144
   9.3   Addition and multiplication   146
   9.4   Computer memory   149
   9.5   Machine language   152

10   DO ROBOTS SLEEP?   162

   10.1 Stacks and subroutines   163
   10.2 Managing tasks   168
   10.3 Multithreaded robots   172
   10.4 Allocating resources   178
   10.5 Metaphorically speaking   184

11   UNDER THE HOOD   185

   11.1 Client-server model   186
   11.2 Acronym city   189
   11.3 Alphabet soup   191
   11.4 Smart milk cartons   193

12 ANALYZE THIS   196

   12.1 Analyzing algorithms   197
   12.2 Computational limitations   205
   12.3 Theory that matters   210

13 FOREST FOR THE TREES   213

   13.1 Graph theory   214
   13.2 Graph algorithms   217
   13.3 File systems as graphs   228
   13.4 The web graph   230
   13.5 Pianos and robots   232

14 SEARCHING THE WILD WEB   237

   14.1 Spiders in the web   237
   14.2 Measuring similarity   240
   14.3 Measuring authority   248
   14.4 Searching for exotic fruit   254

15 DARWIN'S DANGEROUS ALGORITHM   257

   15.1 Competing hypotheses   258
   15.2 Genetic algorithms   259
   15.3 Survival of the fittest   263

16 AIN'T NOBODY HERE BUT US MACHINES   271

   16.1 Machine intelligence   272
   16.2 Other minds   277
   16.3 Freedom to choose   281
   16.4 Carrying on   285

Bibliography   289

Index   295

Preface

Computers are changing almost every aspect of our lives. They're changing how we relate to one another and even changing how we think of ourselves. The very idea that my brain is a biological computer that could be, in some fundamental mathematical sense, no more powerful than the laptop on which I'm typing these words is mind-boggling. The fact that I can program a computer to control a robot, play chess, or find a cure for disease is tremendously empowering.

This book is organized as a series of essays that explore interesting and fundamental topics in computer science with the aim of showing how computers and computer programs work and how the various aspects of computer science are connected. Along the way I hope to convey to you some of my fascination with computers and my enthusiasm for working in a field whose explosive growth is fueled in no small measure by the ability of computers to support collaboration and information sharing.

While not meant to be exhaustive, this book examines a wide range of topics, from digital logic and machine language to artificial intelligence and searching the World Wide Web. These topics are explored by interacting with programs and experimenting with short fragments of code while considering such questions as:

- How can a computer learn to recognize junk email?
- What happens when you click on a link in a browser?
- How can we program a robot to do two things at once?
- What can evolutionary biology teach us about computation?
- How can we find what we're looking for on the World Wide Web?

You can read this book without ever touching a computer, but I think you'll have a lot more fun and learn more if you follow along by running the code fragments in the text. Think of each fragment as a thread in a complex pattern; I try to unravel the thread and explain how it relates to the larger pattern. Then, by making small changes to a code fragment, you can explore some of the nearby threads and test your understanding of the concepts.

Reading a book is different from attending lectures, but a book, like a lecture, adopts a style of teaching and assumes a style of learning. My style in this book is to start with examples and introduce general principles as they seem appropriate. For the most part, I'm hoping that the general principles will come peeking through the examples without my being too heavy-handed. The numerous code fragments invite you to experiment on your own.

I've included snippets of code from a variety of languages: C, Java, Perl and Scheme. I've tried hard to help you see past the differences in syntax to the basic underlying computations. Despite what you may have heard about introductory courses, computer science has little to do with arcane syntax; instead, it's all about thinking about problems computationally. Syntax is just a means to the end of communicating with computers, and here we focus first on what we want to say and only second on how to say it.

But it's no fun if you can't communicate with the computer, and so you'll meet lots of code and lots of syntax in this book. I don't, however, include a comprehensive introduction to programming. You'll need additional sources of information if your experiments deviate significantly from the programs presented here. Fortunately, much of what you need as supplementary material is available online.

Many of my examples involve communicating directly with the operating system by using interactive programs called shells. Shell programs are available for most modern operating systems including Unix, Linux, Solaris, and the Apple and Microsoft operating systems. Shells provide commands for accessing a great deal of online documentation. For example, `man` formats and displays the online manual pages for all the basic commands; `info` provides similar services with a somewhat nicer interface.

Of course, you've got to know where to look and how to call up all this wonderful information. The Web site for this book (www.cs.brown.edu/~tld/talk/) is a good place to start. It lists resources for setting up shells for different operating systems as well as pointers on installing the other programs mentioned in the book. The Web site also lists various online forums and news services that you can subscribe to and post your own questions and suggestions.

Despite all the legends about isolated hackers, programming is a primarily social activity. Programmers use, build on, and improve programs written by others.

Programmers learn by talking with other programmers and reading one another's code. Learning to program can be accelerated by learning with others. Even if you don't initially have close friends who share your programming interests, the Web makes it easy to meet other programmers at all skill levels. If you're shy you can start by reading newsgroups, but don't miss out on all the fun of sharing programs and interacting with other programmers face to face and online.

Acknowledgments

I've talked for years with students considering majoring in computer science who are curious what it's about. I really enjoy these conversations, and invariably as the student gets ready to leave I suggest some book that I think might extend our conversation. I've always wanted to name a book that explores a wide range of topics while remaining grounded in real and useful programs. I want students to experience firsthand the power of computing and gain some appreciation of its many applications. This book was inspired by those conversations and is dedicated to those students.

I couldn't have written this book without the encouragement and patient feedback of many friends and colleagues. I especially want to thank John Bazik, Roger Blumberg, Tom Doeppner, John Hughes, Philip Klein, Shriram Krishnamurthi, Martha Pollack, Bart Selman, Eli Upfal, and Joel Young. Lauren Cowles at Cambridge University Press helped refocus my initial draft and then provided concrete suggestions on how to improve every chapter. And there's not a paragraph that didn't benefit from Trina Avery's careful and insightful editing; Trina made the often tedious process of copyediting mostly interesting and frequently fun.

But most of all, I want to thank my students for their enthusiasm, their creativity, and their friendship. I wish I could list them all, but I especially want to thank Kalin Agrawal, Candace Batts, Nick Beaudrot, Sarah Bell, James Brock, Christine Davis, Michelle Engel, Erika Faires, Sam Hazlehurst, Kate Ho, Aron Holzman, Eliot Horowitz, Albert Huang, Danielle Karr, Roger Lederman, Katrina Ligett, Luke Ma, Gideon Mann, Paul Melnikow, Curran Nachbar, Bryant Ng, Brian O'Neil, Leah Pearlman, Ana-Maria Popescu, Brock Pytlik, Seema Ramchandani, Susannah Raub, Jennifer Rosenbaum, Brandon Roy, Maryam Saleh, Gloria Satgunam, Caitlyn Schmidt, Andrew Schulak, Tracy Schultz, Ravi Sitwala, Damien Suttle, Anisa Virji, Stacy Wong, and Thomas Wooldridge.

CHAPTER ONE

Talking with Computers

Hardly a day goes by that I don't write at least one short computer program: a few lines of code to explore an idea or help organize my thoughts. I think of it as simply talking with my computer, and more and more often there is a computer available to talk with, often several of them joining in the conversation simultaneously. Each time you click on a link in a browser, you cause a sequence of computations involving dozens if not hundreds of computers scattered all over the world.

Making a computation happen is not, however, the same thing as programming. There are lots of powerful programs written by talented programmers that you can call up with a click of a mouse or few keystrokes. These programs animate computers, breathing life and spirit into lumps of metal and plastic. Even if you know what's going on inside computers and computer programs, it's easy to imagine that programs are spells and the programmers who create them are sorcerers. When you click on the icon for a program, you invoke these spells and the spells conjure up spirits in the machine. But this book isn't about invoking the spells of others; it's about creating your own spells and conjuring spirits of your own design.

This is not to say I won't encourage you to use code written by other programmers. Quite the contrary: an important part of the power of computing is that good spells can be reused as often as needed. Programming is about weaving together the spells of others, conjuring your own spirits, and animating the computer to dance to your bidding. This book is about practical conjuring, about revealing what's behind some of the magic associated with computing while at the same time learning to create your own magic. And the best way to begin a book about computing and computer programming is to sit down in front of a computer and start programming.

1.1 COMPUTERS EVERYWHERE

The laptop computer on our breakfast table is connected to a wide-area network (usually called the World Wide Web or the Internet) through a local-area wireless network (our house) and a broadband connection supported by a local cable television company. I leave the laptop on the table so I can read the headlines from the online news services or check the weather while I eat breakfast. I also use it to write and run small programs.

I use a program on my laptop (it's called ssh for "secure shell") to tunnel through the firewall protecting the computers in the computer science department at Brown and open a shell (a special program that lets me interact more or less directly with the operating system – a variant of Unix in this case) on the machine sitting in my office (its name, by the way, is "klee" for the artist Paul Klee – see Figure 1.1 for the inspiration for this naming – and its symbolic address on the Internet is "klee.cs.brown.edu").

When I say "open a shell," I mean that I make a window appear on my laptop screen into which I can type commands to be interpreted by the shell program. When I say that a program "interprets" a command, I mean that the program reads the command I've typed and converts it into instructions that the computer can carry out, thereby executing the command. The results of executing the command, usually one or more lines of text, are then displayed in the same window as the command was typed. The shell lets me write and run programs to do all sorts of routine tasks from checking football statistics to keeping track of all of my email messages, digital photos and music files.

The program ssh allows me to work remotely on computers that "trust me" in such a way that the information sent back and forth between my laptop and klee can't be deciphered by someone with access to the wires on which the information is transmitted and doesn't allow a malicious hacker to break into either my laptop or klee. I could open a shell on any of several hundred machines residing within the firewall, but I generally choose to do it on my own machine rather than slow down or "steal cycles" from a machine being used by someone else.

The time will soon come however when it won't make much sense to talk about "my machine" – computation will become as pervasive as indoor plumbing. The Internet has blurred the distinction among individual computers. I'm almost always connected to the Internet, but most of the time I don't think about what computer I'm talking with. When I'm in the department at Brown but not in my office, I walk around with my laptop connected to the department wireless network, which connects to a wide-area network and then to the Internet. Right this minute I'm working at my laptop, typing into a shell that's running on the

Figure 1.1: Paul Klee's "Twittering Machine" (1922) ©2003 Artist Rights Society (ARS) New York, VG Bild-Kunst, Bonn Digital Image ©The Museum A Modern Art/Licensed by SCALA/Art Resource, NY

computer in my home office a few feet away, but in another window running on my laptop I'm connected to klee. For all I know, the data that's flowing between these computers may be circling the globe, zipping through cables under the ocean and bouncing off satellites along the way. Indeed, I could pretty easily force the data to go through Zurich, Seattle or Tokyo.

Given the current state of the art, though, I do have to think a bit about where I am, or rather where the program is that's currently interpreting my keystrokes. The reason I have to know which computer I'm working on is that different machines have different software, offer different services and have access to different sources of data. I'm pretty confident that I won't lose data that's stored on the machines in the department because I trust the folks who maintain those machines and perform the backups on the file system there. But I have to do the backups on my laptop and the machine in my home office myself, and I know I'm not very careful about doing them.

Eventually, with the exception of very specialized programs and services, I won't have to worry about what computers are running the programs I need. This is already true to a certain extent if you restrict your computing to what you can do within a web browser, and yes, you can do a lot of useful computing within a web browser. Some people don't even distinguish between their web browser and their computer; they do everything – email, news, shopping, entertainment and education – from within their web browser.

For the last twenty years, I've been using programs to work on computers thousands of miles away. In the early '90s, it seemed miraculous to be sitting in a Paris hotel room running programs on the computer in my office in Providence or telling a computer at Stanford to transfer files to the portable computer on my bed in the hotel room. Today, most "netizens" take this amazing connectivity for granted and, though they may not know the magic incantations that animate these processes, they routinely run programs on remote computers and fetch files with the click of a mouse.

1.2 EVERYDAY MAGIC

I want to give you some examples of everyday programming, not fancy programming, just examples of talking with computers and getting them to do interesting things. I'll use the phrase "invoking a program" to mean making a program run, usually by typing its name and then zero or more expressions or "arguments" that provide additional direction or information. Invoking programs with specific arguments is one of the simplest ways to talk with a computer.

In summer 2002, I kept a journal to record ideas for this book. I put the journal entries in a collection of files and directories on klee. Here I'm invoking a program called wc (for "word count") by typing into a shell running on klee in order to see how much I wrote in my journal during August:

```
/u/tld/email/book % wc -l ./journal/02/08/*/*.txt
    465 ./journal/02/08/01/day.txt
    323 ./journal/02/08/02/day.txt
    207 ./journal/02/08/04/day.txt
```

```
 445 ./journal/02/08/08/day.txt
 215 ./journal/02/08/12/day.txt
 299 ./journal/02/08/16/day.txt
 700 ./journal/02/08/24/day.txt
 335 ./journal/02/08/30/day.txt
 857 ./journal/02/08/31/day.txt
3846 total
```

The /u/tld/email/book % part was printed by the shell. It's called the "prompt" and when I'm in the shell window (the portion of my computer screen dedicated to the shell) the cursor is positioned at the end of the prompt waiting for me to type something. I've modified the shell – the shell is itself programmable – so that the prompt always displays the default directory in which the shell looks for files.

When I'm finished typing I signal the shell, usually by hitting the "return" (or "enter") key on my keyboard, to interpret what I just typed. The directory /u/tld/email/ is where I generally store files related to my daily activities. /u/tld/email/book/ is the temporary directory I created for files related to working on this book.

I typed wc -l ./journal/02/08/*/*.txt and then hit the return key as part of my conversation with the shell and so indirectly with the operating system running on klee. More often than not when you invoke one program, that program invokes another program, and that program another, and so on, with some programs possibly invoking several other programs at once. A computer operating system is just another program, really a collection of many programs written (and rewritten) by many different people. You can think of the operating system as the accumulated wisdom of a host of very clever programmers who packed it with everything they felt was fundamentally useful for building other programs.

Other programs, applications such as web browsers and word processors, are run "on top of" or "under the control of" the operating system. The operating system sees all and controls all; it's only through the operating system that your programs can get information from the outside world (through a local network or the World Wide Web) or send files to printers or grab data stored on disks or CDs. If this seems mysterious, don't worry; it really is complicated. The good news is that for the most part you don't have to understand the details, since the operating system hides a lot of the computer's complexities from the programmer. This ability to hide complexity is essential in developing large complicated programs and makes learning to program much easier.

The specific command I typed told the shell to run the program wc to count lines (the -l argument) in the files specified by the pattern ./journal/

02/08/*/*.txt, where * is a "wildcard" that matches any string of characters. With no perceptible pause, the shell printed out the next ten lines, which you can think of as the answer to my question or the result of the computation. The specified pattern matched nine files. Each of the first nine lines contains the name of a file that matched the pattern preceded by the number of lines of text in that file. For the first file listed, the first * matched 01 and the second * matched day. The last line is the total number of lines of text in all of the files.

Let me say a few words about file systems and the strange strings of characters containing slashes (/). A slash with no preceding text indicates the "root" directory; as far we're concerned, everything is stored under the root of the file system. The u in /u/ is a symbolic link to the /home/ directory on the Brown file system where the directories and files of computer users like me are stored. For the most part, symbolic links are invisible to users but allow system managers to handle large file systems more efficiently and transparently. The /u/tld/ designates my home directory, where all my files are stored; my login name is tld for the initials of my name, Thomas Linus Dean.

Most computer file systems are organized hierarchically. So, for instance, my email directory /u/tld/email/ is one of many files and directories stored in my home directory, and the directory /u/tld/email/book/ is one of many files and directories stored in my email directory.

Files can be named *absolutely* with respect to the root directory or *relatively* with respect to some other starting directory. When you're in the directory /u/tld/email/book/, ./journal/02/08/30/day.txt is a shorthand reference (or *relative path name*) for /u/tld/email/book/journal/02/08/30/day.txt, which is the full name (or *absolute path name*) for the file. I keep all files for journal entries written in 2002 in ./journal/02/, all files for August 2002 in ./journal/02/08/, and all files for 30 August 2002 in ./journal/02/08/30/. If I had typed wc -l ./journal/02/*/01/*.txt, the shell would have reported on all journal entries written on the first day of some month in 2002.

Absolute and relative path names can be confusing until you've played with them a bit, and even then you can easily get lost in a file system consisting of thousands of directories, in the same way that you can get lost navigating in a collection of web pages. For the most part, however, the nested, hierarchical directory structure makes it relatively easy to keep track of where you are and is a useful way to organize all sorts of data (including web pages). Consider these files from my journal directory:

```
/u/tld/email/book/journal/02/year.txt
/u/tld/email/book/journal/02/year.htm
/u/tld/email/book/journal/02/08/month.txt
```

```
/u/tld/email/book/journal/02/08/month.htm
/u/tld/email/book/journal/02/08/30/day.txt
/u/tld/email/book/journal/02/08/30/day.htm
/u/tld/email/book/journal/02/08/31/day.txt
/u/tld/email/book/journal/02/08/31/day.htm
/u/tld/email/book/journal/02/09/month.txt
/u/tld/email/book/journal/02/09/month.htm
/u/tld/email/book/journal/02/09/01/day.txt
/u/tld/email/book/journal/02/09/01/day.htm
/u/tld/email/book/journal/02/09/02/day.txt
/u/tld/email/book/journal/02/09/02/day.htm
```

When listed this way, it's hard to discern the organizational structure inherent in calendars, though it's there in the absolute path names if you look hard enough. The underlying structure is similar to a tree, with files corresponding to leaves and directories corresponding to branches. Figure 1.2 shows these files as a tree (or, rather, the branch of the tree called /u/tld/email/book/journal/02/). You can think of Figure 1.2 as grafted onto the tree rooted at / at the branch /u/tld/email/journal/. The same basic tree-like structure that underlies hierarchical file systems in most modern operating systems appears again and again in computer science.

The incantation wc -l ./journal/02/08/*/*.txt really is a program of sorts, albeit a short and rather cryptic one. That this short program called another program wc is not at all unusual: most programming languages provide access to all sorts of specialized programs. Even + in a language that allows 1 + 2 is a program (and not a simple one if you understand how computers handle arithmetic).

Shells and other means of interacting with operating systems offer a wide range of powerful programs that can be orchestrated to perform tasks. For example, the next program (called a *shell script*) renames all files with the extension html to have the extension htm. The HTML ("hypertext markup language") files that comprise web sites are conventionally identified using either the three-letter extension htm or the four-letter extension html. Both conventions are common in practice. Unfortunately, some programs require one or the other exclusively and if your files are in the wrong format, you have to convert them. I used the program ls (for "list directory contents") to list all of the files in the current directory prior to executing the program to rename the files. After executing the program, I used ls again to show that the shell script worked as advertised. In the remainder of this chapter, I've simplified the prompt to just %; each appearance of % signals the beginning of another typed command.

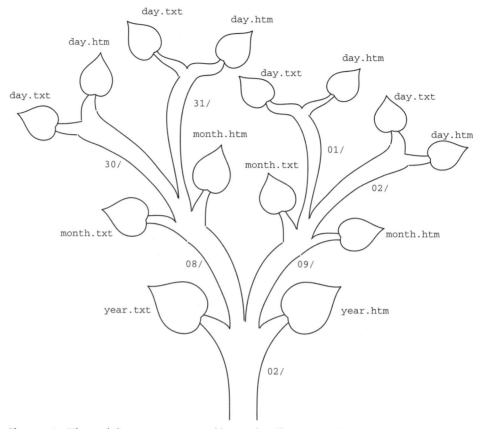

Figure 1.2: Files and directories organized hierarchically in a tree-like structure

```
% ls
home.html       syllabus.html
% ls | sed 's/html//' | awk '{print "mv " $1 "html " $1 "htm"}' | sh
% ls
home.htm        syllabus.htm
```

The program starts by listing the set of files with the extension html.[1] Unix programmers call the vertical bars (|) "pipes": they convert the output of one program, ls in this case, into the input to another program. The sed 's/html//'

---

[1] In this example, all the files in the current directory have the extension html. If they didn't, we could modify the shell script by telling ls to list only files with the extension html. For example, substituting ls *.html for ls would do the trick here. We'll learn more about shells and shell scripts in Chapter 2.

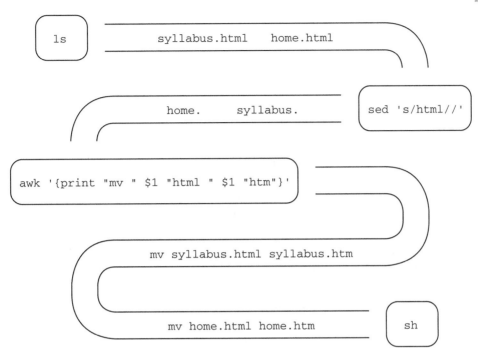

Figure 1.3: Intermediate results flowing through pipes connecting one command to the next in a shell script

part of the program takes each file name in turn and rips off the html part; the output of sed 's/html//' is two truncated file names home. and syllabus.. The next | causes these file names to be piped into the program fragment awk '{print "mv " $1 "html " $1 "htm"}' that essentially writes two little programs that are themselves shell scripts and look like mv home.html home.htm and mv syllabus.html syllabus.htm (mv is the "move" or "rename" command and requires you to specify both the original and the new names of the file you're renaming). The output of awk '{print "mv " $1 "html " $1 "htm"}' is fed into the program sh (yet another shell – remember we're already typing to one shell) via the last |. Figure 1.3 illustrates how the intermediate results from the different steps in this computation are piped from one step to the next.

If you think about it, this little program is pretty interesting despite its simple task. The program actually wrote a couple of littler programs, started up a shell and submitted those programs to the new shell to run, producing the desired outcome. Programs that write and run other programs and even replicate or improve upon themselves are relatively common, for example, computer viruses.

With a few simple modifications, this program could change the names of thousands of files stored in any number of directories and on any number of computers. With just a little more work, you could write a program that would go *inside* each of these files and change any reference in the text to a file with extension html to have the extension htm. If you were maintaining a web site with thousands of web pages spread across hundreds of directories, you might end up writing and running similar programs frequently.

By the way, there's always more than one way to solve any given programming problem, and I certainly don't claim that this shell script is the most elegant or efficient way of handling renaming. We could, for example, eliminate awk from our script and manage everything using sed, as in ls | sed 's/\(.*\)html/mv \1html \1htm/' | sh. However, the most compact program is not always the best: I find the original script clearer and more appealing, though I admit this is an aesthetic judgment.

Let's try something a little more complicated. Many web masters use a language called Perl both to maintain web pages and to do computations for visitors to their web pages. Suppose a bunch of your text files refer to dates in the format mm/dd/yy and you want to change them so as to name months explicitly, perhaps to avoid confusion with the alternative format dd/mm/yy. You might also want to try to clear up the ambiguity of the century implied when only two digits are used for the year. I just created a short text file of the sort I'd like to modify and I'll get the shell to print it out using cat, a Unix command for creating, displaying and stringing together (or *concatenating*) files:

```
% cat dates.txt
The date 1/1/00 should be changed,
as should 12/31/1999 and 1/1/2002,
but not the file /usr/local/bin/.
```

I've written a little Perl program in a file called program.pl to perform the conversion, and again I get the shell to print it out:

```
% cat program.pl
@month = (Jan, Feb, Mar, Apr, May, Jun, Jul, Aug, Sep, Oct, Nov, Dec);
while ($_ = <ARGV>) {
  s"\b(\d\d?)/(\d\d?)/(?:19)?(\d\d)\b"$month[$1-1] $2, 19$3";
  s"\b(\d\d?)/(\d\d?)/(?:20)(\d\d)\b"$month[$1-1] $2, 20$3";
  print "$_";
}
```

Finally, I invoke my program indirectly by calling a program called `perl` with the name of the file in which I've stored my program as an argument. The `perl` program knows how to interpret programs written in the Perl language and `program.pl` has become another command that I can execute from the shell. Now I tell `perl` and the shell – in some cases several programs are reading and processing what I type – to take as input the contents of the file `dates.txt` and to store the output of the program, the result of executing the print statement in `program.pl` multiple times, in a file called `dates.out`:

```
% perl program.pl dates.txt > dates.out
```

I'll tell the shell to print `dates.out` so we can see what the program did:

```
% cat dates.out
The date Jan 1, 1900 should be changed,
as should Dec 31, 1999 and Jan 1, 2002,
but not the file /usr/local/bin/.
```

Not too exciting, and I'll bet that `program.pl` will get the year wrong as often as it gets it right, but you get the general idea. It's not important that you understand the exact syntax of the Perl program except to note that it uses a loop (the part of the program that begins with `while`) to read each line of the file, makes substitutions where appropriate and then prints out the line with the substitutions. The syntax for specifying substitutions is particularly terse in large part because Perl programmers use it so often. Programming languages, like natural languages, typically have short ways of saying things you want to say often.

My Perl program was long enough that I couldn't type it out on a single line, or at least not conveniently, so I put it in a file and submitted the file to the Perl interpreter, `perl`. The Perl interpreter is a program that converts programs written in Perl into commands that are carried out by other programs (such as those comprising the operating system) and ultimately into instructions that run directly on the hardware of a particular machine. You may have heard that computer programs have to be "compiled" into some other form before they can be "executed" but, while this is true, it's largely beside the point. The exact manner in which a piece of syntax such as `while ($_ = <ARGV>) { ... }` is converted into a form that can be handled by the primitive hardware of a particular machine is very complicated, and you don't need to know it in order to be an effective programmer.

Some people distinguish between programs called compilers and programs called interpreters. However, they both do basically the same thing: convert programs in one format into a different format that is more readily available for performing computations. Usually a programmer works in a *programming environment* made up of tools for editing, debugging, testing, using, and packaging programs. I prefer programming environments that let me interact easily with my programs while I'm developing them. Most modern programming environments allow some sort of interaction, and often there is little distinction between writing, running and using programs. Writing programs and using the tools that are part of a programming environment are just how you get your work done, whether you're working in biotechnology, analyzing data from an archaeological dig, or building a web site for your startup.

Different programming languages and programming environments support different styles of programming, different modes of interaction and different ways of thinking about computation. Here are some other languages and environments I use frequently.

1.3 HACKING IN MATHEMATICS

I use the Mathematica programming environment for all sorts of programming that involves mathematics. Most of the time I use the fancy graphical front end that lets me create two- and three-dimensional graphics. It's great for visualizing mathematical functions and analyzing data. But I also occasionally invoke Mathematica in a shell and use it as a fancy calculator. Mathematica can solve algebraic equations much better than I can with paper and pencil, and it can do symbolic differentiation and integration in a snap. It doesn't replace a good mathematics education so much as it augments it.

When I invoke the Mathematica program, called `mathematica` on my computer, it takes over from the shell and interprets what I type. Mathematica displays the prompt, `In[n]:=`, after interpreting the first $n-1$ commands, thereby inviting me to type my nth command, and it then reads each subsequent line I type until it encounters a "shift return" (hold down the shift key and simultaneously hit the return key). At this point Mathematica attempts to make sense of my command, prints out the prefix `Out[n]=`, and displays the result of interpreting the nth command:

```
% mathematica
In[1]:= Solve[ x^2 - 4 == 0, x ]
Out[1]= {{x -> -2}, {x -> 2}}
In[2]:= Solve[ x^2 + 2 x - 7 == 0, x]
Out[2]= {{x -> -1 - 2 Sqrt[2]}, {x -> -1 + 2 Sqrt[2]}}
```

```
In[3]:= D[ x^3, x ]
Out[3]= 3 x^2
In[4]:= Integrate[ Cos[x], x]
Out[4]= Sin[x]
```

This exchange doesn't begin to show off what Mathematica can do, and the standard graphical user interface that most people use to interact with Mathematica is amazingly powerful; other products such as Maple and Matlab provide similar functionality. The neat thing about all these programs is that some very smart programmers have developed powerful tools that let us exploit their knowledge of mathematics.

You may have heard some pontificating math instructor berate students with "I've forgotten more mathematics than you'll *ever* learn," but at times I feel I've forgotten more mathematics than I ever learned. I barely remember that the indefinite integral $\int \cos \theta \, d\theta$ is equal to $\sin \theta$ and I have to think for a minute to calculate the roots of equations like $x^2 + 2x - 7 = 0$, but programs like Mathematica allow me to handle these problems and all sorts of mathematical gymnastics without retaining tomes of esoteric mathematical knowledge. Using Mathematica doesn't make me as good as a practicing mathematician, but I'm a lot better off than I would be with just a library of math textbooks.

Programs like Mathematica act as intelligence amplifiers, combining the functionality of supercalculators with that of electronic encyclopedias that place huge amounts of knowledge at your fingertips.[2] Just as a diesel engine amplifies physical strength and a telescope amplifies visual acuity, so carefully crafted programs can amplify intellectual power. We'll see several examples in the following chapters of how programs like Mathematica can help in writing programs that rely on mathematical concepts.

1.4 PROGRAMMING IN LOGIC

Prolog is a programming language in which programs are specified using statements in logic. Prolog is great for writing programs that depend on complex rules

---

[2] In 1945, Vannevar Bush, Director of the United States Office of Scientific Research and Development, wrote an *Atlantic Monthly* article called "As We May Think" that, anticipating the Internet, outlined how computers could be used to supplement our memories, provide ready access to all human knowledge, and amplify our mental abilities. J. C. R. Licklider (1960) espoused a similar view with further embellishment in his very readable "Man-Computer Symbiosis." Both these articles are now available in several history-of-computing archives on the World Wide Web, as anticipated by Bush and Licklider.

and relationships. If I were writing a program that computed employees' medical benefits or depended on the tax laws, I'd definitely write it in Prolog. Even if you never use Prolog to write a practical program, learning about it teaches you strategies for solving problems such as those involving complex rules. Indeed, programmers working on large programs written in Java or C++ often write a mini version of Prolog as part of the large program just to handle the parts of the problem involving complex rules. It's also not uncommon for a program written in one language to provide input to and accept output from a program written in another language; in this way a programmer can use the most appropriate language for the problem at hand.

Here we'll create a Prolog *database* by first asserting three simple facts: Fred is one of Anne's parents, Anne is one of Lucy's parents and Lucy is one of Bill's parents. Next we specify two general rules indicating that your parents are your ancestors, as are their parents. Then we query the database to see if Prolog gets it right.

Terms that begin with lowercase letters, like `fred`, are constants and those that begin with uppercase letters, like X, are variables. If you don't know the difference between constants and variables, think back to when you learned algebra: constants were typically numbers and variables were often denoted by letters like *x* or *y*. Variables in Prolog don't behave exactly like the variables in algebraic formulas (nor, for that matter, like the variables in other programming languages), but the analogy to algebra will work for our present purposes. Instead of *x* and *y*, in Prolog we'll use X and Y.

In the next interaction, the part corresponding to the assertion of the three facts and two rules should be pretty clear – I typed the strings beginning with `assert` and ending with a period. The period tells Prolog that I'm finished typing and that it should go ahead and try to interpret whatever preceded the period. Statements of the form `assert(expression)` correspond to assertions that end up in the Prolog database, and all other statements are interpreted as queries or requests for Prolog to answer questions about the information contained in its database.

Prolog responds to each individual assertion with "yes." The rule `ancestor(X, Y) :- parent(X, Y)` can be read as "X is the ancestor of Y if X is the parent of Y". The `:-` corresponds to "if." Similarly, `ancestor(X, Y) :- parent(X, Z), parent(Z, Y)` can be read as "X is the ancestor of Y if X is the parent of Z and Z is the parent of Y". The comma separating `parent(X, Z)` and `parent(Z, Y)` means "and."

The line `ancestor(fred, X)` is a query requesting Prolog to find assignments to the variable X, for example, assigning X the constant anne, so that, if you substitute the assigned constants for the indicated variables, the resulting expression, say `ancestor(fred, anne)`, would be true. We use this query to ask Prolog to list all Fred's descendants.[3] In response to this line, Prolog prints out a variable assignment, say `X = anne`, followed by a ? asking if this assignment is the one I was looking for. In response to each ?, I typed "no" and thereby made Prolog look for another assignment.

```
% prolog
| ?- assert( parent(fred, anne) ).
yes
| ?- assert( parent(anne, lucy) ).
yes
| ?- assert( parent(lucy, bill) ).
yes
| ?- assert( (ancestor(X, Y) :- parent(X, Y)) ).
yes
| ?- assert( (ancestor(X, Y) :- parent(X, Z), parent(Z, Y)) ).
yes
| ?- ancestor(fred, X).
X = anne ? no
X = lucy ? no
no
```

By repeatedly typing "no" to each assignment, I forced Prolog to print out all the answers to my query that it could find as facts in the database or derive from the rules. The final "no" printed by Prolog indicates that it couldn't find any more assignments. Did it get them all? Almost, but our second rule wasn't as general as it could have been. We expect Fred to be one of Bill's ancestors, but our rule doesn't cover this case. A query containing no variables, for example, `ancestor(fred, bill)`, just asks Prolog to verify if the statement corresponding to the query is true. So if we ask Prolog about Fred and Bill, it simply returns "no":

```
| ?- ancestor(fred, bill).
no
```

---

[3] The relations "ancestor" and "descendant" are said to be *inverses* of one another. We could have written `descendant(anne, fred)` instead of `ancestor(fred, anne)` but it's not necessary to assert both facts: The query `ancestor(X, anne)` finds all of Anne's ancestors and the query `ancestor(anne, X)` finds all of Anne's descendants. If you really want to use both the ancestor and descendant relation explicitly, you can define the descendant relation in terms of the ancestor relation by adding the rule `descendant(X, Y) :- ancestor(Y, X)`. This is a good example of how Prolog makes it easy to think about logical relationships.

We could add a rule

```
ancestor(X, Y) :- parent(X, Z), parent(Z, W), parent(W, Y).
```

but that would only be a stopgap. What we need is a rule that captures the fact that X is the ancestor of Y if X is the parent of Z and Z is the ancestor of Y. This is a *recursive definition* because we define the notion of ancestor in terms of itself. In this case it seems quite natural: your ancestors are your parents plus their ancestors. When we add this rule we get the answer we're expecting:

```
| ?- assert( (ancestor(X, Y) :- parent(X, Z), ancestor(Z, Y)) ).
yes
| ?- ancestor(fred, bill).
yes
```

Prolog is handy for specifying relationships between people and things, especially when it makes sense to define those relationships implicitly through recursive rules as we did here. It would be a real pain to have to explicitly write down all of the facts of the form `ancestor(fred, lucy)`, `ancestor(anne, lucy)`, and so on; indeed, this would be impossible if there were an infinite number of such facts.

Another important computational idea hidden in Prolog is easy to motivate in terms of one of the most frequently used but under-appreciated utility programs in all of software engineering. Application programs in large software projects are typically built and maintained with a program called make that uses so-called *makefiles* to keep track of how the components of large programs depend on one another.

In a large project involving hundreds if not thousands of component files, *building* the application program involves issuing a long sequence of commands that create and update files so that commands involving a component, call it *c*, occur later in the sequence than commands involving the components that *c* depends on. Since this sort of building is done many times in developing and testing an application, it's important to manage it efficiently.

The make program traces backward through the dependencies to determine what commands, if any, must be issued to build an up-to-date version of the application program. It then works its way forward, executing only those commands needed to update all the component files. This technique of working backward through a set of dependencies is called *dependency-directed backtracking* (or simply *backward chaining*), and it is central to how Prolog operates. Prolog is perhaps the purest and most general use of backward chaining in a programming language.

To get a better idea of how Prolog might accomplish what make does, suppose your project consists of five components, one, two, three, four and five, and suppose these rules describe all the dependencies you would find in a makefile for this project:

```
make :- up_to_date(five).
up_to_date(five) :- up_to_date(four), up_to_date(three), update(five).
up_to_date(four) :- update(four).
up_to_date(three) :- up_to_date(two), up_to_date(one), update(three).
up_to_date(two) :- update(two).
up_to_date(one) :- update(one).
```

For example, the second rule indicates that component five depends on three and four, so if you're going to update five, make sure that three and four are updated first. Now suppose we add another rule: when Prolog is asked to determine if update(*component*) is true, instead of checking the database it issues a command to the shell (such a rule is easy to formulate in Prolog). Finally, suppose that the facts up_to_date(four) and up_to_date(two) are in the Prolog database. Now when we type the query make to the Prolog interpreter it executes the sequence of commands, update(one), update(three), update(five) – exactly as required to build the project.[4]

The make command and its many variants are probably invoked millions of times a day to build and rebuild all sorts of projects. I even use make to manage relatively small projects such as keeping track of the several hundred files that comprise the various drafts of this book and building different versions of the book for colleagues, editors, reviewers and typesetters. You don't need to understand Prolog in order to use make or understand how it works, but Prolog shows a particularly pure form of the basic computational principle that make relies on.

1.5 SCHEMING IN LISP

Here's another member of my pantheon of useful programming languages: Lisp and its dialects. After Fortran, Lisp is the oldest programming language still in

---

[4] In a complete implementation, you might arrange that whenever Prolog successfully executes an expression of the form update(*component*) it also asserts the fact up_to_date(*component*) to the Prolog database. In addition, whenever someone modifies *component*, thus possibly requiring the updating of other components, Prolog removes the fact up_to_date(*component*) from the Prolog database. Alternatively, you might use information about the last time a file was modified to keep track of whether components are up to date, as is done in many versions of make used for building large systems.

current use. I don't know if that seems to you a reason to learn it or to avoid it, but I assure you that the current dialects of Lisp are industrial-strength programming languages with all the modern amenities. A dialect of a programming language is simply a language that adheres to many of the basic ideas in the original language but varies in some details. While languages like Fortran ("formula translation") were designed with number crunching in mind, the original dialect of Lisp ("list processing") was designed for manipulating symbols – think chess pieces, not sines and cosines.

It so happens that large parts of the editor in which I'm writing this book (GNU Emacs) are written in Lisp, and I can easily define Lisp functions (a Lisp function is just a special-purpose program) and assign them to key sequences so that when I type those sequences the function is called. You can't see any evidence of it as you read this paragraph, but as I ended the previous sentence I typed Meta-q (the escape key followed by the lowercase Q), which called my special paragraph-formatting function to adjust how this paragraph appeared in my editor window. I've made lots of functions to do special tasks while I'm writing and debugging programs or responding to email – all of which I do in Emacs.

My favorite dialect of Lisp, Scheme, is used in Abelson and Sussman's *Structure and Interpretation of Computer Programs*, one of my favorite books on programming. I just opened a shell on klee and looked around for programs that support various Lisp dialects. I found a couple of versions of Common Lisp, a relatively recent dialect, and several versions of Scheme, including one that a student wrote in Java. Remember that the programs that make sense of programs written in Prolog, Mathematica, and Scheme as well as Java and C are just that, programs, and they have to be written in some language. Students in our introductory courses at Brown write Scheme interpreters in Java and Java interpreters in Scheme. Scheme is an excellent language in which to create and experiment with new languages and we'll use it often in subsequent chapters.

During a recent trip my wife and I took to California to visit Yosemite and Kings Canyon National Parks, I kept track of our daily expenses and used Scheme to play with the data as we flew back to the east coast. When I'd reduced the data to seven numbers, one for each day of the trip, here's the sort of thing I was able to do using Scheme. Here `length`, `+`, `/` and `max` are functions that, respectively, compute the number of items in a list, sum two or more numbers, divide one number by another, and compute the maximum of two or more numbers. With a little thought, you'll figure out what `define` and `apply` are good for. Here I compute the total expense for the trip, the average daily expense and the maximum daily expense:

```
% scheme
> (define days '(150.50 137.17 102.00 189.70 75.00 144.50))
(150.5 137.17 102.0 189.7 75.0 144.5)
> (length days)
6
> (apply + days)
798.87
> (/ (apply + days) (length days))
133.14
> (apply max days)
189.7
```

Statisticians are always looking at data every which way, trying to find interesting patterns. Statistics programs include a wide range of functions for examining data, but sometimes you just need to write a little program to make the patterns evident.

Now I'll play with the data to compute the largest one-day-to-the-next change in daily expenses. This interaction with Scheme will be a bit harder to figure out, but I'll give you some hints: reverse reverses a list so the last item is first, second-to-last item is second, and so on, cdr takes a list and returns a list consisting of all the items in the original list except the first, abs computes the absolute value of a number, and map ... well, map is kind of like apply, but different in a way that's similar to how determining the age of *each* person in an audience given the birthday of each audience member (a map-like thing to compute) is different from determining the average age of an audience given the age of each audience member (an apply-like thing to compute).

```
> (define firsts (reverse (cdr (reverse days))))
(150.5 137.17 102.0 189.7 75.0)
> (define seconds (cdr days))
(137.17 102.0 189.7 75.0 144.5)
> (map - firsts seconds)
(13.33 35.17 -87.7 114.7 -69.5)
> (map abs (map - firsts seconds))
(13.33 35.17 87.7 114.7 69.5)
> (apply max (map abs (map - firsts seconds)))
114.7
```

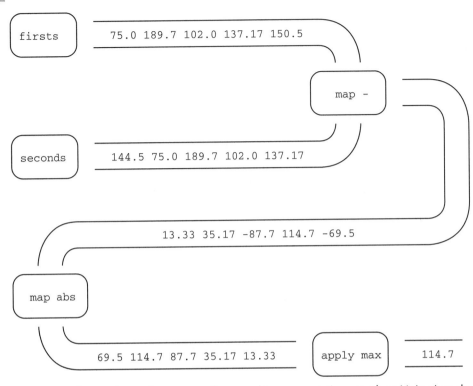

Figure 1.4: The `apply` and `map` operations combine computations much as Unix pipes do in a shell script

The `apply` and `map` operations in Scheme let us connect functions like `abs`, `max`, and `-` in much the same way as the Unix pipes we used in writing programs for the shell let us connect programs like `awk` and `sed`. Figure 1.4 illustrates how the intermediate results in our Scheme calculations flow from one function to the next. If you follow the numbers as they travel along the paths in Figure 1.4, you'll get a good idea of how the `apply` and `map` operations work.

So the difference between our expenses on the fourth day and the fifth was over $100. A statistician might wonder whether one or both of the numbers on these consecutive days was entered incorrectly. In fact, the numbers are right; one night we treated ourselves to Yosemite Lodge, and the next we spent in an unheated tent in Curry Village.

If I were really analyzing a lot of data, I'd use Mathematica, Matlab, or a statistics package made specifically for the purpose. I'd probably have to write some small programs to prepare the data for analysis, and languages like Scheme, Perl or the scripting languages built into statistics packages are all perfectly suitable for this purpose. The details of the languages change but the basic mechanisms for computation remain the same.

However, the different programming languages mentioned in this chapter let us think about computation from very different perspectives. In one case, the language encourages us to think like mathematicians, in another case, like logicians; there are even models in which the programmer thinks a bit like a pipe fitter. It's not surprising that most good programmers are familiar with several different languages and models for thinking about programming. In the next chapter, we'll look more closely at using shells and writing shell scripts to support a highly interactive and exploratory approach to programming.

CHAPTER TWO

The Shell Game

Programming languages come in all shapes and sizes and some of them hardly seem like programming languages at all. Of course, that depends on what you count as a programming language; as far as I'm concerned, a programming language is a language for specifying computations. But that's pretty broad and maybe we should narrow our definition to include only languages used for specifying computations to machines, that is, languages for talking with computers. Remember, though, that programmers often communicate with one another by sharing code and the programming language used to write that code can significantly influence what can or can't be easily communicated.

C, Java and Scheme are so-called general-purpose, high-level programming languages.[1] Plenty of other programming languages were designed to suit particular purposes, among them the languages built into mathematical programming packages like Maple, Matlab and Mathematica. There are also special-purpose languages called *scripting* languages built into most word-processing and desktop-publishing programs that make it easier to perform repetitious tasks like personalizing invitations or making formatting changes throughout a set of documents.

Lots of computer users find themselves constantly doing routine house-cleaning tasks like identifying and removing old files and searching for documents containing specific pieces of information. Modern operating systems generally provide nice graphical user interfaces to make such house-cleaning easier, but many repetitive tasks are easy to specify but tedious to carry out with these fancy interfaces. Sophisticated users and the programmers who manage large computer

---

[1] Some programmers would argue that C is not a high-level language because it gives the programmer ready access to the underlying hardware and to the most sensitive parts of the operating system (the parts that, if you muck with them, you're likely to bring the whole system down). For some programmers, this low-level access is an advantage and for others it's an invitation to disaster. In practice, it depends a lot on what you're trying to do.

systems use programs called *shells* that let them talk more directly with the operating system.

The core programs making up an operating system are located in what is commonly called the *kernel* of the operating system. The programs in the kernel are responsible for juggling multiple programs, allocating memory and dealing with everything from detecting keyboard and mouse input to reading from and writing to disks. A shell is a program surrounding the kernel that makes it easy for the user to do useful work while at the same time protecting the user (and all the other users in a multiple-user operating system) from doing anything stupid or malicious. Applications are built on top of the shell but you can access the shell directly.

Most operating systems support multiple shells and programmers often have strong opinions on which ones they think are best. Almost by definition, a shell requires a programming language, sometimes called a *command language*, in order to make the operating system perform useful work. These languages are general-purpose languages and are often used to write sizable programs. However, shell programs also allow an interactive or conversational programming style that makes it quite easy to write short programs for specialized tasks.

When most people think about programming a computer, they think about writing large programs consisting of many lines of code, but other styles of communication are possible. Writing a sizable program is like sending a letter to a friend: the message has to be largely self-contained and you have to be careful to make sure you're not misunderstood. You may not have a chance to clarify and if your friend ends up confused (or worse misled) it may be some time before you have a chance to set her straight.

When you interact with a shell, on the other hand, you talk directly with the operating system. Here again you don't want to be misunderstood, but shells are designed to allow opportunity for feedback. Often the commands you submit to the shell have options that make them query you before doing something that can't be easily undone (other options turn off all prompts and warnings and let you accept the risks of, say, deleting everything in your home directory if you so choose). The shell acts as an interpreter – the analog of a human interpreter seems particularly appropriate here – intercepting your commands, prompting you for clarification if need be and performing any necessary adjustments and translations before sending them along to the operating system.

In addition to providing a general-purpose programming language, most shells include a set of powerful commands that are themselves programs of considerable complexity. The most common of these commands are used for such tasks as searching and modifying files and are available in most shells. Some of these commands are so powerful that one must use command-specific mini-programming languages in order to exploit them fully. If all this sounds frighteningly complex, it is, but don't imagine that everyone who makes good use of a shell knows everything about that shell – that's not true, not by a long shot. Luckily, you can learn to be quite effective programming a shell without knowing all the ugly details of several programming languages.

2.1 SHELL PROGRAMMING

There are lots of shells to choose from, bash, csh, ksh, sh and tcsh being the most popular and readily available. The bash shell owes its name to Steven Bourne at AT&T Bell Laboratories who developed one of the first shells for the Unix operating system, variants of which are still popular today. bash, the "Bourne again shell," is intended as the shell for the GNU operating system. The csh shell or C-shell, written by Bill Joy at the University of California at Berkeley, is the choice of many C programmers. The tcsh shell is roughly csh with various niceties such as file-name completion[2] and command-line editing.[3] ksh is a public-domain version of the Korn shell developed by David Korn at AT&T Bell Laboratories. The Korn shell is upward-compatible with the Bourne shell and includes many of the features of csh.

These shells run under most modern operating systems including many variants of Unix, Linux and the Apple and Microsoft operating systems. On some systems sh is a version of the original Bourne shell but on others it is a default or generic shell; it is likely to correspond to different shells on different machines. Sampling machines around my department, I found sh corresponding to bash on one machine, ksh on another and to various hybrids on other machines. Here I'll use tcsh but stick to a command subset common to most shells.

A program written to run in a shell is called a *shell script*. We already met a couple of such scripts in Chapter 1; now we'll look shells and shell scripts in more detail. Shell scripts typically deal with objects like files and running programs called *processes* and operations like starting and stopping processes and creating, deleting and modifying files.

---

[2] With file-name completion, if I type part of a file or command name and then hit tab the shell completes the name if the part I typed is unambiguous; what is ambiguous or not depends on the particular commands and files on the system.

[3] Shells supporting command-line editing make available backspace, delete and simple line-editing commands so that you can correct typing errors, cut and paste text and generally speed up typing commands and short programs.

To stretch the language metaphor somewhat, you can think of programs and commands as verbs and file and directory names as nouns. We'll also encounter analogs for adverbs and adjectives, conjunctions, and, of course, punctuation (in the form of seemingly arbitrary, annoying and easily mistyped syntactic conventions). My objective here is not to teach you shell programming but rather to tempt you to learn it on your own and to give you some idea of what shell programming languages are good for.

Before we look at some specific instances of shell programs, let's think about what you generally need in specifying computations. Programs are typically broken down into smaller components called, variously, procedures, functions, programs, methods or commands. Each component is designed to carry out some specific computation; thus a sorting component puts lists in some specified order, say, alphabetic or numeric. Programming languages provide the means of orchestrating the various computations that result from invoking components by stringing them together and enabling them to pass information among themselves.

The term "flow of control" refers to various ways of stringing computations together, for example, as sequences – do this and then do that, conditionals – if such and such is true then do this otherwise do that, and loops – do this again and again until such and such is true. Information can be passed between components by allowing one computation to take as input the result (or output) of another computation, or, more generally, by allowing one component to store information in a convenient place so that it can be used by some subsequent computation.

Some of the most common mechanisms for information passing and flow of control in shell programming languages are rare in other programming languages. The methods of orchestrating computations in shells suit a particular type of computing and a particular class of computations. Understanding these methods is useful in itself and also gives some insight into the advantages and disadvantages of other methods and other programming languages that we'll explore in subsequent chapters.

Files are one of the most convenient ways of keeping track of information. They provide a very useful way of thinking about computer memory that connects directly to almost everything you're likely to do involving computers – files for important documents, web pages, and email messages, as well as digital music, photos and movies. Not surprisingly, shells provide lots of operations for manipulating files and the directories that contain them.

We'll start with one of the most useful commands, `ls`, for listing the contents (the names of files and nested directories) of the specified directories. In these exchanges with the shell, the prompt is the % character followed by a space; I typed everything to the right of the prompt. The intervening lines until the next prompt appears are the shell's responses, the output resulting from a command. The command `ls` appearing by itself is a request to list the contents of the current working directory.

```
% ls
bolts.txt nails.txt nuts.html
```

To find out what the current working directory is you can use the command `pwd`, which returns the absolute pathname of the current working directory. We talked about absolute and relative pathnames in Chapter 1 and we'll talk about navigating in a hierarchy of directories in Chapter 13, but for the remainder of this chapter the current working directory remains fixed.

```
% pwd
/u/tld
```

Shell command *options* are typically specified by a dash, -, followed by one or more characters. In the next exchange, `ls` is invoked with the "long-format" option:

```
% ls -l
total 0
-rw-r--r--  1 tld   staff   0 Dec   3 07:42 bolts.txt
-rw-r--r--  1 tld   staff   0 Dec   3 07:42 nails.txt
-rw-r--r--  1 tld   staff   0 Dec   3 07:42 nuts.html
```

The long-format option makes `ls` list information that's handy for lots of purposes, from sharing files with your friends (or protecting your files from the prying eyes of those who are not your friends) to remembering when you created a file. Other options allow you to list files sorted by time or size, distinguish directories from files and extract all sorts of useful information.

Commands like `ls` take *arguments* in addition to options. Options are like adverbs: they modify a command and tell the shell how something is to be done. Arguments are like the objects of imperative sentences: they indicate what or whom the command applies to. Commands can take any number of arguments, which are entered as sequences (or *strings*) of characters and typically separated by *whitespace* (spaces, tabs and, in some cases, carriage-return and new-line characters).[4] Here

---

[4] Whitespace seems a simple and innocuous concept until you realize that it is largely invisible and the characters that compose it are anything but obvious. Spaces are pretty straightforward, but you can't tell the difference between a tab and one or more spaces just by looking: a tab can appear as any number of spaces depending on the program displaying the text, though it's typically displayed as

are two invocations of `ls` with different arguments:

```
% ls bolts.txt
bolts.txt
% ls bolts.txt tacks.html
ls: tacks.html: No such file or directory
bolts.txt
```

In the first case, the single argument `bolts.txt` simply makes `ls` list the specified file if it's in the current directory and complain otherwise. In the second case, two arguments are supplied and we see `ls` complain that it can't find a file named `tacks.html` in the current directory; it does, however, indicate that `bolts.txt` is present by listing the file name.

Distinctions between options and arguments and the analogies to different parts of speech should be taken lightly. The shell isn't going to wince the way your grade-school teacher did if you use an adjective instead of an adverb. However, shells, like most programming languages, are syntactically less forgiving than even the strictest grammarian. Generally speaking, options modify the behavior of a command (often by specifying the format of the output) and arguments determine the primary input to the computation performed by a given command – what the computation computes on, as it were.

The computations performed by a shell correspond to more than the computations performed by commands. Recall that the shell is itself a program that reads lines typed by the user and interprets them. When a shell reads the arguments following a command, it is free to perform computations involving those arguments before passing them (or its own interpretation of them) to the program corresponding to the command. Consider these two invocations of `ls`:

```
% ls *.html
nuts.html
% ls *.txt
bolts.txt nails.txt
```

In the first invocation, we are asking `ls` to list any files that end with `.html`. As we saw in Chapter 1, the `*` is called a *wildcard* and matches any sequence of

---

four or eight spaces. The appearance of a new line of text is signaled differently in different operating systems; DOS (for "disk operating system", the first operating system in widespread use on personal computers) uses a carriage-return character followed by a new-line character, while Unix requires only a new-line character; other programs employ still other conventions. Chapter 11 talks about the effort to promulgate standards that eliminate or at least tame this and other sources of confusion as the World Wide Web increasingly requires different programs to share information.

characters.[5] Most shells employ a pattern-matching language that allows a great deal of control over matching. For example, the pattern `*.???` matches any file consisting of any sequence of characters followed by a period followed by exactly three characters. The pattern `[nt]*.txt` matches any file that begins with an "n" or a "t" followed by zero or more characters followed by `.txt`. The shell looks at each argument in turn, matches the pattern (think of `nuts.html` as a particularly simple pattern that matches only one possible file name) against the names of the files in the directory, and then passes those names to the command.

This pattern matching on file names is just one example of the sort of computations performed by the shell before passing information on to commands. If you're curious about what gets passed to a command after the shell is finished with its interpretation (or *preprocessing* as it's called) of the arguments, the command `echo` simply prints out what the shell would send on to a command. `echo` is useful for all sorts of purposes and we'll exploit it often in the rest of this chapter.

```
% echo *s.txt tacks.html
bolts.txt nails.txt tacks.html
```

Playing around with `echo` can give some additional insights into the shells computations in preprocessing arguments. Arguments are specified as strings that you type to the shell but not all the arguments correspond to the names of files or patterns specifying the names of files. Consider this invocation of `echo` with two arguments:

```
% echo '*.* expands to' *.*
*.* expands to bolts.txt nails.txt nuts.html
```

In the first argument corresponding to the string `'*.* expands to '`, the part of the string `*.*` is treated literally; the single-quote marks (which don't appear in the output) tell the shell *not* to do any preprocessing on the string enclosed by the single quotes. The single quotes also tell the shell to treat spaces as part of the enclosed string and, in particular, not to treat them as whitespace separating

---

[5] Well, not quite. `ls` without any options doesn't actually list *all* files in the current directory; specifically, it doesn't list so-called *dot* or hidden files that begin with a period, like `.login`. Dot files are used by the operating system for inscrutable purposes and for the most part we don't need to know they exist. The "list-all" option, `ls -a`, lists all the files in the current directory including the dot files. There are some dot files that you may want to become better acquainted with as you become more proficient working with shells. In particular, the `csh` and `tcsh` shells look in your home directory for a file named `.cshrc` that can contain commands customizing your favorite shell to your personal specifications.

arguments. You can think of the single quotes as telling the shell to turn off all preprocessing.

2.2 SHELL VARIABLES

It's often useful to set aside information about the current state of a computation in order to use it later. While you can store information in files for later use, it's often convenient to use a more readily available *shell variable* to keep track of a name, a number or a list of items.

For our purposes, shell variables correspond to typed sequences of alphanumeric characters, for instance, `tmp`, `VAR` or `files`, that can be assigned values and whose assigned values can be read in shell scripts. A special case of shell variables is the so-called *environment variable* that operating systems use to track your preferences for printers, user names, and the like. For example, `USER`, `HOME`, `PWD` and `SHELL` correspond, respectively, to my user name, home directory, current working directory (the value returned by the `pwd` command) and the absolute path of the shell program I'm using:

```
% echo $SHELL
/bin/tcsh
```

In preprocessing arguments, the dollar sign ($) tells the shell to interpret the characters immediately following as a variable name and substitute the value of the variable in the expression. As you might expect, `ls $PWD` does the same as `ls`, whereas `ls $HOME` lists the files in your home directory no matter what your current working directory. If the characters following the dollar sign don't correspond to a variable with an assigned value, the shell protests:

```
% echo $NOT
NOT: Undefined variable.
```

This is the shell's attempt to be helpful – a pretty feeble attempt, but as you gain experience programming, you'll come to appreciate the challenges of getting a shell or any other programming environment to do the right thing in response to an ambiguous or garbled command. For example, you might imagine that if you had a variable `NOTE` it might make sense for the shell to infer that you'd inadvertently left off the `E` and to go ahead and just make the substitution. Sounds obvious in this particular case, but until shell programs become more intelligent, it's probably better for them to play dumb.

If we embed a dollar sign in a string set off by single quotes, its special meaning is ignored and the shell doesn't treat the subsequent characters differently from any other characters appearing in the string:

```
% echo 'my shell is $SHELL'
my shell is $SHELL
```

If, however, we refer to a variable in a string set off with double quotes, the shell looks up the value of the variable and inserts it into the string before passing it on:

```
% echo "my shell is $SHELL"
my shell is /bin/tcsh
```

The double quotes tell the shell to interpret a string selectively, treating some characters, such as spaces, literally, but preprocessing others as though the quotes were not there. As usual, the full story concerning single and double quotes, and the many other special characters recognized by the shell, is complicated, but plenty of quite able shell programmers get along fine without understanding the story completely.

To read a variable as an argument you append the dollar sign to the name of the variable. To assign a variable you use set and =. Here we set the variable tmp to have a value corresponding to a simple string:

```
% set tmp = "a simple string"
% echo $tmp
a simple string
```

So far the strings we've typed as arguments to commands are largely passive; they specify fodder for computation but not the computations themselves. Wouldn't it be interesting to create programs that construct strings out of bits and pieces of other strings and then, when a computation is fully constructed, cause that computation to be carried out, perhaps just once but possibly many times?

To construct a string encoding a computation, you have to control how characters are interpreted, suppressing interpretation in some cases and forcing it in others. This example uses both single and double quotes to create a simple computation that is assigned to be the value of a variable and is later invoked using the eval command, which treats its arguments as though they were typed directly to the shell:

```
% set myshell = "echo 'my shell is $SHELL'"
% echo $myshell
```

```
echo 'my shell is /bin/tcsh'
% eval $myshell
my shell is /bin/tcsh
```

In the first line assigning the variable myshell, the shell reads the entire line. The single quotes are interpreted literally, ignoring their special meaning, but the dollar sign is recognized and the value of SHELL is inserted into the string. If we reverse the use of quotes, substituting single quotes for double quotes and vice versa, we end up specifying a different computation even though the result, in this case, turns out to be the same:

```
% set nowshell = 'echo "my shell is $SHELL"'
% echo $nowshell
echo "my shell is $SHELL"
% eval $nowshell
my shell is /bin/tcsh
```

If we change the value of SHELL, the difference between the two programs becomes apparent:

```
% set SHELL = /bin/bash
% eval $myshell
my shell is /bin/tcsh
% eval $nowshell
my shell is /bin/bash
```

These simple examples illustrate the interchangeability of programs and data. You can encode a program in a string, carry it around in a variable, change the program by altering the string and evaluate it whenever the mood strikes. And as we saw in Chapter 1, even very simple programs can write and run other programs.

A computer virus is a program that disguises itself as data, insinuates itself into your file system by embedding itself in an email message or web page, and then tricks the operating system into believing it's one of your programs; the operating system then runs the virus and allows it to wreak havoc on your computer. Viruses often manifest both their program and data personae simultaneously by rewriting themselves to avoid detection and escape being harvested by antivirus programs.

Often invoking a program can involve multiple levels of interpretation and code generation. Figuring out what happens when, as in determining when the variable SHELL is evaluated, can get complicated, but having the flexibility to control when computations take place (and indeed *where*, once we consider computations on networked computers) is essential in working with modern computer systems.

As you learn more about programming, you'll meet lots of programs that take other programs as input and generate still other programs as output. Variously called compilers, interpreters, assemblers, disassemblers, virtual machines, preprocessors, postprocessing back ends, bytecode compilers, cross compilers and macro-expansion packages, all these programs transform a specification for a computation in one form into a specification for a different but related computation in another form. These program-transforming programs can optimize the performance of programs, specialize programs to run on particular machines, generalize programs to run on a range of machines, or customize programs to run in conjunction with complementary programs.

2.3 INFORMATION PASSING

Let's return to orchestrating computations in shell scripts. So far we've seen only a few component computations in the form of commands like `ls` and `echo`. More often than not we'll perform a computation as part of a more complicated computation in order to obtain an intermediate result for use in a subsequent computation. To create a personalized phone book, say, we might first list the names of all our friends, including their nicknames. We might then look up their names in an online telephone directory, producing a new list that includes phone numbers in addition to names and nicknames. Finally, we might sort the list by nicknames and then print it out.

Suppose you are the system administrator for a large network of computers and suppose you want to find out how many people are using each of the different shell programs we mentioned earlier: `bash`, `csh`, `ksh`, `sh` and `tcsh`. In most operating systems that support shells, you can specify a default shell by setting the SHELL environment variable in the `.login` file in your home directory. For example, if you want `tcsh` to be your default shell program, you can include the line `set SHELL = /bin/tcsh` in your `.login` file.

In a computer network for a business or a university, users typically visualize the files and directories of all users on the network as a single file system. The fact that files reside on many different hard drives connected to one or several networked computers is hidden from the user. The executable binary files for commonly used programs are often found in the directory `/bin/` and the home directories for individual users are likely to be in a directory called `/u/` (or `/users/` or `/home/`). Since my login name is `tld`, my home directory is `/u/tld/`. I could use the `ls` command to list all users' `.login` files:[6]

```
% ls /u/*/.login
/u/dhl/.login      /u/jfh/.login      /u/jsb/.login
/u/jwc/.login      /u/lpk/.login      /u/tld/.login
```

In order to figure out what these users prefer for their default shells, however, we'll have to look inside these files. The `grep` command and its many variants are perfect for this job. We'll take a closer look at `grep` in Chapter 3, which is devoted to searching through files. For our immediate purposes, `grep` takes a pattern and a file specification and returns all lines that contain a string matching the pattern in all files indicated by the file specification. If the file specification indicates multiple files, then the matching lines are prefixed with the name of the file in which the line appeared. Here's how we would extract all the lines in all the `.login` files that set the SHELL environment variable:[7]

```
% grep "set SHELL" /u/*/.login
/u/dhl/.login:set SHELL = /bin/ksh
/u/jfh/.login:set SHELL = /bin/tcsh
/u/jsb/.login:set SHELL = /bin/bash
/u/jwc/.login:set SHELL = /bin/bash
/u/lpk/.login:set SHELL = /bin/tcsh
/u/tld/.login:set SHELL = /bin/tcsh
```

This is the first intermediate result in a multistage computation. To use this result in subsequent stages, we're going to store it in a file. Files are an obvious choice for storing information, and text files have a simple structure that can be used to organize data. A file consists of zero or more lines of text and each line of text can be further subdivided into words, numbers or other distinct data items

---

[6] Files and directories in a multiple-user system of networked computers are typically protected so that users can keep information private as they see fit. Different communities often adopt different conventions for sharing personal information. For example, professional programmers and faculty and students in computer science departments often let anyone read their `.login` files as a way of sharing programming knowledge and keeping others informed about their preferences. System administrators typically can read any file if absolutely necessary, but it is assumed that they will exercise discretion and not violate others' privacy. In the present exercise, we're assuming that individual users have made their `.login` files readable to all other users.

[7] You can also set the SHELL environment variable using the `setenv` command, for example, `setenv SHELL /bin/tcsh`. To find all the lines of all the `.login` files that use either `setenv SHELL` or `set SHELL =` to specify a default shell, you can use a somewhat more complicated invocation of `grep`, say `grep "set SHELL\|setenv SHELL" /u/*/.login`, in which two patterns are separated by a backslash followed by a vertical bar. The vertical bar is used to indicate disjunction; the backslash tells `grep` to interpret the next character as other than its literal meaning.

separated by whitespace or other forms of punctuation. In our examples so far, the output of commands like `ls` has simply been printed to the shell (or, as it's often called, the *standard output*). Alternatively, we can force the output of a computation to be sent to a file using the *redirect output operator*, >:

```
% ls > ls.txt
% cat ls.txt
bolts.txt
ls.txt
nails.txt
nuts.html
```

Here we've redirected the output of the `ls` command to be sent to a new file `ls.txt`.[8] Listing the contents of `ls.txt` using the `cat` command, we see the names of all the files in the current working directory at the time we called `ls`, including `ls.txt`. If you experiment with `ls` in directories containing lots of files, you'll find that the output sent to the standard output and displayed by the shell is formatted in accord with your display window. In redirecting output to a file, individual items such as file names are listed one item to a line; this turns out to be handy in using such output files as input to other computations. We can redirect the output of `grep` to create a file – which we'll call `login.txt` – in the same way as we did with `ls`:

```
% grep "set SHELL" /u/*/.login > login.txt
```

The file `login.txt` contains the information we need but not in a form we can readily use in order to tabulate how many users prefer each shell. As our next step, we'll get rid of all the extraneous information in the file `login.txt` by using another program called `sed`. The name of this program derives from "stream editor" but here "text filter" is a more appropriate description. We'll use `sed` to filter the file, eliminating the parts we don't want and leaving only those parts we do. In general, `sed` takes strings corresponding to lines of text from files and returns versions of those strings with various additions, deletions and substitutions. `sed` is a complex program with its own commands and its own specialized programming language. We'll use just one of `sed`'s commands to filter `login.txt`. You can do a lot with this one command, and indeed many shell programmers get by fine

---

[8] By the way, if you're experimenting with this on your own and try to redirect output to the same file using > in two consecutive shell commands, you're likely to encounter resistance from the shell. If you try to redirect output into an existing file using >, the shell will refuse you. If you don't want the old contents of the file, then delete the file and try again. If you want to *append* new results to an existing file, then you can use another output redirection operator, >>.

knowing only this command. (If this seems strange, think about how few people know how to use all the options on their television remotes, VCRs, automotive cruise controls, kitchen appliances or even Swiss Army knives.)

A sed command of the form s"pattern"replacement"g substitutes the string specified by replacement for all strings matching pattern.[9] If you leave off the g (for "global") at the end of the command, it replaces only the first string matching the pattern. So, for example, sed 's"java"scheme"g' old.txt > new.txt would create a file new.txt that looks like old.txt except that all occurrences of the string java in old.txt are replaced by the string scheme in new.txt. Usually it's important to establish some context for substitutions; in our case, we're looking for the string that follows /bin/. We'll also have to do some gymnastics to keep track of the parts of the string that we want to keep. Take a look at sed in action and then we'll consider more carefully how it did what it did.

```
% sed 's".*/bin/\([a-z]*\)"\1"' < login.txt
ksh
tcsh
bash
bash
tcsh
tcsh
```

Let's look at a single line of input from login.txt. Given the string /u/jsb/.login:set SHELL = /bin/bash, the .* part of the pattern matches /u/jsb/.login:set SHELL = , the /bin/ part matches /bin/ to establish the context for extracting the shell name, and the [a-z]* part matches bash. The \(and \) operators save whatever is matched by the pattern between them. In general, the first pair of \(\) saves its matched string into \1, the second pair into \2, and so on. In the present use of sed, the string bash is saved into \1, and so the entire line set SHELL = /bin/bash is replaced simply by bash.

So far we've also specified the inputs to computations as arguments typed to the shell or, in this case, the *standard input*. Inputs can also be redirected using

---

[9] The sed command allows considerable flexibility in using separators for delimiting the pattern and replacement strings. I used s"pattern"replacement"g instead of the more common s/pattern/replacement/g since the pattern I wanted to search for contains forward slashes. By using double quotes instead of forward slashes, I avoided having to use escape characters to turn off the special meaning of the forward slashes appearing in the pattern so that they are treated literally. sed treats the first character appearing immediately after the s in a substitution command as the separator delimiting the pattern and replacement strings. This sort of flexibility contributes to the difficulty of learning programs like sed while at the same time making them that much more useful to experts.

the redirect input operator, <. For the next step in our multistage computation, we take the input from the last step in `login.txt` and redirect the output to a new file called `shell.txt`:

```
% sed 's".*/bin/\([a-z]*\)"\1"' < login.txt > shells.txt
```

Now if we could just count the number of occurrences of each shell program we'd be done. Unfortunately, there isn't a standard program for doing this, so we'll use two additional commands in a two-step trick that you'll probably see often if you look at a lot of shell scripts. First we sort the lines in `shells.txt` using the sort command:

```
% sort < shells.txt
bash
bash
ksh
tcsh
tcsh
tcsh
```

We'll need to save that result and so we redirect sorted lines into the file `sorted.txt`:

```
% sort < shells.txt > sorted.txt
```

The next command, `uniq`, eliminates identical adjacent lines in the input. Repeated lines in the input that are not adjacent are not detected – this is why we sorted the list before submitting it to `uniq`. This command unadorned won't do us much good, but `uniq` with the "count-identical-adjacent-lines" option, specified with –c, is exactly what we need to get the answer we wanted:

```
% uniq -c < sorted.txt
    2 bash
    1 ksh
    3 tcsh
```

The trick of using sort followed by `uniq -c` is definitely a hack, albeit a hack known to lots of shell programmers. We saw another, more elegant trick in Chapter 1 for passing information between commands, and now we're going to use it to simplify computing user shell preferences.

We have the answer we're looking for, but in the process we generated three files, `login.txt`, `shells.txt` and `sorted.txt`, to keep track of intermediate results that we now have no use for. The folks at AT&T who developed the Unix operating system created a very elegant abstraction that lets us dispense with the creation and subsequent elimination of files for storing intermediate results. It's an abstraction because it hides the details of how information is passed from one computational component to another. Indeed, we no longer have to even think about files. Unix *pipes*, denoted by vertical bars (|), allow us to take the output produced by one command and "pipe" it into the input for another command.

Here's a shell script that uses the Unix plumbing abstraction to perform our example task of listing user shell preferences:

```
% grep "set SHELL" /u/*/.login | sed 's".*/bin/\([a-z]*\)"\1"' | sort | uniq -c
   2 bash
   1 ksh
   3 tcsh
```

But there's more to pipes than merely eliminating temporary files. In the temporary-file approach, we created the entire file containing all the intermediate results, one line at a time, before invoking the next command that used those results. Why not send along each line of text as soon as it's ready? Why not have all the commands running simultaneously and working on lines of text as soon as they become available? That's exactly what the abstraction of pipes allows.

The pipe abstraction supports the idea of lines of text flowing through pipes being processed by various plumbing fixtures (commands) along the way (see Figure 1.3 for a sketch from this plumber's perspective). As soon as the first line of text is processed by the first command, the second command can start working. Once a line is written to a file, it's not going to change, so why not start working on it? The abstraction doesn't require pipes to be implemented in this way, but it allows it, and that's why it's such a powerful way of thinking about computation.

2.4 ASYNCHRONOUS PROCESSES

In order to make the most of the plumbing abstraction, however, we need another abstraction, that of *asynchronous processes*. Executing a command in a shell could easily require thousands if not millions of more primitive instructions. Modern operating systems allow multiple programs to run *asynchronously* by interleaving the execution of their instructions – for example, first run a couple of instructions from program one, then a couple from program two, and then go back and give program one another chance. This interleaving happens so quickly that the different programs appear to run in parallel. Modern operating systems typically run dozens of programs quietly in the background, where you're not even aware of them, to do all sorts of tasks (much as your body has all sorts of subsystems that manage breathing, heart rate, digestion and the like).

Your operating system often runs a program by starting a new process. A *process* is just a computation that can be run simultaneously with other computations. A running program that initiates a new process is itself running as a process, called the *parent process* of the newly initiated process. A parent process can initiate multiple child processes and its children can initiate their own child processes. The shell is also a program running in a process. Every time the shell reads a command you've typed, it starts up a new child process to run the program corresponding to that command. It's the operating system's job to manage all these processes.

The best way to learn about processes is to create a bunch of them and watch what they do. The Unix `sleep` command takes a single integer argument specifying how many seconds the process in which the command is running should sleep for. To illustrate, we'll introduce another flow-of-control mechanism for sequencing commands. A shell script of the form one ; two, where one and two are commands, first executes one and then two – the commands are executed in sequence. What do you expect to happen in the this example?

```
% sleep 10 ; echo done
```

When you run this script, there is a pause of about ten seconds and then the shell prints "done". In the next example, the shell starts two separate processes, one for each of the two commands. What do you think happens next?

```
% sleep 10 | echo done
```

The shell almost immediately prints out "done" and then there is a pause of about ten seconds at the end of which the prompt reappears.

How can we determine what's going on? One of the commands the shell provides for managing processes is the *process status* command ps, but there's a problem in using this command to inspect processes such as those generated by this shell script. To inspect running processes, I have to be able to type commands to the shell. The problem is that a running shell script takes over the standard input and output, preventing me from interacting with the shell. To get around this, I can use the & operator, which allows me to run a script in the *background* and returns control over input and output to the shell.[10] Note what happens when I

[10] What do you think would happen if you start running a shell script in the background that produces a lot of output? If you want to find out, try typing a command immediately after executing `repeat 1000 echo "hello" &`.

run this simple script terminated by an &:

```
% sleep 10 | sleep 20 &
[1] 1453 1454
```

The 1 in [1] is the number of the *job* associated with the command. You can see the jobs you have running in the background by using the jobs command:

```
% jobs
[1]  + Running                     sleep 10 | sleep 20
```

The other two numbers, 1453 and 1454, are the *process identifiers* or PIDs of the two processes created by the shell and used to run the two commands sleep 10 and sleep 20. We can examine these processes with the process status command:

```
% ps -o "pid command"
  PID  COMMAND
  893  -bin/tcsh
 1453  sleep 10
 1454  sleep 20
```

The -o option lets me tell ps exactly what status information to list. The unadorned ps command lists several pieces of status information in addition to the process identifier and command. You can learn more about ps by invoking man ps or info ps from the shell (although, some of the documentation may be incomprehensible without a course on operating systems).

By the way, if you ever create a process and then decide you don't want it, you can get rid of it by using the kill command. I could get rid of the second sleep command by typing kill 1454. Processes in their final death throes can hang around, however, and kill 1454 with no options is not as strong (or as terminal) as kill -KILL 1454.

The ability of an operating system to handle multiple processes enables a word-processing program to keep up with your typing at the same time it's checking your spelling, or an office delivery robot to look for nameplates on office doors at the same time it's avoiding obstacles in the hallways. In Chapter 10 we'll talk about processes that really make your computer work hard and thus better show off the advantages of running multiple processes.

Unix processes are called *asynchronous communicating processes*. The 'asynchronous' part refers to the fact that the individual instructions comprising the programs associated with the different processes can be executed in any order. But even asynchronous processes occasionally need to coordinate their efforts – that's the 'communicating' part. This is especially true when one process depends on input from another.

For processes to communicate with one another, they need some way to synchronize their behavior. The operating system provides synchronization machinery so that processes that must send information to another process can do so and get on with whatever else they're doing without waiting for the other process to accept or acknowledge receipt. The same machinery allows processes that need information from other processes to go to sleep and ask to be awakened when it becomes available. In Chapter 10 we'll see how this machinery keeps robots from getting confused and banks from giving you more (or less) money than you're entitled to.

Pipes support unidirectional flow of information. Other interprocess communication and synchronization mechanisms support bidirectional exchanges of information between processes. One such mechanism, *sockets*, is used to enable processes on different machines to exchange information and supports the client-server model that in turn supports the World Wide Web. We'll look at the client-server model in some detail in Chapter 11.

You can learn a lot about shell programming by reading the online documentation available on your system or on the web. Sometimes, however, it's comforting to have a nice fat book full of examples to guide you through the maze of arcane syntax and technical terms. Ellie Quigley's *Unix Shells by Example* provides a good general introduction to shell programming with side-by-side comparisons of the most popular shells. I also recommend Kochan and Wood's *Unix Shell Programming* as an introduction and general reference.

Computer scientists are notorious for mixing metaphors and seeing computation in all sorts of strange places. In some respects, shell programming languages are pretty tame stuff, not nearly as exotic as programming models like object-oriented programming. Still, orchestrating computations using files, pipes and processes is a powerful basis for computation and we've barely scratched the surface of what you can do within a shell. In the next chapter, we'll see some more simple shell scripts that are useful for everyday computing tasks.

CHAPTER THREE

Keeping Track of Your Stuff

One consequence of inexpensive computer memory and storage devices is that much less gets thrown out. People who normally wouldn't characterize themselves as packrats find themselves accumulating megabytes of old email messages, news articles, personal financial data, digital images, digital music in various formats and, increasingly, animations, movies and other multimedia presentations. For many of us, digital memory serves to supplement the neural hardware we were born with for keeping track of things; the computer becomes a sort of neural prosthetic or memory amplifier.

However reassuring it may be to know that every aspect of your digital lifestyle is stored on your computer's hard drive, storing information doesn't do much good if you can't get at what you need when you need it. How do you recall the name of the restaurant your friend from Seattle mentioned in email a couple of years back when she told you about her new job? Or perhaps you're trying to find the recommendation for a compact digital camera that someone sent you in email or you saved from a news article. It's tough remembering where you put things and you'd rather not look through all your files each time you want to recall a piece of information.

In 1999, when NASA launched the first of its Earth Observing System (EOS) satellites, they knew they would have to do something with the terabytes (a terabyte is a billion bytes) of data streaming down from these orbiting observers. EOS satellites collect data for the long-term study and monitoring of our planet including its atmosphere, oceans and biosphere. NASA scientists realized that there was too much data to store on fast-access disk drives and it simply wouldn't do any good to put it on some long-term-storage media like CDs because no one would really know what was on them. Using CDs would have been like your throwing a decade's worth of your financial data in unmarked boxes in your basement.

To make sure that scientists would be able to use the EOS data, NASA engineers devised strategies for cataloging and summarizing it as it streamed down from the satellites, and developed software for searching these catalogs and summaries to help scientists find what they're looking for. Just as a library would be much harder to use without a card catalog, so the EOS data would be almost useless without a way to search it efficiently. Let's consider some techniques and programs for keeping track of our digital data.

3.1   FINDING STUFF

Simple text files are particularly convenient for storing data, whether it's dessert recipes, sports scores or your old email messages. Even if your data is in some special format, you can often convert it to raw text by using an appropriate *filter* (a program that takes a file in one format and converts it to another format). One of the dangers of storing data in special formats is that, by the time you get around to using it, the program that created it may no longer work. Another problem is that different programs use different formats and often enough you'd like to search across files generated by different programs. For example, in trying to recall that digital camera recommendation, you might want to look at files generated by your email program, your word-processing program and your web browser.

One simple way to catalog and summarize all your data is to use filters to convert the text parts of all your files into raw text files. These text summaries would omit images, audio clips and graphical information, but the text remaining is likely to provide useful clues about the non-text content. The NASA engineers working on EOS didn't have much text in their satellite data but they did have information about the time the data was generated, where the satellite was positioned in its orbit and therefore what it was looking at, and what sorts of cameras and sensors were used to produce the data, all of which could be very useful to someone searching for information relevant to a particular study.

Let's look as some basic but powerful tools for searching text files. Suppose you have a lot of text files (indicated by the extension `txt`, as in `java.txt`) in which you've stored various email messages and news articles about programming languages. How would you go about searching in these files for, say, an article that talks about both Java and Scheme? A host of programs make it relatively easy to search through files and whole file systems.

To demonstrate one such program, suppose that we have five files each consisting of one line each. I'll list their contents using `cat`:

```
% ls
1.txt 2.txt 3.txt 4.txt 5.txt
% cat 1.txt
Here we have Java and Scheme appearing on the same line.
% cat 2.txt
Scheme appearing on the same line but followed by Java.
% cat 3.txt
Java followed by Scheme after fewer than 20 characters.
% cat 4.txt
Java with more than 20 characters before Scheme appears.
% cat 5.txt
Java on a line without that word that rhymes with scream.
```

The original text editor provided in Unix provides an operation, g/re/p, which searches globally (hence the g) for strings matching a given pattern (called a regular expression – hence the re) and then prints (the p) out the lines containing those strings. This operation was used so often that it was packaged into the command grep that can be easily invoked from a Unix shell. Versions of grep are now available for every operating system I know of. Here's how to use grep to find all lines in all our text files containing the word Java:

```
% grep Java *.txt
1.txt:Here we have Java and Scheme appearing on the same line.
2.txt:Scheme appearing on the same line but followed by Java.
3.txt:Java followed by Scheme after fewer than 20 characters.
4.txt:Java with more than 20 characters before Scheme appears.
5.txt:Java on a line without that word that rhymes with scream.
```

In this invocation, grep takes two arguments: a search pattern, Java in this case, and a file specification, *.txt. grep prints out the file name, for example, 1.txt, and the line of text separated by a colon.

Let's try something a little more complex. Here's a way to find all lines in all text files containing the words Java and Scheme:

```
% grep Java *.txt | grep Scheme
1.txt:Here we have Java and Scheme appearing on the same line.
2.txt:Scheme appearing on the same line but followed by Java.
3.txt:Java followed by Scheme after fewer than 20 characters.
4.txt:Java with more than 20 characters before Scheme appears.
```

Here we used Unix pipes to feed the results from one program, grep Java *.txt, into another, grep Scheme. The pipe packages up the results from the first invocation of grep as a (virtual) file so that it becomes the second argument (the file specification) to the second invocation.

You can also tell grep that you want to *exclude* all lines that match a pattern by using the -v (for "veto") option. Here's how you'd find all lines in all text files that contain the word Java but *not* the word Scheme:

```
% grep "Java" *.txt | grep -v "Scheme"
5.txt:Java on a line without that word that rhymes with scream.
```

We can get similar results by making more sophisticated use of the language of regular expressions to specify search patterns. But, as so often in modern programming practice, we're going to find ourselves trying to make sense of different languages and different syntax even within a single call to grep.

The pattern language for specifying lists of files to search as the second argument to grep is not as sophisticated as the language for specifying regular expressions used in the first argument to grep. The former is part of the shell language and common to all commands; the latter is part of grep. To complicate matters, grep uses a different pattern language for regular expressions.

In specifying files, the shell uses ? to match any single character and * to match any sequence of zero or more characters, so that *.??? matches text.txt but not program.pl. grep uses a different method for matching single characters that doesn't involve ? at all and uses * in a related but disorientingly different method for matching multiple characters.

As the first argument in an invocation of grep, the pattern "Java.*Scheme" matches any string consisting of Java followed by zero or more characters (except the so-called newline character) followed by Scheme. In specifying files in the shell, the . was treated literally, but in the regular expression the . indicates what can match (any character except newline) and the * indicates how often it can match (zero or more times).

This regular expression language lets you be very precise about what can match and how many times. For example, \d* matches zero or more digits (0,...,9), \s+ matches one or more whitespace characters (spaces, tabs, carriage returns), and [a-zA-Z]{2,5} matches at least two and no more than five alphabetic characters (A,...,Z and a,...,z). This command finds any line in which Java appears followed by Scheme:

```
% grep "Java.*Scheme" *.txt
1.txt:Here we have Java and Scheme appearing on the same line.
```

```
3.txt:Java followed by Scheme after fewer than 20 characters.
4.txt:Java with more than 20 characters before Scheme appears.
```

This is not the same as finding any line that contains both Java and Scheme; we can manage that search by using a somewhat more complicated regular expression:

```
% grep "Java.*Scheme\|Scheme.*Java" *.txt
1.txt:Here we have Java and Scheme appearing on the same line.
2.txt:Scheme appearing on the same line but followed by Java.
3.txt:Java followed by Scheme after fewer than 20 characters.
4.txt:Java with more than 20 characters before Scheme appears.
```

The vertical bar, which means "pipe" elsewhere in Unix, means "or" in this context. The backslash, \, preceding the bar is an "escape" character that tells Unix not to interpret the bar in the usual way. Curly brackets, { and }, also have to be "backslashified" to avoid being misinterpreted by the shell, as in this next invocation, meant to find all lines in all text files containing the word Java followed by the word Scheme separated by no more than 20 characters:

```
% grep "Java.\{0,20\}Scheme" *.txt
1.txt:Here we have Java and Scheme appearing on the same line.
3.txt:Java followed by Scheme after fewer than 20 characters.
```

The need to prefix characters like |, { and } with backslashes so annoyed some programmers that they modified and extended grep's regular expression language so that they could use these and other characters without a slash. If you find yourself similarly annoyed, use egrep (for "extended" grep) to search your files:

```
% egrep "Java.{0,20}Scheme" *.txt
1.txt:Here we have Java and Scheme appearing on the same line.
3.txt:Java followed by Scheme after fewer than 20 characters.
```

How, you might ask, could anyone have invented such an arcane set of conventions for invoking one relatively simple program? Even though it's not really simple, most folks will agree that it's fairly Byzantine in its rules of engagement. There are a number of factors at play here. Programming languages, like natural languages, evolve to suit the purposes of those who use them. It makes sense to have short ways of saying things that'll be said often. The most succinct ways of saying things, short character sequences, are few and hence they tend to get reused with different meanings in different contexts. You wouldn't translate "La palabra española para 'said' es 'dicho' " as "The Spanish word for 'said' is 'said'." Quotes, backslashes and other conventions for escaping characters establish the appropriate context for interpretation and enable a program that uses one set of conventions to invoke a program that uses a different set.

It's not at all unusual to have a program written in one language call a program written in another that calls a program written in a third. A web page written in HTML, which is interpreted by your web browser, may cause a program written in Perl or Scheme to run on the web server (another program) hosting the web page, which in turn causes a Java program to be downloaded to your web browser and run in the Java Virtual Machine (still another program). Often enough the calling program needs to pass information to the program being called using the language of the calling program.

Here's an example illustrating how useful it is for one program, the shell, to convey information to a second program, grep in this case. The shell command alias lets you define new commands corresponding to short programs (to save typing or to customize your environment). The alias command takes two arguments: the name of the new command and its definition. Even though the definitions are pretty short, it's handy to put them in a special file that's loaded every time you fire up a shell. Usually in a shell command the name of the command is followed by one or more arguments. And so, in defining new commands using alias, it's convenient to be able to refer to the arguments; alias uses the convention that \!* refers to all the arguments appearing on the command line (there are other conventions for referring to individual arguments).

Suppose I want to define a new command whose arguments are inserted into the pattern or file specification arguments passed to an invocation of grep. I could use the definition:

```
% alias self 'grep "\!*" \!*.txt'
```

The new command self invokes grep to search through a text file whose name (minus the .txt extension) is specified as the only argument to self and print out all lines in which the name of the file appears. Here's a simple example showing the new command applied to a self-referential file:

```
% cat refers.txt
This file refers to its name in the text.
% self refers
This file refers to its name in the text.
```

You can probably guess that 'grep "\\!*" \!*.txt' would yield something very different: lines containing the string \!*. With a little more work, I could define a command that would rename a file and then change all internal references to the old name of the file to the new name of the file; this is very useful for maintaining lots of web pages. But I'm not trying to teach you everything about grep or alias, and I'm the first to admit that every time I do anything nontrivial combining these two programs I have to look up the documentation to get the silly conventions right. The point is that the conventions aren't quite as silly as they first appear and when you are doing a lot of grepping through files looking for stuff, escape characters and cryptic (but easy to type) sequences suddenly make a lot of sense. Well, maybe not a *lot* of sense, but certainly some sense.

Programs like grep are amazingly useful for searching your own stuff, largely because you have some idea of what's in your own stuff. You know what you tend to call things; moreover, you know the names of your friends, familiar places and favorite things that you can use in arguments to programs like grep to find what you're looking for. Other sources of data, however, can require more effort to organize.

3.2 ORGANIZING YOUR STUFF

In the case of the Earth Observing System, we imagined associating text files with chunks of satellite data. These text files would be even more useful if the information in them appeared in a particular order and a consistent format, say:

```
% cat data/EOS-078879.txt
Spacecraft: QuikSCAT
Date: 2002-08-24T14:10:00-05:00
Latitude: 44.67 North
Longitude: 63.58 West
Measurement: Phytoplankton and Dissolved Organic Matter
Instrument: Moderate-Resolution Imaging Spectroradiometer (MODIS)
```

The date is specified in an international standard, ISO 8601, the location in terms of latitude and longitude and the measurement and instrument in terms of known types identified by NASA. The associated data could consist of a few numbers or an image file of many megabytes. For an example a little closer to earth, imagine creating a format to keep track of all your music files:

```
% cat song/1739.txt
Title: Raccoon Cat
```

```
Artist: Bill Frisell
Album: Gone, Just Like A Train
Genre: jazz
Year: 1998
Track: 14 of 16
```

These files contain a very simple form of structured data that's easier to search than "unstructured" data: because the information is tagged consistently, you can easily pick out, say, the title and track of a song. It should be pretty obvious that, given a collection of such files, we could use grep or some other such program to find all jazz songs about raccoons performed by artists named Bill on albums whose names mention trains.

That's just the beginning; we could also create a set of files containing information about individual artists. Here's what a file for Bill Frisell might look like:

```
% cat artist/0427.txt
Name: Bill Frisell
Birthdate: March 18, 1951
Born: Baltimore, Maryland
Instrument: guitar
```

Combining the files for songs and the files for artists, we could search for all artists born in Baltimore after 1950 who produced more than one jazz album between 1900 and 2000. We'd need more than just grep, but it wouldn't be very difficult to write a short shell script for such a search.

If we're really into keeping and analyzing a lot of data, there are plenty of programs out there to help. These programs, called database management systems or databases for short, are used to keep track of bank accounts, customers, payrolls, employee benefits, purchases, inventory, scientific data, train schedules, computer accounts, college applications, student grades, course registrations, medical records, and so on. Name a type of data – someone probably keeps track of it in a database somewhere. If suddenly all the database programs in the world stopped working, business would grind to halt and most stores would close their doors; planes wouldn't take off and government agencies wouldn't be able to function.

In addition to being indispensable in this information age, databases are very interesting programs, and often they're just the thing for keeping track of your stuff. In Chapter 1, we played briefly with the logic programming language Prolog. Prolog lets you assert relationships like "Fred is Anne's parent", expressed in Prolog syntax as `parent(fred, anne)`. We could use Prolog to describe all our song and artist data. We stored everything we knew about Bill Frisell's song "Raccoon Cat" in a file called `1739.txt`. We could use this file name as a unique name to refer to the song and then express the data in terms of several binary relationships, for example, `genre(1739, jazz)` and `year(1739, 1998)`. Modern databases, often called relational databases, can express much the same information as Prolog but they use a somewhat different format and are designed to handle huge amounts of data – say, all the account information for American Express or the parts inventory for the Ford Motor Company.

In database lingo, the song and artist files are called records. Songs and artists are different types of records. Each record consists of a set of binary relationships that assign values or *instances*, for example, 1998 and jazz, to attributes, for ex- ample, year and genre. Each record has one attribute, called its *primary key*, that distinguishes it from every other record of the same type. Here this could be the song's title, but since we're talking about recordings or song tracks we could easily have songs of the same title performed by several artists or even the same artist at different times. Often the primary key is just an integer unique among records of the same type.

A collection of records of a given type, such as the collection of all songs or the collection of all artists, is called a *table*. A database is just a collection of tables. Usually there are several ways of organizing your data and it's quite tricky to set up the records, attributes and instances so as to anticipate all the ways you might ultimately want to think about them. If you really want to go crazy with your music database, you'll probably want record types for albums, recording labels, concerts, groups of artists such as bands and orchestras, and other people involved in the music business such as producers and recording engineers. People with a knack for organizing data are paid very good money for structuring data in commercial applications.

Let's call up a database program and try to get some idea of what it means to create and use a database. Modern database systems have all sorts of fancy graph- ical front ends but, as usual, we'll interact with this database program using a relatively low-level programming language, here a variant of SQL (for "structured query language"). Programmers who write database programs typically start with a subset of standard SQL and then add special syntax to take advantage of function- ality that distinguishes their program or product. I've got a couple of open-source database programs, MySQL and PostgreSQL, installed on my home computer ("open-source software" and "free software" are not synonymous but they're close enough as long as you're just using the programs for your own purposes). I'll use MySQL.

First I'll create a new database named "music" and indicate that I want all the tables and records I'll create to be stored in it:

```
> CREATE DATABASE music ;
OK
> USE DATABASE music ;
OK
```

I'm going to create separate tables for artists and songs, starting with the artist table. Artist records will have an integer identifier (the primary key) plus attributes for the artist's first name, last name, birthdate and birthplace. In addition to the names of the attributes, I indicate the type of the attribute values, integers, variable length sequences of characters; for the artist's birthdate, I use a special DATE type that has associated functions for referring to a DATE's year, month and day. NULL is a special attribute value and I've used the AUTO_INCREMENT feature so that the database program provides integer identifiers numbered from 1 to however many artist records I create. All the terms in capital letters are either part of SQL, so-called reserved words, or MySQL extensions. The MySQL interpreter conveniently lets me use multiple lines for a command as long as I observe the correct syntax and end the command with a semicolon.

```
> CREATE TABLE artist (
> id SMALLINT UNSIGNED NOT NULL AUTO_INCREMENT,
> first VARCHAR(20),
> last VARCHAR(20),
> birthdate DATE,
> birthplace VARCHAR(40),
> PRIMARY KEY (id) ) ;
OK
```

The DESCRIBE command lets us look at the fields of a specified table. I usually do this just to make sure I didn't mistype anything.

```
> DESCRIBE artist ;
```

Field	Type	Null	Key	Default
id	smallint(5)		PRI	NULL
first	varchar(20)	YES		NULL
last	varchar(20)	YES		NULL
birthdate	date	YES		NULL
birthplace	varchar(40)	YES		NULL

The output following the invocation of the DESCRIBE command depicts a table using various characters (+, − and |) to produce the horizontal and vertical lines separating rows and columns. It's kind of old fashioned, but it's convenient for interacting with a database without a fancy graphical user interface.

Next we INSERT a bunch of records into the artist table. I use NULL for anything I don't know or want the program to fill in for me, in this case, the record number.

```
> INSERT INTO artist VALUES
> (NULL, 'Bill', 'Frisell', '1951-03-18', 'Baltimore, Maryland'),
> (NULL, 'Bonnie', 'Raitt', '1949-11-08', 'Burbank, California'),
> (NULL, 'Melvin', 'Taylor', '1959-03-13', 'Jackson, Mississippi'),
> (NULL, 'Robert', 'Cray', '1953-08-01', 'Columbus, Georgia'),
> (NULL, 'Keith', 'Jarrett', '1945-05-08', 'Allentown, Pennsylvania'),
> (NULL, 'Sue', 'Foley', '1968-03-29', 'Ottawa, Canada') ;
OK
```

3.3 DATABASE MANAGEMENT

Now that there's some data in the database, let's see how SQL lets us manage it. First, we'll use an SQL query to list all the artist records sorted by last name:

```
> SELECT * FROM artist ORDER BY last ;
+----+--------+---------+------------+-------------------------+
| id | first  | last    | birthdate  | birthplace              |
+----+--------+---------+------------+-------------------------+
|  4 | Robert | Cray    | 1953-08-01 | Columbus, Georgia       |
|  6 | Sue    | Foley   | 1968-03-29 | Ottawa, Canada          |
|  1 | Bill   | Frisell | 1951-03-18 | Baltimore, Maryland     |
|  5 | Keith  | Jarrett | 1945-05-08 | Allentown, Pennsylvania |
|  2 | Bonnie | Raitt   | 1949-11-08 | Burbank, California     |
|  3 | Melvin | Taylor  | 1959-03-13 | Jackson, Mississippi    |
+----+--------+---------+------------+-------------------------+
```

Once you get the hang of translating them, SQL queries read a little like natural language. This one might be translated as "select all (the * acts as a wildcard) the attributes from the artist table and then print them out, one record to a line, ordered by the last name of the artist." MySQL displays the result as a table. Indeed, in addition to the tables specifically defined by CREATE TABLE, every SQL query creates a new virtual table that can be used anywhere an explicitly defined table can be used.

Let's make a more interesting request: a table with two columns listing the name and birthdate of those artists born before 1950:

```
> SELECT last, birthdate FROM artist
> WHERE birthdate < '1950-01-01' ORDER BY birthdate ;
+---------+------------+
| last    | birthdate  |
+---------+------------+
| Jarrett | 1945-05-08 |
| Raitt   | 1949-11-08 |
+---------+------------+
```

Regular expressions and pattern matching are just too useful for them to be unavailable for SQL queries. Unfortunately, MySQL has a different pattern syntax from grep; in the next query % matches zero or more characters. To create a table with three columns listing the first name, last name and birthplace of any artist born in Mississippi, I say:

```
> SELECT first, last, birthplace FROM artist
> WHERE birthplace LIKE "%Mississippi%" ;
+--------+--------+---------------------+
| first  | last   | birthplace          |
+--------+--------+---------------------+
| Melvin | Taylor | Jackson, Mississippi |
+--------+--------+---------------------+
```

We can also create tables that relate records within the same table. Suppose we're interested in finding artists born in the same month. We could create a table with four columns that lists the last name and birthdate of one artist and the last name and birthdate of a second artist if both artists were born in the same month. Previous queries concerned only one table, specified by the FROM keyword, and so we could refer to attributes by name without ambiguity. To avoid confusion when referring to separate records from the same table, we use the AS keyword in the next query to introduce local aliases, one and two, so as to distinguish between the two references. In queries involving more than one table or referring to the same table multiple times, we refer to attributes by prefixing the attribute names with their respective table names or designated aliases (for multiple references to the same table).

The first line of this query takes advantage of functions for referring to the year, month and day of an attribute value of type DATE. The last line of the query is a bit of a hack, but imagine what would happen if you left it off: you'd find out a bunch of facts such as that Robert Cray was born in the same month as Robert Cray and ditto for Keith Jarrett and Keith Jarrett. We could eliminate this sort of useless information by requiring the records to be different; however, you'd still be told that Melvin Taylor and Sue Foley were born in the same month and – surprise, surprise – Sue Foley and Melvin Taylor were born in the same month. So this final line ensures that an artist is not listed as being born in the same month as him or herself and that pairs of artists born in the same month are listed only once.

```
> SELECT one.last, one.birthdate, two.last, two.birthdate
> FROM artist AS one, artist AS two
> WHERE MONTH(one.birthdate) = MONTH(two.birthdate)
> AND one.last > two.last ;
+---------+------------+---------+------------+
| last    | birthdate  | last    | birthdate  |
+---------+------------+---------+------------+
| Taylor  | 1959-03-13 | Frisell | 1951-03-18 |
| Frisell | 1951-03-18 | Foley   | 1968-03-29 |
| Taylor  | 1959-03-13 | Foley   | 1968-03-29 |
+---------+------------+---------+------------+
```

This query is a special case of a *join*. When a database program (or *engine*) processes a join of two tables, it creates a new temporary table with one record for each possible combination of a record from the first table and a record from the second table. The new records are the concatenation of the attributes of the two records from which they were created. If there are n records in the first table and m in the second, then there are $n * m$ combined records in the temporary table. Since there are six records in the artist table and the artist record has five attributes, the next query would display a table with 10 columns and 36 records:

```
> SELECT * FROM artist AS one, artist AS two ;
```

Here the database engine goes through each new record in the new temporary table using the specification in the WHERE portion of the query to determine what gets included in the final table resulting from the SELECT. To join a table containing thousands of employee records with itself in order to find groups of people living in the same area who might want to carpool, you'd have create a temporary table consisting of millions of records. In practice, database engines are clever enough that they seldom have to construct the full temporary table.

Such cleverness is even more important with queries joining many tables. In general, the size of the temporary table resulting from a join of multiple tables is the product of the sizes of the tables; thus a join of three different tables consisting of a thousand records each would yield a temporary table with a billion records. A lot of effort is applied to designing algorithms that optimize the performance of database engines.

Most databases contain many different tables. In running a business, you might need a table for your employees, another for customers, another for inventory items, and yet another for keeping track of every business transaction. Queries involving joins of multiple tables would be required in generating the payroll, billing customers, and figuring out which products to stock and which to discontinue.

Let's create another table for songs with records that have identifier, title, artist, album and year attribute values:

```
> CREATE TABLE song (
> id SMALLINT UNSIGNED NOT NULL AUTO_INCREMENT,
> title VARCHAR(100),
> artist SMALLINT UNSIGNED NOT NULL REFERENCES artists,
> album VARCHAR(100),
> year VARCHAR(4),
> PRIMARY KEY (id) ) ;
OK
```

And let's create a few song records just to experiment with:

```
> INSERT INTO song VALUES
> (NULL, 'Let Me Drive', '6', 'Love Comin\' Down', '2000'),
> (NULL, 'Two Trains', '6', 'Love Comin\' Down', '2000'),
> (NULL, 'Gone, Just Like A Train', '1', 'Gone, Just Like A Train', '1998'),
> (NULL, 'Lowdown Dirty Shame', '3', 'Blues On The Run', '1982'),
> (NULL, 'Monkey Business', '2', 'Silver Lining', '2002') ;
OK
```

Now we find all artists who've produced a song with the word "Train" in the title:

```
> SELECT artist.last, song.title FROM artist, song
> WHERE song.title LIKE "%Train%"
> AND artist.id = song.artist ;
+---------+------------------------+
| last    | title                  |
+---------+------------------------+
| Foley   | Two Trains             |
| Frisell | Gone, Just Like A Train |
+---------+------------------------+
```

And this last query finds all artists born before 1950 who produced an album after 2000:

```
> SELECT artist.last, song.album
> FROM artist, song
> WHERE artist.id = song.artist
> AND artist.birthdate < '1950-01-01'
> AND song.year > '2000' ;
+-------+---------------+
| last  | album         |
+-------+---------------+
| Raitt | Silver Lining |
+-------+---------------+
```

Databases are great for keeping track of lots of highly structured data in a format carefully designed with particular applications in mind (check out Ullman (1988) or Silberschatz, Korth, and Sudarshan (2001) for a more comprehensive introduction to the theory and practice of database systems). In some cases, large databases are even *mined* to discover interesting trends and unsuspected relationships. In mining the sales data for a chain of convenience stores, it was discovered that customers who purchase disposable diapers also often purchase beer. In an effort to encourage this trend, the store owners were advised to put the disposable diapers and the beer close to each other so as to remind forgetful customers. The programs that mine the data rely on methods from statistics and artificial intelligence, but they depend on powerful database engines to answer queries efficiently. Indeed, most SQL queries are generated not by humans typing or using fancy graphical interfaces but rather by other programs dynamically generating queries and then using the results to perform additional computations that give rise to still more queries.

SQL and its variants are basically programming languages. Any given commercial database product has extensions that let you do almost anything you could do in any other programming language. Many programmers, however, prefer to handle calculations that don't involve inserting or extracting data in some other programming language such as C++; in this case, the C++ code generates SQL queries involving INSERTs and SELECTs, sends them off as "foreign function calls" to the database program, and receives the results back so it can perform additional calculations.

A program responsible for handling online orders might generate a SQL query to find out all the items a customer has put in his or her electronic "shopping cart," generate another SQL query to determine where the customer lives, use C++ code to tally up the cost of the items and add state tax as appropriate, call another program to manage the necessary credit-card transaction, and issue a request to shipping to pack and ship the items. Such complex programs are made much simpler by the fact that the data is highly structured, so the programmer knows exactly which records contain information about purchases, billing, shipping and the like.

Not all data is so conveniently structured to suit our purposes. Most of us aren't going to take the time to organize our files (email messages, recipes, financial records) so they can be put in a database and conveniently accessed by SQL queries. One advantage in searching through your own stuff is that you generally know what you call things and may even have some idea of where you put them – music in one directory, favorite artists in another and so on. You also have some idea of what your personal data does and, more importantly, doesn't contain. For example, you'd probably know if you had a recent consumer review on digital cameras among your files. Neither of these advantages is likely to hold if you're searching in other people's stuff.

With the advent of the World Wide Web, ordinary people, not just computer professionals, are storing large amounts of unstructured data on computers so that anyone, anywhere in the world can get at that information with a click of a mouse. We'll return to the topic of searching through this information in Chapter 14, after learning more in Chapter 11 about the basic machinery that makes the World Wide Web possible.

CHAPTER FOUR

Don't Sweat the Syntax

Programming languages, like natural languages, have a vocabulary (lexicon) and rules of syntax (grammar) that you have to learn in order to communicate. Just as unfamiliar grammatical conventions can make learning a new natural language difficult, unfamiliar programming-language syntax can make learning to program difficult. English speakers learning Japanese have to get used to the fact that Japanese verbs generally come at the end of the sentence. With computer languages, the problem is made worse by the fact that computers are much less adept at handling lexically and syntactically mangled programs than humans are at grasping the meaning of garbled speech.

If you want to talk with computers, however, you're going to have to learn a programming language. Just as you learn new natural languages to communicate with other people and experience other cultures, you learn a programming language to communicate with computers and other programmers and to express computational ideas concisely and clearly. The good news is that learning one programming language makes it a lot easier to learn others.

When you start learning to program, you may find yourself consumed with sorting out the lexical and syntactic minutiae of the programming language. You'll have to look up the names of functions and operators and memorize the particular syntax required to invoke them correctly. You may end up spending obscene amounts of time tracking down obscure bugs caused by misplaced commas or missing parentheses. This is really too bad, because fooling around with commas and parentheses is not what computer programming is all about; furthermore, these annoyances can usually be avoided by using a text editor that checks for syntactic errors – dealing with such details is one of the things that computers are good at.

What is computer programming all about? It's about solving problems with computers. Unfortunately, that may not be immediately apparent in an introductory course. More often than not in beginning programming assignments, instructors tell you what you're supposed to compute – they solve the problems – and your job is simply to translate what you've been told into whatever language you're learning.

4.1   SPECIFICATIONS AND IMPLEMENTATIONS

A programming assignment might describe a computation in terms of a recipe – first do this, then do that, and so on. Such a recipe is called an *algorithm*. Programming assignments are also likely to include descriptions of various computational objects called *data structures* that organize the information needed for a computation and calling conventions called *interfaces* that specify how to use the programs you're writing. Algorithms, data structures and interfaces can be described in natural language, and the resulting description is called a *specification*. The result of translating a specification into a given computer language is called an *implementation*.

The strategy of giving beginning programmers a specification and asking them to provide an implementation has some merit. Once you've mastered the conventions of a given programming language you can start writing programs and interacting with the computer, and the more quickly you can start interacting with the computer, the more fun and positive feedback you're likely to get. However, this strategy can discourage some people who might otherwise go on to become excellent programmers and encourage others who really aren't well suited to programming. The problem is that a facility for mastering the syntax of programming languages is neither necessary nor sufficient to become a good programmer.

The hardest part of programming is transforming an initial, often vague description of what you want to do into a clear specification. If the specification is precise enough, then producing an implementation is relatively straightforward. Good programmers are, first and foremost, good problem solvers. If you like solving problems but are having some trouble getting over the initial hurdle of arcane syntax, don't get discouraged, you can overcome the syntactic irritations with a little perseverance.

Here is an example of the problem-solving part of programming. You've probably heard dire warnings about letting interest charges on credit cards accumulate. The basic idea is that compounding interest can cause an initially small unpaid balance to balloon so that the next thing you know you're up to your ears in debt. Suppose you want to understand this phenomenon more quantitatively. Specifically, you want to calculate what you would owe the credit card company after some number of months given an initial balance, a fixed interest rate, an estimated monthly payment, and an estimated monthly amount of new charges.

One approach is to think about the computation as simulating the process whereby payments are made, interest accumulates and new charges appear on your monthly statement.

Here's a natural language specification for this computation. Break the problem down into two cases. In the first case, there are no months left to simulate. This is the trivially easy special case in which you want to calculate what you owe after zero months. If the number of months is zero, then your computation should return the current balance. In the second case, there is at least one month left to simulate. To handle this case, you calculate a new balance, taking into account the interest, payments and charges for one month, and then consider the new problem of calculating what you would owe after *one month less* than originally specified, starting with the new balance.

This is called a recursive definition (recall our introduction in Chapter 1 to recursive rules in Prolog) because you repeatedly break a problem down into smaller parts and apply the same method to all the parts. Eventually the parts are so simple there is no need to break them down any further. In our example, each time you recursively consider the problem, the number of months decreases until eventually you reduce the problem to the trivially easy case.

Implementing this specification in the syntax of a given programming language may seem daunting at first, but it's really just a matter of using some admittedly rigid conventions to make sure that a linguistically challenged, literal-minded computer does the right thing. You have to specify a name for the procedure that performs the calculations – call it debt. You also need names for the arguments referring to problem parameters such as the current balance, interest rate, estimated payment, estimated charges and number of months – call them, respectively, balance, rate, payment, charges, months. Finally you have to specify the logic and flow of control for the computation. Here a simple if-then-else construction will work fine. The recursive call requires some simple math functions to compute the balance after one month, but they're relatively straightforward once you're clear about the calculations.

Here's what the full specification might look like in natural language:

Define the procedure debt as follows: The procedure is called with five arguments, balance, rate, payment, charges and months. If months is equal to zero, then exit the procedure, returning the value of balance. If months is not equal to zero, begin by introducing two new variables, new-balance and remaining-months. Let new-balance be the sum of charges plus balance plus balance times one-twelfth the interest rate minus payment. Let remaining-months be months minus one. Call the procedure debt recursively with the arguments new-balance, rate, payment, charges, and `remaining-months`. The value returned from this recursive call to `debt` is the value returned to the initial call to `debt`.

Once you've got the specification in this form, the next step really is easy, or rather will become so with some practice in the language you've chosen for implementation. Here's an implementation written in the Scheme language we introduced in Chapter 1; it lacks some bells and whistles (for example, it might be a good idea to check that months is a non-negative integer), but you get the basic idea:

```
(define (debt balance rate payment charges months)
  (if (= months 0)
      balance
    (let ((new-balance (+ charges
                          balance
                          (* balance (/ rate 12))
                          (- payment)))
          (remaining-months (- months 1)))
      (debt new-balance
            rate
            payment
            charges
            remaining-months))))
```

If I were writing this for my own use, I would dispense with the intermediate variables `new-balance` and `remaining-months`, inserting the expressions for their values (as specified in the `let` statement) directly in the recursive call as shown in the next definition. If the calculations are complicated enough, however, I generally do like to introduce intermediate variables to make the code more readable. Many programmers aspire to writing code that's as readable as natural language.

```
(define (debt balance rate payment charges months)
  (if (= months 0)
      balance
    (debt (+ charges
             balance
             (* balance (/ rate 12))
             (- payment))
          rate
          payment
          charges
          (- months 1))))
```

Just to test it out, if you start with an initial balance of zero and a fixed interest rate of 18% per year, and expect to pay $50 per month on $100 worth of purchases per month, then after four years or 48 months, you'll owe:

```
> (debt 0 0.18 50 100 48)
3478.2609643766245
```

a little over $1000 of which is interest:

```
> (- (debt 0 0.18 50 100 48) (* 50 48))
1078.2609643766245
```

You'll probably get this program wrong the first time, but even so, if the specification is correct, then you're well on your way to solving the problem. My point is that the last step, converting the problem specification into an implementation in a particular programming language, is (or will soon become as you work with the language) the easiest and most automatic part of the whole process.

It's also important to realize computer programming is as much about reading programs as it is about writing them. It's useful to learn how to scan a program, even one in an unfamiliar language, in order to extract the gist. This ability to scan and extract summaries of technical specifications has its analog in every scientific and engineering discipline, whether the relevant specifications are text-based or graphical.

Think about how you'd make sense of the schematic in Figure 4.1 illustrating Thomas Newcomen's steam engine used in the 1700s to pump water from mines. You can probably figure out how the up-and-down action of the piston on the right translates into an up-and-down action of the shaft on the left pumping water from the mine. However, you might have to look at the diagram carefully and draw on your understanding of physics to understand the role of steam in supplying the motive force.[1]

Some programmers think about programs linguistically. They analyze or *parse* programs in terms of sentences, words and parts of speech and think of constants as proper nouns, variables as pronouns or generic nouns that have different meanings depending on context, and procedures as imperative verbs. They develop an ability to squint at unfamiliar syntax, scan for the verbs and nouns and ignore the analogs of the "uhs" and "umms" punctuating everyday speech. Every parenthesis and

---

[1] Newcomen's engine, like that of James Watt, was an "atmospheric" engine. As the piston is raised by the force of gravity pulling the heavy pump shaft down, a valve opens admitting slightly pressurized steam into the lower part of the cylinder. When the piston reaches the top, the steam valve closes and a second valve opens, spraying cool water into the cylinder. This condenses the steam back into water, creating a vacuum that pulls the piston down and thereby raises the pump shaft.

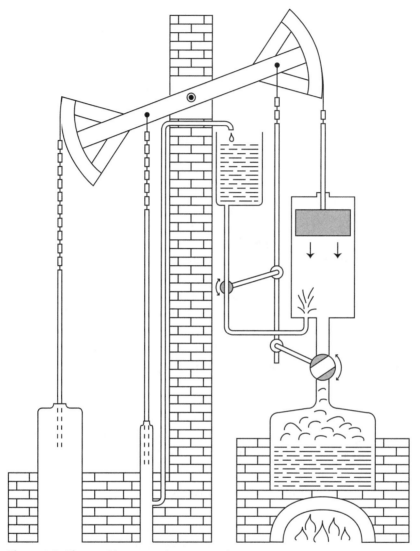

Figure 4.1: Thomas Newcomen's steam engine

semicolon in a computer program conveys some meaning, but some of the syntax doesn't contain enough information to bother puzzling over.

With practice, you'll get used to extracting the gist of unfamiliar syntax. Hardly a day passes that some piece of arcane syntax doesn't whiz past as I'm invoking, installing, compiling and otherwise talking with machines. Happily, I rarely have to go back and figure out what the mysterious character sequences mean.

4.2 SYNTACTIC VARIATIONS ACROSS LANGUAGES

I can't say, however, that a facility for working with different programming languages and hence an ability to deal with syntax is unimportant. Professional programmers often have to deal with several languages in developing a given application. After a while, you learn to look past the syntax to the underlying meaning.

Let's take a particularly simple program written in Scheme and consider its syntax in more detail. The factorial function, notated $n!$ and spoken "n factorial," takes a non-negative integer as its only argument and returns 0 for $n = 0$ or the product of $1, 2, 3, \ldots$, up to n, for $n > 0$; thus, $4! = 1 * 2 * 3 * 4 = 24$. Practically speaking, $n!$ is the number of ways of ordering n items. Most large programs rely on libraries full of mathematical functions like factorial for everything from document formatting to financial planning.

Here's how we might write factorial in Scheme:

```
(define (factorial n)
    (if (= n 0)
        1
        (* n (factorial (- n 1)))))
```

As in the earlier example, I've defined factorial recursively. Mathematical expressions in Lisp and Scheme in particular are written in *Polish notation*, with the operator appearing first; thus instead of writing (3 + (3 * 3)), where the parentheses are optional, you would write (+ 3 (* 3 3)) and the parentheses are required by Scheme syntax.

Let's make sure that our implementation works:

```
> (factorial 3)
6
> (factorial 4)
24
> (factorial 5)
120
> (factorial 6)
720
```

Seems OK, but given my earlier warning you might be suspicious about negative numbers. The factorial of a negative integer is rarely useful and you'll usually generate an error if you try to compute -3 factorial in, say, a financial program. If you tried to compute (factorial -3) as defined, the computation would not terminate or would terminate with an error. A better implementation would test for a negative argument and terminate the computation with an informative error message, but we won't worry about such niceties now. For present purposes, our simple definition is easy to understand and illustrates some points about Lisp syntax in particular and programming language syntax more generally.

In the definition of `factorial`, the `define` tells the computer that we're about to define a function. The expression `(factorial n)` immediately following the `define` specifies the name of the function – `factorial`, the number of arguments – one in this case, and how the arguments are to be referred to in the function definition – the single argument is referred to as n. The expression `(if (= n 1)` `1 (* n (factorial (- n 1))))` is the function definition and specifies how the computation is to be carried out. In English, the specification reads as follows: if n is equal to 1 then return the value 1, otherwise return the value of n times the value returned by recursively calling `factorial` with the argument n minus 1.

Here's a variation on factorial in which we've adopted a different syntax for calling functions, `function( arguments )` instead of `(function argu-ments)`, infix notation `(n == 1)` instead of prefix notation `(= n 1)`, and different primitive functions and predicates, `==` instead of `=` for numerical equivalence. We've eliminated the `define` so we'll have to make sure that the computer doesn't confuse this definition with some other sort of specification.

```
factorial( n )
   if ( n == 0 )
      1
      n * factorial( n - 1 )
```

Without indentation, this definition could be interpreted in a number of ways. In particular, without indentation, it's not clear which expressions correspond to the various parts of the if-then-else statement. In the next variation, we use curly brackets and semicolons instead of parentheses to set off statements and larger blocks of code, and we use the keyword `else` to identify the else part of the if-then-else statement:

```
factorial( n ) {
   if ( n == 0 )
      1;
      else n * factorial( n - 1 );
}
```

Many languages require the programmer to specify the *type* of each variable and the type of the values returned by each function. For example, integer, string and character are primitive types available in most programming languages. Scheme doesn't require such a specification. Also, some languages require that a function definition explicitly indicate what the function returns. In the next variation, we make use of the `return` keyword and introduce a variable `result` to keep track of the returned value of the factorial function. We use the `int` type specifier to indicate the type of n and `result` as well as the type of the result returned by `factorial`. Note that `==` is a predicate used to test for equivalence, while `=` is the assignment operator (not to be confused with the Scheme predicate) that assigns the variable appearing on the left-hand side of the operator to the value of the expression on the right-hand side. Finally, the indentation and formatting of the function definition have been adjusted slightly to suit the prevailing conventions for this sort of syntax.

```
int factorial( int n ) {
        int result;
        if ( n == 0 )
           result = 1;
        else result = n * factorial( n - 1 );
        return result;
}
```

We've transformed our Scheme definition of `factorial` into code written in a different language. This program fragment would work as part of a program in Java or C. We'd need to wrap it in some additional syntax to run it, but the actual definition is complete.

Here's how the code fragment might appear in a complete Java program that simply prints out the value of 3!:

```
class Factorial {
   public static void main( String[] args ) {
      System.out.println( factorial( 3 ) );
   }
   public static int factorial( int n ) {
      int result;
      if ( n == 0 )
         result = 1;
      else result = n * factorial( n - 1 );
      return result;
   }
}
```

Running this program takes a few additional steps. Assuming that the code resides in a file called `Factorial.java`, now I display the code using the Unix cat command, compile it using the Java compiler javac, and then run it using the Java interpreter java (I typed everything to the right of the % prompt and the various programs are responsible for the rest):

```
% cat Factorial.java
class Factorial {
    public static void main( String[] args ) {
        System.out.println( factorial( 3 ) );
    }
    public static int factorial( int n ) {
        int result;
        if ( n == 0 )
            result = 1;
        else result = n * factorial( n - 1 );
        return result;
    }
}
% javac Factorial.java
% java Factorial
6
```

If I were working in C, the wrapper code would be somewhat different and the steps of compiling and invoking the program would be different, but not that much:

```
% cat factorial.c
main () {
    printf("%d\n", factorial( 3 ) );
}

int factorial( int n ) {
        int result;
        if ( n == 0 )
            result = 1;
        else result = n * factorial( n - 1 );
        return result;
}
% cc -o factorial.o factorial.c
% factorial.o
6
```

The point is that after a while the syntax won't matter that much to you. You'll use an editor to write programs, you'll submit your programs to other programs, compilers and interpreters that will convert them into a form that can be directly run a computer and then you'll execute those programs. The steps may vary but the basic idea remains the same. The hard part, indeed the creative part, is coming up with the specifications that solve problems. After some years of practice, if you stumble on a program written in a language you're not expert in, say Mathematica,

```
In[1]:= factorial[n_Integer] := If[n == 0, 1, n * factorial[n - 1]]

In[2]:= factorial[3]

Out[2]= 6
```

you'll just squint at the unfamiliar notation and after a couple of lines say, "I get it! It's just the factorial function in yet another syntactic variation – no sweat."

4.3 STYLISTIC VARIATIONS ACROSS IMPLEMENTATIONS

Variations across languages are just one source of variability in implementing specifications. Even within a particular language there are typically many different ways of writing even the simplest of functions. Here's an implementation of the factorial function using the Java/C syntax and employing an iterative rather than recursive strategy:

```
int factorial( int n ) {
      int result = 1;
      for ( int i = 2; i <= n; i++ ) {
          result = result * i;
      }
      return result;
}
```

An integer counter is introduced in the "for loop" to count down from n to 2.

Here's another implementation using a different iterative construct (a "while loop") and making the argument variable do double duty as the counter:

```
int factorial( int n ) {
      int result = 1;
      while ( n > 1 ) {
          result = result * n;
          n = n - 1;
      }
      return result;
}
```

And here's an alternative implementation in Scheme using an additional func-tion to introduce counter and result variables. While the auxiliary function in-cludes a recursive call, this implementation is really more in the spirit of the first of the two iterative implementations:

```
(define (factorial n)
    (aux-factorial 1 1 n))

(define (aux-factorial result i n)
    (if (> i n)
        result
        (aux-factorial (* result i)
                       (+ i 1)
                       n)))
```

In time you'll find a programming style that suits you, probably using different strategies as the situation warrants and your aesthetic sense dictates. Even as writers search for the right word, the phrase that most perfectly conveys their thoughts, so programmers look for the implementation that most elegantly solves the problem. Might not sound like a high art form to you, but programming is definitely a craft with its own aesthetic.

4.4   DEVELOPING A FACILITY FOR LANGUAGE

You might think that to learn a new programming language you buy a book de-scribing its syntax and then slog through the chapters until you understand all the details. Perhaps some programmers learn this way, but most people learn new programming languages the same way they learn new natural languages: by learn-ing to say the things they want or need to say and attending to the differences between languages.

If you're learning C and you know Scheme, you'll probably want to figure out how to translate (define (*function arguments*) *definition*) into *function*(*arguments*) { *definition* }. If you're learning Mathematica and you know C, you'll be interested in turning for (*start*; *test*; *increment*) { *body* } into For[*start*, *test*, *increment*, *body*]. Most of us aren't interested in communicating syntax, we're interested in communicating meaning.

Learning your first programming language is a bit like learning your first natural language; it takes time, patience and a willingness to experiment. And, while the range of meaning you can convey in a programming language is virtually unlimited, expressing a particular idea so that a computer can understand it can be pretty painful. If you want to tell a robot to walk down the hall and turn left at the corridor with the ugly beige carpet, you're going to have to write a lot of statements of the form for (int i = 1; i < n; i++) { ... }.

To program a computer you have translate your way of thinking about the world into primitive operations like adding and multiplying numbers, testing if a number is zero and using if-then conditional statements to control execution. Once you understand how to combine these primitive operations to do more complicated calculations, you're on the road to becoming a computer programmer – the syntax really has very little to do with it. Instead of thinking of the computer as a parent teaching you how to communicate with it, you'll be teaching the computer by building a vocabulary that will let you rise above the primitive operations and enable you to communicate fluidly.

CHAPTER FIVE

Computational Muddles

There is a reason I liken computations to evanescent spirits. They are called into being with obscure incantations, spin filaments of data into complex webs of information, and then vanish with little trace of their ephemeral calculations. Of course, there are observable side effects, say when a computation activates a physical device or causes output to be sent to a printer, displayed on a screen or stored in a file. But the computations themselves are difficult to observe in much the way your thoughts are difficult to observe.

I'm exaggerating somewhat; after all, unlike our brains, computers are designed by human beings. We can trace every signal and change that occurs in a computer. The problem is that a complete description of all those signals and changes does not help much in understanding what's going on during a complex computation; in particular, it doesn't help figure out what went wrong when the results of a computation don't match our expectations.

An abstraction is a way of thinking about problems or complex phenomena that ignores some aspects in order to simplify thinking about others. The idea of a digital computer is itself an abstraction. The computers we work with are electrical devices whose circuits propagate continuously varying signals; they don't operate with discrete integers 0, 1, 2, ..., or for that matter with binary digits 0 and 1. The idea that computers deal with 1s and 0s is an abstraction.

The dependability of this abstraction is a testimony to the many electrical engineers and physicists who developed modern computers. It would complicate things considerably if every once in a while when you add 1 and 0 you got something a little more, say 1.0012, or a little less, say 0.99998, than 1. If you're a digital circuit designer, you can never forget that the signals in computer circuits are continuous; your job is to make them behave according to the digital abstraction. As a programmer you can safely adopt the digital abstraction, but you'll need additional abstractions to develop sophisticated software.

70

5.1 COMPUTATIONAL MODELS

The term *computational model* is often used to describe an abstraction that simplifies thinking about computation. Chapter 1's abstraction of Unix pipes passing information between commands in shell scripts is a computational model. The metaphor of files as fluid flowing continuously through pipes is potentially misleading. However, we can easily weave a somewhat more complicated story around the pipe abstraction to provide a more accurate picture of what's going on during the execution of a shell script.

Think of each command in a shell script as a bureaucrat responsible for some particular paper-shuffling task in a company. Imagine that the bureaucrats are linked to one another via a set of pneumatic tubes of the sort found in 19th-century factories and office buildings. To send a purchase order to the fellow in accounting for approval, you put it in a little capsule and stuff it in the right tube; the capsule is sucked through the system and ends up on the desk of the fellow in accounting in a matter of seconds. The messages thus zip through these pneumatic tubes and land on the desk of one bureaucrat who processes each message in the order in which it arrived and then sends it along to the next bureaucrat by placing it into his outgoing pneumatic tube. A little quaint, perhaps, but easy to visualize and it does a pretty good job of describing reality. With this abstraction, we move from plumbing pipes carrying some sort of fluid (a continuous view of the world) to pneumatic tubes carrying individual messages (a discrete view of the world).

As we move from one-line shell scripts composed of powerful commands whose inner workings we largely ignore to programs consisting of many lines and involving components of considerable complexity whose inner workings we have to comprehend and in many cases design, we need more powerful computational models. But just because these models are more powerful doesn't mean they have to be more complex. In this chapter we'll be looking at some relatively simple models that can be used to understand a broad range of computations. We'll be going back over some of the territory we covered in Chapter 4 but this time with different objectives in mind.

I've heard some computer scientists say that the most important prerequisite for learning how to program is knowing a little algebra. While this is largely true, it is rarely a comfort to students thinking of taking a computer science class. Many people found learning algebra painful, all the more so because it wouldn't go away – you needed it for all sorts of other things. Fortunately, the kind of algebra required to carry out basic programming tasks is of a particularly benign sort. Those of you who aced algebra, however: don't get too excited, because being good

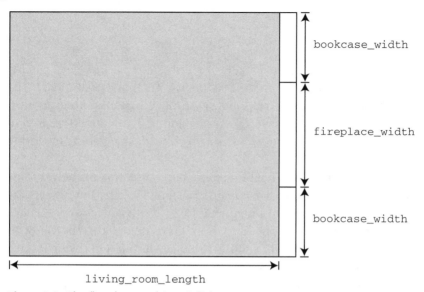

bookcase_width

fireplace_width

bookcase_width

living_room_length

Figure 5.1: The floor layout of Anne's living room

at algebra is not the only skill you need to become a good computer scientist or programmer.

To follow the connection from algebra to programming, consider this simple word problem like those you met in grade school:

> Anne wants to buy carpeting to cover her living-room floor. The room is rectangular and 8 meters long. At one end of the room, there is a 3-meter-wide fireplace flanked by two identical bookcases that, together with the fireplace, take up the entire width of the room. The bookcases are 2 meters wide each. The fireplace and two bookcases are built into the wall and don't cover any of the floor space. The carpeting Anne wants costs $5 per square meter. How much will Anne have to pay for her new carpet?

How would you solve this problem? I usually start by drawing a diagram like the one in Figure 5.1; we want to calculate the shaded area. Next you'll have to recall the mathematical relationship involving area and the dimensions (length and width) of a rectangle. Algebraically, you would write this down as a formula involving three variables or terms that we specify using easily remembered (mnemonic) names:

```
living_room_area = living_room_length * living_room_width
```

Following a convention common in programming languages, the * here stands for multiplication. For simplicity, all the terms in our formulas will be *unitless*, which means we'll have to be careful not to add a term specified in meters to one specified in kilometers.

You'd also write down the the specified quantities and relationships in the word problem, introducing additional terms as needed:

```
living_room_length = 8

bookcase_width = 2

fireplace_width = 3

cost_per_square_meter = 5

living_room_width = fireplace_width + (2 * bookcase_width)
```

and the formula for answering the question posed:

```
total_cost = cost_per_square_meter * living_room_area
```

Now to calculate the answer, you just "plug and chug", as engineering students like to say. Starting with the basic formula

```
total_cost = cost_per_square_meter * living_room_area
```

you proceed by substituting (the "plug" part) the appropriate formulas and values for the terms in the formula and simplifying (the "chug" part) by performing arithmetic operations (addition, subtraction, multiplication) as appropriate:

```
total_cost = cost_per_square_meter *
             living_room_length * living_room_width

total_cost = cost_per_square_meter *
             living_room_length *
             (fireplace_width + (2 * bookcase_width))

total_cost = cost_per_square_meter *
             living_room_length * (fireplace_width + (2 * 2)))

total_cost = cost_per_square_meter *
             (living_room_length * (fireplace_width + 4))
```

```
total_cost = cost_per_square_meter * (living_room_length * (3 + 4))

total_cost = cost_per_square_meter * (living_room_length * 7)

total_cost = cost_per_square_meter * (8 * 7)

total_cost = cost_per_square_meter * 56

total_cost = 5 * 56

total_cost = 280
```

Note how our original formula

```
total_cost = cost_per_square_meter * living_room_area
```

expanded and contracted as we made substitutions and simplified subformulas.

In a language like Scheme, we'd specify the entities and relationships much as we did here, though we'd have to adhere to Scheme's syntax, which takes a little getting used to. In Scheme, an expression like

```
(define living_room_length 8)
```

tells the Scheme interpreter that we are defining the term `living_room_length` to be 8. If we subsequently ask Scheme to "evaluate" `living_room_length`, it looks up this definition and returns the "value" 8. Here's what interacting with the Scheme interpreter looks like:

```
> (define living_room_length 8)
> living_room_length
8
```

The first typed expression was interpreted as a request to make the indicated definition; Scheme had nothing to say about this so the prompt immediately reappeared. The second typed expression was interpreted as a request to "evaluate" the expression, which Scheme did by printing out the result. (This form of interaction is called a "read, evaluate and print loop" for obvious reasons.) We can continue to define the other terms in our word problem:

```
> (define bookcase_width  2)
> (define fireplace_width 3)
```

```
> (define cost_per_square_meter 5)
> (define living_room_width (+ fireplace_width (* 2 bookcase_width)))
```

The last line is bit different: The definition is a compound expression that involves previously defined terms as well as mathematical operators in Polish notation (operators precede their arguments). When Scheme sees an expression of this compound form, it evaluates it by replacing the values of the terms in the expression with their values as defined previously and then simplifying to obtain a value to use as the definition of the new term, `living_room_width` here. If we submit this term to the interpreter now, it looks up the newly minted definition, as you might expect:

```
> living_room_width
7
```

The next definition is a very different animal:

```
> (define (total_cost unit_cost quantity) (* unit_cost quantity))
```

Scheme behaves very differently when it encounters an attempt to define an expression of the form (*some-term args*), where *some-term* is a placeholder for the name of a "function" (also called a "procedure") and *args* is a placeholder for one or more terms called "formal parameters" (also called the "arguments" to the function). Unlike the earlier definition in which Scheme evaluated the compound expression, when a function is defined, Scheme stores both the calling pattern, here (`total_cost unit_cost quantity`), and the function definition, (`* unit_cost quantity`). It doesn't evaluate the function definition as it did *expression* in a definition of the form (`define` *name expression*). A definition of the form (`define` (*name args*) *expression*) is special in that it provides a general recipe for performing a computation, a recipe that is carried out whenever Scheme is asked to evaluate an expression of the form (*name args*).

We use this form of definition again to specify one last formula:

```
> (define (living_room_area width length) (* width length))
```

Now that we've defined all of the relevant terms and formulas, we can ask Scheme to evaluate an expression corresponding to the answer to the word problem:

```
> (total_cost cost_per_square_meter
              (living_room_area living_room_width
                                living_room_length))
```

Here are the steps Scheme takes to evaluate this expression:

```
(total_cost cost_per_square_meter
            (living_room_area living_room_width
                              living_room_length))
(total_cost 5
            (living_room_area living_room_width
                              living_room_length))
(total_cost 5
            (living_room_area 7
                              living_room_length))
(total_cost 5 (living_room_area 7 8))
(total_cost 5 (* 7 8))
(total_cost 5 56)
(* 5 56)
280
```

To be more precise, this is just one possible sequence of steps that a Scheme interpreter might take in order to evaluate the expression. In writing code for a Scheme interpreter, a programmer has two primary goals: first, to make sure that the interpreter evaluates expressions according to the semantics of the language and second, to make sure that those evaluations are done quickly. The semantics of a language specifies the meaning of expressions formed in accord with the syntax of that language. Scheme has a formal and an informal (intuitive) semantics and I'll rely entirely on the latter in this chapter. As with a spoken or natural language, an intuitive semantics for a programming language explains the meaning of more complex expressions in terms of the meaning of simpler ones; for example, the meaning of (+ 1 2) is 3. In general, we'll use our understanding of arithmetic and algebra in deciphering the meaning of Scheme expressions.

As an alternative to our first specification and to make the Scheme calculations look a little more like our algebraic manipulations, we can define a special-purpose function to replace our previous definition of living_room_width:

```
> (define (living_room_width bookcase_width fireplace_width)
      (+ fireplace_width (* 2 bookcase_width)))
```

In defining this function, as in invoking total_cost, we used more than one line. When functions become longer and more complicated, programmers use indentation and formatting to keep track of arguments and nested expressions. I often line up arguments vertically, as in this alternative formatting of the living_room_width definition:

```
> (define (living_room_width bookcase_width fireplace_width)
    (+ fireplace_width
      (* 2
        bookcase_width)))
```

Formatting is just one way in which programmers try to make code more readable, easier to understand and hence easier to write and modify, both for the original programmer and for other programmers who might want to use or adapt the code later.

5.2 THE SUBSTITUTION MODEL

With our new definition for living_room_width, the computation looks more like the algebraic substitutions and simplifications we saw earlier. The model of computation as a sequence of substitutions and simplifications, called *the substitution model*, is probably the most useful abstraction for thinking about computing. Most programmers, whether they know it or not, use the substitution model every day.

When we first defined living_room_width, we assigned it the number 7, which was the result of a computation. The second time we defined living_room_width we defined it as a function that, when invoked with the proper arguments, computes the width of the living room from a formula (specified in the function definition). Each time living_room_width is invoked with the correct number of arguments, it substitutes the arguments into the formula and evaluates the result.

You may have been puzzled by the fact that the formal parameters to living_room_width have the same names as two terms we defined earlier, bookcase_width and fireplace_width. The whole business of deciphering the meaning of terms and establishing different contexts in which they can have different meanings is important in designing programming languages that can be used to build large programs involving many different programmers. Even a single programmer is likely to use the same term in multiple independent contexts.

The letter "x" must be one of the most frequent variable names in mathematics. In the next exchange, it should be pretty clear what I mean even though I use x twice as a formal parameter, once to assign it a value and once to refer to it as the argument to a function:

```
> (define (square x) (* x x))
> (define (double x) (+ x x))
> (define x 3)
> (define y (double (square x)))
> y
18
```

Here's the new method of calculating the answer to our word program:

```
> (total_cost cost_per_square_meter
            (living_room_area (living_room_width bookcase_width
                                                fireplace_width)
                              living_room_length))
280
```

And here is the series of substitutions and simplifications the Scheme interpreter performed:

```
(total_cost cost_per_square_meter
            (living_room_area (living_room_width bookcase_width
                                                fireplace_width)
                              living_room_length))
(total_cost 5
            (living_room_area (living_room_width bookcase_width
                                                fireplace_width)
                              living_room_length))
(total_cost 5
            (living_room_area (living_room_width 2
                                                fireplace_width)
                              living_room_length))
(total_cost 5
            (living_room_area (living_room_width 2 3)
                              living_room_length))
(total_cost 5
            (living_room_area (+ 3 (* 2 2))
                              living_room_length))
(total_cost 5
            (living_room_area (+ 3 4) living_room_length))
(total_cost 5 (living_room_area 7 living_room_length))
```

```
(total_cost 5 (living_room_area 7 8))
(total_cost 5 (* 7 8))
(total_cost 5 56)
(* 5 56)
280
```

We can use this same trick of substitution to explain the calculations performed by the factorial function in Chapter 4:

```
> (define (factorial n) (if (= n 1) 1 (* n (factorial (- n 1)))))
> (factorial 3)
6
```

Here's the sequence of substitutions and simplifications; we don't simplify any subformulas unless we have to:

```
(factorial 3)
(if (= 3 1) 1 (* 3 (factorial (- 3 1))))
(if #f 1 (* 3 (factorial (- 3 1))))
(* 3 (factorial (- 3 1)))
(* 3 (factorial 2))
(* 3 (if (= 2 1) 1 (* 2 (factorial (- 2 1)))))
(* 3 (if #f 1 (* 2 (factorial (- 2 1)))))
(* 3 (* 2 (factorial (- 2 1))))
(* 3 (* 2 (factorial 1)))
(* 3 (* 2 (if (= 1 1) 1 (* 1 (factorial (- 1 1))))))
(* 3 (* 2 (if #t 1 (* 1 (factorial (- 1 1))))))
(* 3 (* 2 1))
(* 3 2)
6
```

You may have stumbled over interpreting the expression (if (= 3 1) 1 (factorial (- 3 1))). Scheme interprets this as saying: if 3 is equal to 1 then this expression simplifies to 1, otherwise it simplifies to (factorial (- 3 1)). A so-called "conditional" statement of the form (if *test then else*), where *test*, *then* and *else* are expressions, is interpreted as follows: if the *test* expression evaluates to true (#t in Scheme), evaluate the *then* expression and substitute its value for the conditional statement; but if the *test* expression evaluates to false (#f in Scheme), don't mess with the *then* expression at all but instead evaluate the *else* expression by substituting its value for the conditional statement. The `test` statements can be quite complex in general, combining simpler tests using operators such as `or` and `and` and `not`. For example, the expression

```
(if (and test1 (or test2 (not (test3)))) (+ 1 2) (* 1 2))
```

evaluates to 3 (`(+ 1 2)`) if `test1` is true and either `test2` is true or `test3` is false and otherwise to 2 (`(* 1 2)`).

The exact sequence of substitutions and simplifications used in calculating (`factorial 3`) is complicated. To take a somewhat closer look, we'll use a program called a *stepper* that walks us through Scheme's steps in interpreting (`factorial 3`) (at least when viewed through the abstraction of the substitution model). Here is a sequence of transformations in which each transformation has the form *initial expression* => *resulting expression* and the substitutions are highlighted by enclosing the pre- and post-transformation subexpressions in square brackets:

```
[(factorial 3)] =>
[(if (= 3 1) 1 (* 3 (factorial (- 3 1))))]

(if [(= 3 1)] 1 (* 3 (factorial (- 3 1)))) =>
(if [#f] 1 (* 3 (factorial (- 3 1))))

[(if #f 1 (* 3 (factorial (- 3 1))))] =>
[(* 3 (factorial (- 3 1)))]

(* 3 (factorial [(- 3 1)])) =>
(* 3 (factorial [2]))

(* 3 [(factorial 2)]) =>
(* 3 [(if (= 2 1) 1 (* 2 (factorial (- 2 1))))])

(* 3 (if [(= 2 1)] 1 (* 2 (factorial (- 2 1))))) =>
(* 3 (if [#f] 1 (* 2 (factorial (- 2 1)))))

(* 3 [(if #f 1 (* 2 (factorial (- 2 1))))]) =>
(* 3 [(* 2 (factorial (- 2 1)))])

(* 3 (* 2 (factorial [(- 2 1)]))) =>
(* 3 (* 2 (factorial [1])))

(* 3 (* 2 [(factorial 1)])) =>
(* 3 (* 2 [(if (= 1 1) 1 (* 1 (factorial (- 1 1))))]))
```

```
(* 3 (* 2 (if [(= 1 1)] 1 (* 1 (factorial (- 1 1)))))) =>
(* 3 (* 2 (if [#t] 1 (* 1 (factorial (- 1 1))))))

(* 3 (* 2 [(if #t 1 (* 1 (factorial (- 1 1))))])) =>
(* 3 (* 2 [1]))

(* 3 [(* 2 1)]) =>
(* 3 [2])

[(* 3 2)] =>
[6]
```

The stepper gives us a close look at a Scheme computation as seen through the lens of the substitution model. Very few programmers want to look at a complex computation at this level of detail, but in trying to find a problem with program (a process called *debugging*) they may look this closely at selected parts of a computation. For instance, you could tell the stepper to step through only the transformations for selected functions and summarize all other computations – for example, use [(factorial 3)] => [6] to summarize the computations of the factorial function. As much detail as there is in this sequence of transformations, as much or more is abstracted away; at the level of primitive instructions executed directly by the CPU, the computation involves many more steps than those few shown here.

5.3 SYNTAX AND STYLE REVISITED

In defining the factorial function, I used a powerful method that sometimes throws students for a loop (pun intended, as you'll soon discover). The definition of factorial is *recursive*, meaning that I used factorial to define factorial: the term being defined appears in or "recurs" in the definition.

```
(define (factorial n)
    (if (= n 1)
        1
        (* n
           (factorial (- n 1)))))
```

I promise you that this really isn't a big deal and it seems perfectly natural to lots of students, particularly when they see how it works and aren't scared off by a teacher who feels recursion is somehow "abnormal." Some folks think that the "normal" way of computing factorial runs something like this:

```
int factorial( int n ) {
        int result = 1;
        for ( int i = 2; i <= n; i++ ) {
            result = result * i;
        }
        return result;
}
```

This is the same syntax for the factorial function that we met at the end of Chapter 4. In prose form, it would read something like: to compute the function n factorial, first assign the variable `result` to be equal to 1, then begin a loop in which the "iteration" variable i is first set to 2 (`i = 2`) and then incremented by 1 (`i++`) on each iteration until i is equal to n; on each iteration in which the body of the loop is executed (those iterations in which i is assigned one of 2, 3, ..., n - 1), reassign the variable `result` to have its old value times the value of the iteration variable, i. Finally after you've completed the loop, return the last assigned value of `result`.

Asked to calculate `factorial(3)`, this program first sets the variable `result` to 1, then starts through the "for loop," setting `result` to be `result` times 2 (`result` is now equal to 2) on the first iteration, and `result` to be `result` times 3 (`result` is now equal to 6) on the second and last iteration, before returning the final value of `result`, which is 6 in this case. Each time through the loop, the program checks to see if i is greater than 3; if so, it exits the loop without executing the body. In C, the body of a loop is set off with curly brackets { and } following the keyword `for` and the iteration variable specification (`int i = 2; i <= n; i++`), so that, in the last definition, the body is just the single statement `result = result * i`. This is a perfectly good way of calculating factorial and I have no problem whatsoever with it, but the recursive definition is also fine and, to my mind, simple and elegant.

You might worry that a recursive definition would keep calling itself indefinitely, and indeed this is a concern in writing recursive function definitions. The trick is to arrange things so that some argument (assignment to a formal parameter) in the recursive call steadily gets closer to the terminating condition, (= n 1) in the case of factorial. It takes a little practice, but once you get the hang of it, designing recursive definitions with appropriate terminating conditions becomes pretty easy. If you really have an aversion to recursion (or experience some dissonance with assonance), then there are always other languages that are less elegant and less cool ... just kidding; most dialects of Lisp support other methods of iteration besides recursion.

Indeed, Lisp programmers often use the equivalent of C `for` loops. The Scheme do construct is a general iterative construct. When an expression of the form (`do` (`var-init-step-expressions`) (`test exit`) `body`) is evaluated, each variable mentioned in the list of `var-init-step` expressions is bound to the result of evaluating the variable's corresponding `init` expression, then the termination condition `test` is evaluated. If the termination condition evaluates to true (#t), then any `exit` expressions are evaluated. If the termination condition evaluates to false (#f), then the expressions in the `body` are evaluated. On each subsequent iteration, each of the variables is updated using its corresponding `step` expression if present. The Scheme expression (`do` ((i 1 (+ i 1))) ((= i n)) `body`) is essentially equivalent to `for` (int i = 1; i < n; i++) { `body` } in C or Java.

Here's a translation of the "normal" implementation of factorial to Scheme using do:

```
(define (factorial n)
  (let ((result 1))
    (do ((i 2 (+ i 1)))
        ((> i n) result)
      (set! result (* result i)))))
```

We won't explore `let` (it's used to introduce local variables) or `set!` (it's an assignment operator) until the next chapter, but you should have a pretty good idea of how this implementation works. You may prefer this to the recursive definition; however, it's worthwhile becoming comfortable with both styles, as you're likely to encounter both in reading code.

While we're on the subject of preferences, if you went off and got a programming job today, you'd probably end up using Java, C, C++, various web-page formatting languages like HTML and various scripting languages like JavaScript, Perl and PHP. In a couple of years, perhaps C#, Python and XHTML will be the hot languages to know. At this stage, though, don't worry too much about which language to program in, just learn to program and have some fun at it. If you end up programming for your own professional or recreational purposes, almost any language with a reasonably large and dedicated following will do just fine. And if you learn to program well, picking up a new language will be relatively easy.

By the way, the substitution model works fine for understanding any program written in any programming language. However, to have a completely general model, we'd need to extend the model to handle assignments, for example, i = 1 in Java or C and `set!` in Scheme, loops and other flow-of-control mechanisms. We'd also have to extend it to handle programming concepts like object-oriented programming. Discussing these extensions would take us too far afield from my aim of giving you a high-level overview of interesting computational ideas. So let's leave the substitution model behind and explore some different computational models, including some that lead us to an object-oriented view of programming.

CHAPTER SIX

Getting Oriented

On the morning I began this chapter, I was driving into work and passed a sign near a grade school advertising a "Bug Safari". When I got to work, I found out from the Web that "Butterfly Walks", "Spider Safaris", "Pond Dips" and similar excursions are regular fare at summer camps and neighborhood activity centers. This intrigued me: who would lead these tours? I initially thought that the most likely candidates would be trained entomologists or specialists such as lepidopterists. An entomologist studies bugs, beetles, butterflies, spiders and the like (not to be confused – as I usually do – with the similar-sounding etymologist, someone who studies the derivation of words), while lepidopterists specialize in lepidoptera, butterflies and moths.

But then I realized that it's a rare specialist who can resist being distracted by his or her own specialty. I thought about what this tendency might portend for my attempt to speak to a general audience about concepts in computer science. By most accounts, I'm an expert in computer science and a specialist in artificial intelligence. But just as a trained and practicing physicist is not an expert in all matters spanning the length and breadth of physics, from quantum electrodynamics to cosmology, so I'm not an expert in all areas of computer science.

In this chapter, I'll be talking about programming languages, an area of computer science about which I know a fair bit but certainly am not an expert. As your guide for today's "Computational Safari", I'll introduce you to some interesting programming-language flora and fauna, but don't be surprised if my interest in artificial intelligence biases my choice of topics. Programming languages often spring from the needs of particular areas of computer science, and artificial intelligence has been a driving force in the creation of many languages including Lisp, Scheme and, as we'll see, various object-oriented languages.

6.1 STRUCTURING LARGE PROGRAMS

In Chapter 5 we encountered the substitution model. In a purely theoretical sense, this model provides all the power or "expressiveness" you'll ever need. Computational models are often characterized in terms of their expressiveness, the extent to which they allow you to express or specify computations. One model, call it the plain vanilla model, is less expressive than a second model, call it vanilla with savory chocolate bits, if, say, you can specify how to add numbers of any size in the vanilla-with-chocolate-bits model but only how to add numbers less than 1,000 in the plain vanilla model.

Although the substitution model is as powerful as any computational model can be, models have characteristics apart from power that differentiate them. Paramount among these characteristics are simplicity, comprehensibility, and the ability to organize or *structure* large programs. The substitution model is certainly simple to learn and easy to comprehend, but it doesn't help particularly in structuring large programs.

The first thing you should realize when considering a large program is that any program of, say, several tens of thousands of lines of code is likely to have been written by more than one programmer. Even if it was written by one person, most merely mortal programmers can't keep all the details in a large software project in their heads at the same time, so it's almost as though there are several programmers. The way most professional programmers deal with large amounts of code is to break it down into smaller chunks, called variously libraries, packages, classes, and modules.

Each chunk is designed to provide a particular service or solve a particular part of the overall problem. The application programming interface (API) of a given chunk specifies how programs can use the functionality provided by that chunk. The API for a library that supports drawing geometric diagrams might include instructions on how to draw rectangles or circles on your screen; these parts of the geometry library are made "public" so that other programmers can use them.

In order to implement a geometry library you might also need a lot of support functions, say functions that use trigonometry to rotate and redraw rectangles, that aren't part of the library's interface. These trig functions are considered "private." The programmer using a library knows only the public procedures specified in its API. The author of a library is free to rewrite the internals of the library and, in particular, to rewrite or rename its private functions.

In addition to hiding unnecessary detail from the programmer, this method of breaking large problems into bite-sized chunks allows groups of programmers to work together, share code (APIs at least) and improve existing libraries without interrupting one another. In theory, a team of programmers can partition a large project into a bunch of interacting modules, specify the interfaces for the modules and then go off and work independently to write the internals of their respective modules. In practice, large software projects require almost constant communication among the developers.

Libraries and modules also establish a discipline for naming things. Within a library you can use any names you like for private functions as long as you're consistent within that library. Someone else writing the internals of another library can use the same names with no fear of confusion. Two libraries can use the same public name. For example, both the `geometry` library and the `euclid` library may have functions called `circle` that perform different operations. If you want to use both libraries in the same program, you have to disambiguate your use by indicating the context somehow, say by appending the library name, so that `geometry::circle` is unambiguously different from `euclid::circle`. All this may seem a little picayune when you're just starting out, but such common-sense conventions are essential in building large programs.

This is an example of what happens when you hire a myrmecologist (someone who studies ants) to lead a bug safari and then run into a bunch of interesting moths – you'll probably get some useful information about moths but not the same sort of information you'd have gotten had you hired a lepidopterist. I no longer write large programs, though I commonly write programs that use several libraries. Occasionally I write a library myself; you get a sense after a while of when it makes sense to take a chunk of code and turn it into a separate library. I've never worked as part of a team of programmers to develop a large project as a set of loosely coupled modules whose interaction is completely specified by their respective APIs, but it seems a perfectly reasonable way of proceeding and my students and professional programmer friends tell me it works (much of the time). We'll get back to libraries in Chapter 7, but in the meantime there's a fascinating little ant colony I'd like to explore.

6.2 PROCEDURES THAT REMEMBER

This cursory overview of what's involved in structuring large programs emphasized techniques for avoiding cognitive overload in programmers, avoiding conflicts in naming and separating the public and private parts of larger software components. The substitution model (or at least the simple version in Chapter 5) does little to support our thinking about such issues in part because it assumes such a simple model of memory.

Where does memory come up in thinking about programming? When you type a set of define statements to a Scheme interpreter, you essentially create a set of associations in memory. In the next exchange, I define a function for converting inches to centimeters, specify a conversion rate and invoke the function on my approximate height in inches to obtain my height in centimeters:

```
> (define (inches_to_centimeters x) (* x conversion_rate))
> (define conversion_rate 2.54)
> (inches_to_centimeters 73)
185.42000000000002
```

The function name inches_to_centimeters and the constant conversion_rate are said to be "global" in the sense that they can be seen (referred to) by any other function I might define. What if I wanted conversion_rate to be "local" to inches_to_centimeters in the sense that it was seen only by the inches_to_centimeters function? I could do this by defining inches_to_centimeters as:

```
> (define inches_to_centimeters
    (let ((conversion_rate 2.54))
      (lambda (x) (* x conversion_rate))))
```

There's a lot going on in this little function, so we'll take our time exploring it. As usual, the syntax is a pain but we'll work our way through it. If you paid really close attention in Chapter 5, you might recall some odd facts about define, namely that (define *name body*) evaluates *body* and assigns the result to *name*, while (define (*name args*) *body*) stores *body* along with the calling pattern (*name args*) in the definition of *name* and trots out *body* as a recipe for the computation assigned to *name* whenever Scheme is asked to evaluate something of the form (*name args*). You might want to read that again.

The lambda (referring to the Greek letter and hinting at the mathematical origins of Lisp in theoretical computer science) is like the single- and double-quote mechanisms for controlling evaluation that we met in discussing shell scripts in Chapter 2. lambda says to the Scheme interpreter, "Stop evaluating! I'm a recipe for a procedure; set me aside until you want to apply this recipe to an appropriate set of arguments."

This distinction between "evaluate now" and "store in order to evaluate later" is important, and I admit that it would be nice if Scheme made it more syntactically obvious. The definition (define (*name args*) *body*) is semantically the same as (define *name* (lambda (*args*) *body*)); for example, (define square (lambda (x) (* x x))) and (define (square x) (* x x)) are interpreted in exactly the same way.

So, from what I just said, Scheme will evaluate (let ((conversion_rate 2.54)) (lambda (x) (* x conversion_rate))), but when it gets to the (lambda (x) ...) it'll stop evaluating. What happens when Scheme evaluates the (let (...) ...) part? When Scheme evaluates an expression of the form (let (*variable-value-pairs*) *body*) it sets aside a portion of memory in which to keep track of the variables and their specified values, but these variables are visible only to the expressions in the body of the let statement.

With that lengthy prologue, our definition (define inches_to_centimeters ...) can be paraphrased as follows: I'm defining a function called inches_to_centimeters, and in doing so I'm going to introduce some special terminology so that, only in the context of this definition, the variable conversion_rate refers to the number 2.54. Other functions won't be able to see inches_to_centimeters's local conversion_rate, and indeed they can feel free to define their own local variables with the same name if they so choose. Another way of thinking about this is that I'm allocating some space in my memory for the definition of inches_to_centimeters and, along with the space for the definition, I'm setting aside space for a constant to be seen only by inches_to_centimeters.

Well, the basic idea seems pretty useful but applying it in this particular case doesn't make a whole lot of sense. The way I'm using conversion_rate in inches_to_centimeters, I could have just as easily defined it as:

```
> (define (inches_to_centimeters x) (* x 2.54))
```

But there are other cases in which setting aside a private memory area to keep track of things makes lots of sense. To illustrate, we'll need some way to change the contents of memory. If you think of let as the way of setting aside or allocating portions of memory, then set! is the way to change the contents of portions of memory within the let statement that allocated them. When it comes to memory, we want to be able to forget as well as remember, change our minds as well as make up our minds. Once you can alter memory, things get more interesting.

Just for fun, we're going to make up a tricky little program that multiplies pairs of numbers. The reason it's a bit mischievous is that it returns not the product of the two numbers it's given as arguments but the product of the two numbers that were given the previous time the function was called.

```
> (define behind_the_times
    (let ((x 0) (y 0) (z 0))
```

```
(lambda (a b)
   (set! z (* x y))
   (set! x a)
   (set! y b)
   z)))
```

The (set! *term expression*) allows us to change the contents of memory (the specific location in memory in this case is referenced by *term*) to refer to the result of evaluating *expression*. And so we get this behavior:

```
> (behind_the_times 1 3)
0
> (behind_the_times 2 3)
3
> (behind_the_times 3 4)
6
```

Now a multiplication function that returns the result of multiplying the *previous* pair of numbers it was given is not terribly useful, but behind_the_times is definitely a function with a memory. I'm sure you can imagine a better application – say, a function that keeps track of your bank balance or remembers the answers to particularly difficult problems and returns them instantly when asked again (such functions are said to be *memoized*).

So let allows us to allocate or lay aside portions memory and associate these portions of memory with function definitions, and set! allows us to modify the contents of memory. The lambda syntax is just another way of providing the definition of a procedure (lambda (*args*) *body*), where *body* is the full description of the function. But it also gives us a powerful way of extending functions. What do you think the next definition does?

```
> (define (head contents)
   (let ((memory contents))
      (lambda (what)
         (if (equal? what "more")
            (set! memory (+ memory 1))
            (if (equal? what "less")
               (set! memory (- memory 1))
               (if (equal? what "show")
                  memory))))))
```

I hope the equal? didn't distract you: it's like = except that it checks whether two items are the same when the items are something other than numbers. The notion of equality is complicated even for numbers – is the integer 0 equal to the "real" number 0.0? – but we won't sweat the details here. Using `equal?` we can compare strings, which in Scheme are set off by double quotes.

In any case, `equal?` wasn't the tricky part. The tricky part is that *every* time the function `head` is called it returns a brand-new function with its own specially set-aside portion of memory for storing a local value of `contents`. In order to understand what is really going on in the last definition, it might help to use the alternative syntax for defining functions, (`define` *name* (`lambda` (*args*) *body*)), and think about what gets evaluated when:

```
> (define head
    (lambda (contents)
      (let ((memory contents))
        (lambda (what)
          ... ))))
```

The head function creates other functions:

```
> (define freds_head (head 17))
> (define annes_head (head 31))
> (freds_head "less")
> (annes_head "more")
> (freds_head "show")
16
> (annes_head "show")
32
```

We used `head` to create `freds_head` and `annes_head` as distinct functions with their own separate associated memory. The variable `contents` in the context of `freds_head` is completely different from the variable `contents` in the context of `annes_head`. The two functions `freds_head` and `annes_head` are completely separate and retain a memory of their past in the form of their local version of `contents`.

We can use `head` to create as many of these functions as we like. You can even define functions with their own local functions:

```
> (define cerberus
    (let ((dopeys_head (head -7))
          (sleepys_head (head 0))
          (grumpys_head (head 7)))
      (lambda (which what)
```

```
          (if (equal? which "dopey")
              (dopeys_head what)
              (if (equal? which "sleepy")
                  (sleepys_head what)
                  (if (equal? which "grumpy")
                      (grumpys_head what)))))))
> (cerberus "dopey" "less")
> (cerberus "grumpy" "more")
> (cerberus "dopey" "show")
-8
> (cerberus "grumpy" "show")
8
```

Well, you get the idea. We just defined a function `cerberus` that has as part of its local memory three newly minted head-generated functions, `dopeys_head`, `sleepys_head` and `grumpys_head`, each of which has its own private contents.

Using `lambda` and `let`, you can create functions that are said to be "first-class objects" – objects with their own mutable memories (they're said to have "internal state") and their own varied set of capabilities (called "methods") embodied in their associated functions. Such objects are the basis of a powerful programming model called *object-oriented programming* that supports software engineering in the large, the art and science of building large programs. Objects with internal state and associated methods can create more versatile spirits. Now our procedures can give rise to spirits that persist over time, have memory and can even cast their own spells by creating and invoking new procedures.

6.3 OBJECT-ORIENTED PROGRAMMING

In the previous section, we beefed up procedures to have persistent memory (internal state) and their own specially assigned internal procedures. Using `lambda` and `let`, we can mix and match procedures and internal state. We can define a group of procedures that share state so that any of the procedures can refer to (read) or modify (write) their shared locations in memory but no procedures outside the group can read or write to these locations.

An object in object-oriented programming sometimes behaves like memory and sometimes behaves like a procedure or, rather, a whole passel of procedures. Imagine a procedure called `make_room` that takes two arguments, integers corresponding to the width and length of a room in inches, and returns a "room object":

```
> (define annes_living_room (make_room 7 8))
```

We could ask `annes_living_room` to tell us its width or compute its area:

```
> (annes_living_room "width")
7
> (annes_living_room "area")
56
```

It might even be smart enough to convert its default metric units, say square meters for area, to imperial units, square yards in this case:

```
> (annes_living_room "area" "imperial")
66.98
```

We could change the dimensions of the room, read or write the width and length in any units, ask `annes_living_room` to, say, display itself as a rectangle in a graphical interface or alter how it's displayed, say, by rotating the rectangle a specified angle in a specified direction about its centroid. We could combine the `annes_living_room` object with, say, `annes_kitchen` object to create a composite object with associated composite information and compositing procedures. In general, `annes_living_room` would be a single source for information about Anne's living room and procedures for doing things with and to this information.

This syntax is pretty clunky, but it's just syntax, and the syntax for object-oriented languages like C++ and Java looks pretty clunky the first time you see it. For instance, in Java, we might create a new room and assign it to the variable `annes_living_room` with the incantation:

```
annes_living_room Room = new Room (width.7,length.8) ;
```

refer to the width of this room in a program as:

```
annes_living_room.width
```

refer to (compute in this case) the area of `annes_living_room` as:

```
annes_living_room.area
```

refer to the area in alternative units of measure as:

```
annes_living_room.area("imperial")
```

and perhaps request that `annes_living_room` "rotate itself" 180 degrees counterclockwise (`-Pi` radians) and then "draw itself" at coordinates 500 by 500 in some (unspecified) graphics window as:

```
annesLivingRoom.rotate(- Pi) ;
annesLivingRoom.draw(500, 500) ;
```

The syntax doesn't really matter that much. What matters is that objects have state and can perform all sorts of useful computations; you tend to stop thinking of them as data or procedures and start thinking of them as repositories of a particular sort of knowledge or expertise. Some programmers like to think of objects as entities to which you can send requests to provide services. Objects often refer to other objects and may even have a set of objects exclusively cached away in their internals; for example, a chess-board object might have a collection of objects corresponding to chess pieces. It's a very powerful way of thinking about programs and, as I mentioned in the previous section, it's the basis of an engineering discipline for the design and development of very large programs consisting of millions of lines of code.

There's another aspect of object-oriented programming that I'll mention in passing, as it is often touted as one of the principal useful characteristics of this model of computation. In Java and C++, programs are organized in terms of classes. A class is like a library in that it provides a particular set of capabilities. But not only can you generate instances of a class and thereby directly take advantage of its capabilities, you can also extend the class by adding new capabilities or altering existing ones.

Imagine that we have a class called `Rectangle` that has a width and length and can be drawn in a graphics window, rotated, resized and, perhaps, labeled, shaded and painted different colors. Now I want to create a `Room` class that computes its area, handles conversions, performs functions peculiar to my program, but otherwise behaves like an instance of the `Rectangle` class. Someone probably worked hard to create the `Rectangle` class and it doesn't make sense for me to repeat this work and perhaps not even do as good a job.

In Java, C++, C#, Smalltalk or any number of other object-oriented programming language, I would define the `Room` class as a subclass of the `Rectangle` class that *inherits* most if not all of the capabilities of the `Rectangle` class. An *instance* of the `Room` class such as `annes_living_room` would behave like a `Rectangle` except in cases where I explicitly override a `Rectangle` capability. So I'll be able to draw and rotate a `Room` without ever writing any code for these operations.

This is great if you're smart or lazy or both. Before you write a program to do something, you look for a class that does most of what you want to do and then simply adapt it to your particular purposes by defining a new class that inherits what you want from the original class. Really well-written classes become widely used and programmers end up being much more efficient by reusing other programmers' code.

6.4 PROGRAMMING WITH CONSTRAINTS

You don't need to use an object-oriented programming language to program in an object-oriented style or exploit the ability of object-oriented programming languages to structure large programs. My initial exposure to object-oriented programming came soon after I started using Lisp, first in a dialect called T and then later in a dialect called Zeta Lisp, both of which had object-oriented extensions. At that point, I found the object-oriented viewpoint more useful in understanding existing programs than in structuring my own.

When I discovered how to implement objects in Lisp, the big eye-opener for me was that I could invent my own languages and create my own syntax to suit the problem at hand or my own idiosyncratic perspectives on computing. I loved to create my own Lisp-implemented variants of object-oriented programming languages. Conversely, programming in Smalltalk, an early object-oriented language, changed how I thought about writing programs in Lisp. One of Alan Perlis's "Epigrams on Programming" reads, "A language that doesn't affect the way you think about programming is not worth knowing" and, whether by accident or design, I've persisted in using and learning only languages that provided that added benefit.

Often, in the process of solving a particular problem you end up inventing a highly specialized language. In some cases, that specialized language is subsequently generalized to solve a wider range of problems. In the remainder of this chapter, we'll explore an idea that inspired a new model of computation called *constraint programming* and was an important influence on object-oriented programming languages.

Consider this simple algebra problem, a variant of the one that started us off thinking about the substitution model in Chapter 5:

The living room in Anne's house is 56 square meters. She wants to buy a rug that fits exactly in the room. Along one side of the room is a 3-meter-wide fireplace flanked by two identical bookcases that together take up the entire width of the room. The bookcases are 2 meters wide each. The fireplace and two bookcases are built into the wall and don't cover any floor space. What are the dimensions of the rug that Anne should buy?

We begin by noting the known and unknown quantities:

```
living_room_area = 56

bookcase_width = 2

fireplace_width = 3

living_room_width = fireplace_width + (2 * bookcase_width)
```

We have the same general relationship as before,

```
living_room_area = living_room_length * living_room_width
```

but it isn't quite what we need, and so we do a little algebra to isolate the unknown variables on one side of the equation:

```
living_room_length = living_room_area / living_room_width
```

substitute the appropriate formula for items that have to be computed:

```
living_room_length = living_room_area / (fireplace_width + (2 * bookcase_width))
```

and then do the necessary calculations by plugging in the numbers and substituting the results back into the formula:

```
living_room_length = living_room_area / (fireplace_width + (2 * 2))

living_room_length = living_room_area / (fireplace_width + 4)

living_room_length = living_room_area / (3 + 4)

living_room_length = living_room_area / 7

living_room_length = 56 / 7

living_room_length = 8
```

This is all well and good, but we can't use the same Scheme functions we defined in Chapter 5. Why? Because they handle only one particular case. Given the equation

```
living_room_area = living_room_length * living_room_width
```

and given values for any two of the terms, we can compute the third. Why can't we simply provide this equation and have the computer figure out how to compute the missing value when two other values are supplied? A similar question occurred to Ivan Sutherland back in the early '60s when he was implementing Sketchpad, a system that anticipated a bunch of technologies we take for granted today, including graphical interfaces and an object-oriented programming style.

Sutherland was interested in displaying graphical objects and he wanted to specify general constraints (equations) governing their position and orientation and have the computer figure out the consequences of those constraints in drawing the objects on the computer screen. For example, at one point you might say that two rectangles should be drawn so that one is above the other, and later you might add that the bottom of one should be aligned with the top of the other and both enclosed in a third rectangle. The computer is expected to display these three rectangles so that all of these constraints are satisfied.

Later (1977) Alan Borning used the object-oriented language Smalltalk to develop an elegant design environment for computer simulations based in part on Sutherland's ideas. And still later Abelson and Sussman created a "constraint-oriented" language in Scheme and used it in their book *Structure and Interpretation of Computer Programs*. The code for Abelson and Sussman's constraint-oriented language is available on the MIT Press web site, so I copied the relevant parts into a file called `constraints.scm` and then loaded the file into Scheme:

```
> (load "constraints.scm")
```

I created objects for each of the terms in the next equation, specified that they are related to one another through multiplication, and indicated that the cost per square meter is a particular constant value. The terms in the equation become *connector* objects that connect different constraints. The constraints for this application, called *multipliers* and *adders* for obvious reasons, are attached to the appropriate connectors. Here's the equation:

```
total_cost = cost_per_square_meter * living_room_area
```

and here are the incantations that create the necessary connectors and constraints:

```
> (define total_cost (make-connector))
> (define cost_per_square_meter (make-connector))
> (define living_room_area (make-connector))
> (multiplier cost_per_square_meter
```

```
                    living_room_area
                    total_cost)
> (constant 5 cost_per_square_meter)
```

What would you guess that a multiplier constant does? Think about a multiplier (or adder for that matter) as follows. Suppose that the `living_room_area` connector suddenly wakes up and realizes it knows its "value". Well, that might be important information to send along to the multiplier created in the last exchange, so `living_room_area` wakes up the multiplier and says, "Hey! Here's some new information, see if you can do something with it." Perhaps the multiplier checks and finds out that neither `cost_per_square_meter` nor `total_cost` connectors have values; therefore it can't do anything with the information, so it goes back to sleep. Alternatively, perhaps the multiplier finds that `cost_per_square_meter` has a value but `total_cost` currently doesn't; so the multiplier figures out what the value of `total_cost` should be and tells the `total_cost` object to wake up and see if anyone else cares about this new value.

The multiplier doesn't have to be too smart, just smart enough to handle these three special cases: If `cost_per_square_meter` and `living_room_area` have values, then set

`total_cost = cost_per_square_meter * living_room_area`.

If `cost_per_square_meter` and `total_cost` have values, then set

`living_room_area = total_cost / cost_per_square_meter`.

Finally, if `living_room_area` and `total_cost` have values, then set

`cost_per_square_meter = total_cost / living_room_area`

Now we'll do something very similar with the next equation:

`living_room_area = living_room_width * living_room_length`

which results in the incantations

```
> (define living_room_width (make-connector))
> (define living_room_length (make-connector))
> (multiplier living_room_width
              living_room_length
              living_room_area)
> (constant 8 living_room_length)
```

And again, from the equation

```
living_room_width = fireplace_width + total_bookcase_width
```

we invoke

```
> (define fireplace_width (make-connector))
> (define total_bookcase_width (make-connector))
> (adder fireplace_width
         total_bookcase_width
         living_room_width)
> (constant 3 fireplace_width)
```

And finally, for the last equation

```
total_bookcase_width = number_of_bookcases * bookcase_width
```

we produce

```
> (define number_of_bookcases (make-connector))
> (define bookcase_width (make-connector))
> (multiplier number_of_bookcases
              bookcase_width
              total_bookcase_width)
> (constant 2 number_of_bookcases)
```

All the constraints are related to the other constraints they depend on through the connectors. Abelson and Sussman provide the abstraction of a *probe* that you can attach to a connector as though attaching an oscilloscope or voltmeter probe to a wire in an electrical circuit. The probe then reads off the value of the connector whenever it changes. We'll put a probe on two of the connectors:

```
> (probe "bookcase width" bookcase_width)
Probe: bookcase width = ?
> (probe "total cost" total_cost)
Probe: total cost = ?
```

The reply from the interpreter indicates that the constraint system currently has no values for these terms. So let's set one of them. We'll try the easy case first (corresponding to the case handled by the simple functional solution we implemented in Chapter 5):

```
> (set-value! bookcase_width 2 'user)
Probe: bookcase width = 2
Probe: total cost = 280
done
```

Works as expected. Let's undo that last operation and then set the total cost to see if the constraint system can work backwards:

```
> (forget-value! bookcase_width 'user)
Probe: bookcase width = ?
Probe: total cost = ?
done
```

It looks like the values have returned to being unknown. So, let's set total_cost to be 280 and see if the values propagate backward through the constraints to determine bookcase_width:

```
> (set-value! total_cost 280 'user)
Probe: total cost = 280
Probe: bookcase width = 2
done
>
```

That's the answer we were looking for: propagating the constraints calculates the right values as long as there is enough information to do so. By the way, why do you think that the probes responded in a different order this time? Recall that a probe reads off the value of its connector only when that value changes. The order of computation is determined in all cases by the topology of the connections and constraints.

Figure 6.1 clarifies the order of computation and the way in which the constrained values are propagated through a constraint network. Figure 6.1a shows the constraint system with only the constants assigned values. No constraint propagation is possible in this case. Figure 6.1b shows the propagation that results from setting total_cost to 280, assuming that bookcase_width is not assigned a value. In this case the multipliers are solving for x in $x + y = z$ given y and z, and analogously for the single adder. Figure 6.1c shows the propagation that results from setting bookcase_width to 2, assuming that total_cost is not assigned a value. In this case the multipliers are solving for z in $x + y = z$ given x and y, and analogously for the single adder.

The code fragments used to create and then alter the constraint systems illustrate another model of computation, based on the propagation of constraints

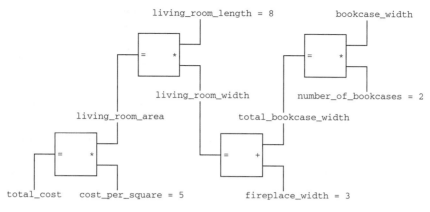

a. Initial state with only the constants assigned values

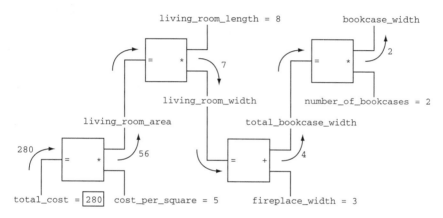

b. Propagation resulting from setting `total_cost` to 280

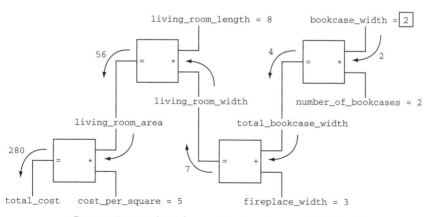

c. Propagation resulting from setting `bookcase_width` to 2

Figure 6.1: Constraint system in three different configurations

and inspired or at least facilitated by thinking in terms of object-oriented programming. In our example, the terms in the equations for our simple algebra problem are animated as objects that can receive instructions, for example, `set-value! 280`, consult their internal state, send instructions to other objects, and set in motion complicated computations that ripple through a set of objects.

As I mentioned earlier, when you hire a myrmecologist as a field guide you're likely to learn more about ants than spiders or bees. I'm more expert in artificial intelligence than in programming languages, but programming languages influence how you think about whatever it is you write programs for. If the programs you write always seem to have the same structure or involve the same blocks of code with only small variations, pretty soon you start thinking about writing a special-purpose language to make writing them easier and more natural.

The fields of artificial intelligence, robotics and computer graphics all involve different ways of thinking about computation. Programming languages based on the propagation of constraints have arisen out of several different fields. Occasionally, some core idea found in a language or a set of related languages cries out to be generalized and codified in a set of syntactic conventions that make it easy to adopt a particular way of thinking about computation. Object-oriented programming is one such core idea; in fact, it comprises a set of core ideas that have wide appeal and turn out to be very useful for software engineering in the large.

CHAPTER SEVEN

Thanks for Sharing

When I use the term "hacker" I mean someone who enjoys programming and is good at it.[1] Hackers in my experience tend to be an opinionated and individualistic lot and they tend to appreciate strong opinions and independence of thought in others. The slogan of the Perl language is "There's more than one way to do it", and most hackers are motivated to exploring different ways of doing the same job. That said, if adopting a standard way of doing something provides leverage for building better software, then most hackers will agree to adopt the standard (after much dickering about the details, of course).

If you write code because you want other people to use it, it behooves you to use a language that others are familiar with, adopt standard conventions for input and output so that others can interact with your code without learning some new set of conventions, and provide your code in a format so that others can use it as a component of a larger project without having to understand all the details of your implementation. The struggle to meet these basic criteria requires the hacker to negotiate, make concessions and, generally, work within a community of potential users to produce, adopt and adhere to reasonable standards.

Building great software requires a great deal of discipline and interpersonal skill – in sharp contrast with the stereotype of a hacker as an unkempt, uncommunicative obsessive compulsive lacking basic hygiene and addicted to highly caffeinated drinks. It also requires adherence to the lessons of modern software engineering practice. I know how to program in Java (more or less) but I generally

---

[1] I love the original definition (actually one of several definitions claimed as the original) of hacker as "someone who makes furniture with an axe", especially since in a former lifetime I made chairs, tables and large sculptures with an axe, hatchet, maul and chainsaw in an unsuccessful attempt to earn a living in rural Virginia.

don't think about programs from the perspective of software engineering. I'm pretty good at designing and implementing solutions for specific, narrowly defined problems, but I stink when it comes to structuring large programs of the sort typically encountered in industry.

Students today, budding software engineers, are being taught how to structure large programs. Most of them will never have to implement a basic utility (say for performing numerical calculations or graphical display) of any complexity except as an academic exercise. Most of the basic utilities that anybody might actually need are already implemented as libraries – or will be as soon as anyone recognizes their value. In designing a new program nowadays, you borrow most of the required functionality by "including" or "importing" utilities from existing libraries. I'll illustrate some lessons from modern software engineering by critiquing some of the Neanderthal coding practices I used when writing code to automate constructing a web site.

I mentioned in the first chapter that in preparing to write this book I kept a journal. At one point, I decided to convert my journal entries into a web site so I could solicit feedback. The plan was to create a separate page for each journal entry and then link them together so a visitor to the web site could jump from one entry to the next in the order in which they were written. Since I'm lazy I didn't want to create all of these pages by hand; instead, I wanted a program to go through all my journal entries and produce a web site with all the requisite web pages, linked appropriately and formatted for a web browser.

Object-oriented programming (or OOP as it's often called) as a programming style and a software engineering discipline is touted as facilitating reuse and sharing of code, encapsulation of expertise and management of information by controlling access to implementation details. You don't need to use object-oriented programming language in order to get these benefits, but the prevailing wisdom is that OOP makes them easier to achieve.

My first introduction to object-oriented programming was an academic exercise in graduate school requiring us to write a program in the language Smalltalk. A little later I had to learn about object-oriented language extensions for a Lisp dialect called Zeta Lisp in order to translate some of my software to run on the Lisp Machine (a computer specially designed to run Lisp, soon made obsolete by low-cost, high-performance commodity PCs).

In neither case did I really learn much about object-oriented programming; I just figured out how to get these languages to do what I usually did, namely implement procedures for solving problems that came up in my research. If I had used these object-oriented programming languages as they were intended or if I had absorbed the lessons revealed by the design of such languages, I might have saved myself a good deal of grief. Let me give you a simple example illustrating the benefits of controlling access to implementation details.

7.1 CODE FOR THE TAKING

In designing the software for building my journal web site, I needed a data structure for storing information about each web page corresponding to a journal entry. This data structure, which I called a *record*, would include a field (the term used to describe the components of a data structure) called the *entry* corresponding to the relevant parts of the path in the file system leading to the files for the journal entry, a field called *previous* corresponding to the path in the file system leading to the files for the chronologically prior journal entry, a field called *next* corresponding ... well, I expect you can guess, and fields for the *date* and *title* of the entry. I needed to be able to create such records, access their fields and modify selected fields.

Here's how I used lists in Scheme to implement the `record` data structure. By way of background, the Scheme function `list` creates a list whose items are initialized to be the values of the arguments in the invocation of the function. Lists in Scheme use zero-based indexes (the first item in the list has the index 0, the second has the index 1 and so on) and (`list-ref` *record n*) returns the *n*th item (zero-based) in the list corresponding to *record*. (`set-car!` (`list-tail` *record n*) *new-value*) assigns the *n*th item (zero-based) in the list corresponding to *record* to be *new-value*. The first function defined creates a new `record` initializing all the fields with values supplied as arguments. The next five functions access the five fields in the `record` data structure and return the value of the specified field. The last two expressions are two of the five functions used to modify the fields in the `record` data structure.

```
(define (make-record entry previous next date title)
  (list entry previous next date title))

(define (record-entry record) (list-ref record 0))
(define (record-previous record) (list-ref record 1))
(define (record-next record) (list-ref record 2))
(define (record-date record) (list-ref record 3))
(define (record-title record) (list-ref record 4))

(define (set-record-entry! record new-entry)
  (set-car! (list-tail record 0) new-entry))
```

```
(define (set-record-previous! record new-previous)
  (set-car! (list-tail record 1) new-previous))
```

You might notice that the prompt is missing in this code. As programs get larger, it becomes convenient to type them into files and then load them into Scheme so the functions can be used in interacting with the Scheme interpreter. In the program listings in the remainder of this chapter, you can assume that if the prompt isn't displayed then I've put the function definitions in a file and loaded them into Scheme. This method of creating files consisting of definitions and other code fragments is the way programs of any size are usually developed. Indeed, large programs are typically composed of hundreds if not thousands of files.

I can also make the record data structure more useful by defining functions for doing things with records. For example, it's often handy to have a print function for data structures that displays their fields clearly:

```
(define (print-record port record)
  (fprintf port
           "Record object:~%~
            Entry path         = ~A~%~
            Previous entry path = ~A~%~
            Next entry path    = ~A~%~
            Entry date         = ~A~%~
            Entry title        = ~A~%"
           (record-entry record)
           (record-previous record)
           (record-next record)
           (record-date record)
           (record-title record)))
```

Now I'll create a new record, modify one of its fields (correcting the mistyped year in the date field), and then print the modified record:

```
> (define test-record
    (make-record "/02/08/24/"
                 "/02/08/16/"
                 "/02/08/28/"
                 "August 24, 2001"
                 "Sharing and Reuse"))
> (set-record-date! test-record "August 24, 2002")
```

```
> (print-record (current-output-port) test-record)
Record object:
Entry path          = /02/08/24/
Previous entry path = /02/08/16/
Next entry path     = /02/08/28/
Entry date          = August 24, 2002
Entry title         = Sharing and Reuse
```

This is all very well, but it uses a lot of code to do something that pro-grammers have to do far too often. Most modern dialects of Lisp have one or more methods of creating data structures. In Scheme, the invocation (define-struct record (entry previous next date title)) does everything my implementation of the record data structure does and more. But my implemen-tation helps illustrate the point I want to make: whatever the merits of this par-ticular implementation, a problem can arise when someone else tries to use my code.

Suppose my friend Sulee Jenerika decides to use my record data structure in her code. Rather than copy my code into her program, she simply puts a require statement in her code that loads the file (or *library*) that I've conveniently provided containing the code that implements my record data structure.

In Sulee's software project, she needs to search for a record containing a particular entry; having looked at my implementation of record, she writes two procedures for operating on records. By way of background, the Scheme function assoc takes an object (a string corresponding to the path for an entry in this case) and a list of lists (a list of records in this case) and finds the first list whose first item is equal to the object. The function cons takes an object and a list and returns a new list whose first item is the object and whose remaining items are the items in the original list.

```
(define (record-lookup entry records)
  (assoc entry records))
(define (record-insert record records)
  (cons record records))
```

This works fine until I discover *vectors*, another primitive data type available in most programming languages and applicable in many of the same circumstances as lists. Let's suppose that I buy some hacker's impassioned argument that I'll get better performance if I implement records using vectors. I do this and then update my record library, expecting everyone using my record data structure to be pleased when their code suddenly runs faster. Here's what the reimplemented `record` data structure might look like:

```
(define (make-record entry previous next date title)
  (vector entry previous next date title))


(define (record-entry record) (vector-ref record 0))
(define (record-previous record) (vector-ref record 1))
(define (record-next record) (vector-ref record 2))
(define (record-date record) (vector-ref record 3))
(define (record-title record) (vector-ref record 4))


(define (set-record-entry! record new-entry)
  (vector-set! record 0 new-entry))
(define (set-record-previous! record new-previous)
  (vector-set! record 1 new-previous))
```

And so on. My other `record` functions, for example `print-record`, work fine as written, but Sulee's `record-lookup` and `record-insert` functions are badly broken: her implementation relies on the details of my initial implementation using lists. If Sulee uses my code in a product and she recompiles her code (including my `record` library) in the next release of her product, her customers are in for some unpleasant surprises.

Is Sulee at fault for writing her extensions based on my initial implementation, or am I at fault for changing my implementation? Clearly there's a need for some sort of a contract between library consumers and library producers that stipulates who is responsible for what. Object-oriented programming languages help enforce such a contract by requiring that a library (called a *class* in object-oriented-programming parlance) producer publish an *interface* specifying exactly how a library consumer is to use a given library, what functions to call and what behaviors to expect. Consumers for their part are expected not to assume anything about a library beyond what is specified in the interface. To enforce this discipline, library producers can make certain parts of a library's implementation *private*, thereby making it impossible for a consumer to access those parts or exploit them in any fashion. As the producer of a library, I can modify the implementation as long as I preserve the interface. And as a consumer of a library, I can rely on a stable interface, both in terms of the calling conventions for invoking procedures (the names of the procedures and the number, order and types of their arguments) and their resulting behavior.

What's good for the goose is good for the gander. A major cause of my software woes over the years has been my tendency to violate contracts with myself. I implement a data structure – typically in a rush – and then exploit its implementation in various, sometimes subtle ways throughout my code. Later, when I realize that I need to improve the implementation to get better performance, I have to find and fix all the places where I exploited the initial implementation – a task both tedious and error prone. I always rationalize my impatience and lack of discipline in coding by saying that it's just a prototype and I'll fix it later, but invariably the prototype code persists and causes problems later.

When I learned Java a few years back, I got frustrated working my way through the recommended two texts, Arnold and Gosling's authoritative *The Java Programming Language* for a description of the language and Budd's excellent *Understanding Object-Oriented Programming with Java* for a balanced introduction to object-oriented programming in Java. My problem was that most of the functionality I was being introduced to I didn't need (or at least didn't think I needed). Why would I want to publish an *interface* describing the procedures I intend to write, why would I want to use or *extend* a *class*, why would I want to make some parts of my implementation *public* and other parts *private*, why would I want *inherit* some parts of a class and *override* others? The answers to all these questions have to do with the benefits derived from sharing and reusing in the context of software engineering in the large – the art and science of writing, maintaining and improving large programs.

I'm still not entirely sold, and I expect I'll always want to implement everything from scratch rather than borrow someone else's code (my attitude here underscores one of the major obstacles to software reuse, as summed up in one of Alan Perlis's epigrams, "It is easier to write an incorrect program than understand a correct one"). But the fact of the matter is, if you're a mere mortal and want to produce any interesting software, you'll probably have to use significant amounts of code written by other people and reuse your own code. Consider: all the compilers, editors, debuggers and other tools are written by others, so why not use well-crafted libraries to expedite and improve your own programming projects? Here's an example illustrating how object-oriented programming facilitates code sharing, again based on my experience building a web site for my online journal.

7.2 CLASS CONSCIOUS

One of the first things you have to deal with in implementing an online journal involves specifying dates in various calendars. I didn't think too much about calendars, having resolved early on to simplify my life and use the Gregorian calendar. To get the flavor of the potential confusion arising over dates in various calendars, consider the date August 24, AD 2002 in the Gregorian (Reform) calendar, one of the days on which I wrote a journal entry.

Nowadays, the letters AD/BC ("Anno Domini"/"Before Christ") are beginning to be replaced by CE/BCE ("Common Era"/"Before Common Era"), and hence our example date is August 24, 2002 CE (the letters now appearing after the year by convention). The year 2002 CE in the Gregorian calendar is 5763 in the Jewish calendar and 1423 in the Islamic calendar. August 24, 2002 CE at 12:00 UT ("Universal Time," sometimes called "Greenwich Mean Time" and abbreviated GMT) is 2452515 JD ("Julian Date") in the Julian calendar, in which dates are computed as a continuous count of days and fraction of days since noon UT on January 1, 4713 BCE. It makes your head swim.

But, having finessed this one aspect by fixing on the Gregorian calendar, I still had plenty of room for ambiguity in dealing with dates. The date format most common in the U.S. is mm/dd/yy, which is easily confused with the European date format dd/mm/yy. There are alphanumeric formats such as August 24, 2002 and 24 Aug 2002. And there is a proposed international standard, ISO 8601, for representing dates and times in which the string 2002-08-24T14:10:00-05:00 corresponds to August 24, 2002 at 2:10PM US Eastern Standard Time, where the -05:00 specifies an offset from Coordinated Universal Time (UTC). Calculations involving dates specified in accord with ISO 8601, say the difference in time between two dates, have to deal with time zones, leap years and even leap seconds. Happily, I was only concerned with years, months and days.

Most object-oriented programming languages, including Java and C++, have libraries, called *classes*, for calendars, dates, time zones, and the like. A class specifies the mutable internal state, stored in *fields*, and the immutable procedures, called *methods*, for all objects or *instances* of the class. The Java Date class provides methods to determine if one instance of the class Date comes before or after another and whether two instances are equivalent. Date methods let the user extract from an instance the year, month, day, hour, minute, second and millisecond.

If I were programming in Java, I'd just type "import java.util.Date;" at the top of my Java program and I'd be in business. But we've been steeped in Scheme syntax with all its lovely parentheses for most of the last three chapters, so let's stick with it just a little longer to give you the basic idea. Keep in mind that object-oriented programming is not about syntax, it's about a particular way of structuring programs and thinking about computation; you can do object-oriented programming in any language.

I could invent my own idiosyncratic syntax for object-oriented programming in Scheme, but there is a much better alternative. The folks at PLT[2] provide a very nice library written in Scheme that implements classes and objects. The PLT library, `class.ss`, mirrors much of the functionality found in Java but uses lots of parentheses instead of curly brackets and semicolons. But just so you won't feel you're missing anything, as soon as we've explained the basic ideas using a Scheme-like syntax, we'll take a look at the same program in Java.

First, let's see what a PLT Scheme `date` class might look like (I'll use the capitalized `Date` for the Java class and the all-lower-case `date` for the PLT Scheme class). This is a simplified version of what's provided in the Java `Date` class. I begin by specifying an `interface` promising that any class implementing this interface provides methods for getting the year, month and day of an instance of the PLT Scheme `date` class and a method for checking whether one instance is `before` another instance:

```
(define date-interface
  (interface () year month day before))
```

The next expression describes the class specifying the various fields of the class (`init-fields` are fields that are initialized when an instance of the class is created) and defining the methods specified in the indicated interface. The function definitions within a class description implicitly take as an argument an object of the class and can refer to the fields of the class directly. The class `date` is said to *inherit* functionality from its *superclass*, which is the base class (the simplest, most basic class possible, referred to here as `object%`). The class description indicates that all the methods specified in the interface are *public* and hence accessible to anyone who *imports* the class. We'll ignore the rest of the syntax for our immediate purposes.[3]

---

[2] PLT Scheme is an umbrella name for a family of implementations of the Scheme programming language and PLT is the group of people who produce PLT Scheme. I recommend Felleisen et al.'s *How to Design Programs* as an excellent introduction to programming in general and programming in Scheme in particular.

[3] The expression (cond ...) is an example of a *generalized if statement*. In an expression of the form (cond ($test_1$ $result_1$) ($test_2$ $result_2$) ... (else $result_n$)), Scheme evaluates each test in order until the first test returns the Scheme equivalent of true, at which point it evaluates the corresponding result. In Scheme, #t evaluates to logically true and #f evaluates to logically false. If no test returns true, then Scheme evaluates the last result ($result_n$) corresponding to the else keyword. Exactly one of the results gets evaluated and is returned as the result of the cond statement. The cond statement, like other generalized conditional operators, for instance case and switch statements, is an example of flow-of-control mechanisms that considerably simplify some types of programming.

```
(define date
  (class* object% (date-interface)
    (public year month day before)
    (init-field (this-year 0))
    (init-field (this-month 0))
    (init-field (this-day 0))
    (define (year) this-year)
    (define (month) this-month)
    (define (day) this-day)
    (define (before that)
      (cond ((> this-year (send that year)) #f)
            ((< this-year (send that year)) #t)
            ((> this-month (send that month)) #f)
            ((< this-month (send that month)) #t)
            (else (< this-day (send that day)))))
    (super-instantiate ())))
```

In the next exchange with Scheme, I create (*instantiate* is the term for creating an instance of a class) a couple of date objects and then invoke the before method, illustrating the somewhat clunky syntax for invoking methods (as we'll see, Java has a much nicer syntax for instantiating and calling methods on objects, but then Java was designed from the ground up as an object-oriented programming language). An expression of the form (send *object method arguments*) invokes the *method* on specified *object* and additional *arguments* (the *object* being an implicit argument in every method definition). Java uses the convenient dot (".") operator, so that this invocation would appear as *object.method*(*arguments*); this seems rather elegant to me but perhaps I've brainwashed myself by looking at more OOP code than is healthy.

```
> (define date-one (instantiate date (2002 8 16)))
> (define date-two (instantiate date (2002 8 24)))
> (send date-one before date-two)
#t
```

In addition to implementing dates there is the messy problem of parsing strings to see if they contain dates and, if so, extracting the dates and converting them into the format needed to create an instance of the Date class. There is also the problem of formatting dates for display purposes. Some of this functionality is handled in the Java DateFormat class. There's lots more to the story of how dates, calendars, locales, time zones and the like are supported in Java; if you're interested, check out out Arnold and Gosling's book for details.

For purposes of illustration, let's pretend that someone else implemented the date class and I just want to use it. I'm going to do so by defining a new class, the journal-date class, that relies on or *extends* the date class. The journal-date class also implements an associated interface, the journal-date-interface, which extends the data-interface. Again, don't sweat the details, but you might be interested to know that super-instantiate refers to the procedure that instantiates the superclass, the date class in this case. Instances of the journal-date class deal primarily with strings and so I have to convert the strings to numbers for use in instances of the date class. This sort of conversion, often referred to as *type coercion* in languages like C, C++ and Java that require explicit type declarations, is quite common in programming. Instances of the journal-date class, besides storing the original strings presumably extracted from my text, also reformat the date according to the ISO 8601 standard:

```
(define journal-date-interface
  (interface (date-interface) iso))


(define journal-date
  (class* date (journal-date-interface)
    (public iso)
    (init-field (year-string ""))
    (init-field (month-string ""))
    (init-field (day-string ""))
    (define (iso)
      (format "~A-~A-~A" year-string month-string day-string))
    (super-instantiate ((string->number year-string)
                        (string->number month-string)
                        (string->number day-string)))))
```

And here's a simple test to make sure everything works as advertised with instances of the journal-date class responding to methods inherited from the date class as well as to those (well, one) implemented in the journal-date class:

```
> (define journal-date-one (instantiate journal-date ("2002" "08" "16")))
> (define journal-date-two (instantiate journal-date ("2002" "08" "24")))
> (send journal-date-one before journal-date-two)
#t
> (send journal-date-one iso)
"2002-08-24"
```

Most real classes are much more complicated than my simple examples suggest. If real classes were this easy to write, there wouldn't be much point in sharing them. A good class is well documented and easy to tailor to the needs of a specific project. It takes effort to understand someone else's code, but the benefits of well crafted and widely used classes in terms of better performing and more easily shared, maintained and extended software can more than offset the disadvantages. Way better than sliced bread.

7.3 IT'S JUST SYNTAX

As I hinted, I feel a little guilty about all that Lisp code in the last section. I talked a lot about the benefits of object-oriented programming but I showed you hardly a scrap of code from languages specifically designed to support object-oriented programming such as Java or C++. I know it's just syntax, but I also know from experience that struggling with unfamiliar syntax can be frustrating – hence my reluctance to code in Java or C++ simply because I'm less familiar with the syntax. Trading parentheses for curly brackets and semicolons and different formatting and commenting conventions and different names for often-used functionality is more than a little disorienting, and sometimes important concepts can get lost in translation. I chose the PLT Scheme `class.ss` library because it captures the most important features of object-oriented programming by mapping object-oriented-programming concepts directly onto appropriate Scheme syntax.

The `class.ss` library introduces syntax to make coding in Scheme seem like programming in an object-oriented programming language. Since the `class.ss` library is written in Scheme, it's obvious that we really didn't need the syntax of `class.ss` in order to program in Scheme in an object-oriented style. So why all the extra syntax? Don't programming languages have enough annoying syntax already?

Syntactic sugar is features added to a language that make it more palatable for humans but don't affect its ability to specify computations (such features neither increase nor decrease the expressiveness of the language). Syntactic sugar is meant to encourage programmers to write better code by hiding both features that are seldom useful and might distract someone trying to make sense of the code and features that are difficult to use and can lead to bugs. In some languages, (x + y) is syntactic sugar for plus(x,y) – the former notation is more familiar and thus makes a programmer less likely to make mistakes in longer, more complicated formulas.

Contrast syntactic sugar with *syntactic salt*, which makes it more difficult to write good code, and *syntactic saccharin* (also called *syntactic syrup*), which introduces gratuitous syntax serving no useful purpose. Some programming-language mavens believe that syntactic sugar can itself be distracting or that the need for it in a programming language is evidence that the language was poorly designed ("Syntactic sugar causes cancer of the semicolon" is another of Alan Perlis's epigrams). And it's true that a programmer addicted to syntactic sugar is less likely to understand or use the features that the sugar sweetens by masking.

The PLT Scheme implementation of classes does abstract away some important features of Java and C++, specifically the requirement of declaring the types of all variables, constants and return values of functions. But these features are not pertinent to object-oriented programming per se, and individual preferences regarding parentheses versus curly brackets are similarly beside the point. Therefore it's my belief that any sugaring in the notation introduced in `class.ss` is of the good sort. However, I'm also sensitive to the criticism that syntactic sugar is *more* syntax and too much of even a good thing can rot your teeth.

So, let's take a look at some "real" object-oriented programming syntax. As an exercise, I translated the classes I designed using the `class.ss` library into Java classes. I was pleased with how easily the translation went and how directly the abstractions in `class.ss` mapped onto standard Java abstractions. Showing off the code will require some tools from the Sun Java Development Kit (JDK), but we've never been reluctant to introduce new tools and inscrutable (and all too briefly explained) notation in the past so I don't know why we should start now. Also, we'll be using a somewhat different style of developing and executing programs from what we're used to in interacting with a Lisp interpreter.

To implement the necessary classes, I created three files: one file for each of the `Date` and `JournalDate` classes and one file for a class called `TestDate` to demonstrate that the code actually works. `TestDate` has no associated instances and exists only so that I can call its `main` procedure to build some instances of the `Date` and `JournalDate` classes and apply methods to these instances to demonstrate that the classes work as advertised.

```
% ls
Date.java    JournalDate.java    TestDate.java
```

Here's what the code for the `DateInterface` interface and `Date` class looks like. Again, we've kept it simple for illustration; the Java code implements the same behaviors as the Scheme code. In Java `Object` is the base class. I use the Unix `cat` program to print the `Date.java` file to my terminal from the shell. I won't explain the Java syntax in any detail except to note that the `DateInterface` describes the interface that the Date class implements and that the Date class defines four methods, year, month, day and before, in addition to explicitly defining the Date instantiator.

```
% cat Date.java
interface DateInterface {
    public int year ();
    public int month ();
    public int day ();
    public boolean before ( Date that );
}

class Date extends Object implements DateInterface {
    protected int year, month, day;
    public int year () { return year; }
    public int month () { return month; }
    public int day () { return day; }
    public boolean before (Date that) {
        if ( year > that.year ) return false ;
        else if ( year < that.year ) return true ;
        else if ( month > that.month ) return false ;
        else if ( month < that.month ) return true ;
        else return ( day > that.day ) ;
    }
    public Date (int y, int m, int d) {
        year = y; month = m; day = d;
    }
}
```

Next we have to compile this code using javac, the Java compiler, which converts the Java source code, for example the contents of the Date.java file, into Java *bytecodes*. Most compilers produce assembly code that is then converted by an assembler into machine code to run on a particular machine. The Java compiler produces bytecodes, which are the machine code for the Java Virtual Machine (JVM), a piece of software that runs on lots of different machines and serves to simulate a virtual or software machine. Java bytecodes run on any machine that has an implementation of the JVM. Let's invoke the compiler.

```
% javac Date.java
```

Now there is a file called `Date.class` in the directory along with `Date.java`. `Date.class` contains the compiled version of the `Date` class.

Next let's look at the file implementing the `JournalDate.java` class. It begins by declaring its dependence on the `Date` class and then proceeds to extend `DateInterface` before getting around to describing the `JournalDate` class. Here, as in the Scheme version, I invoke the instantiator, called `super` in Java, for the superclass `Date`.

```
% cat JournalDate.java
import Date;

interface JournalDateInterface extends DateInterface {
    public void iso ( );
}

class JournalDate extends Date implements JournalDateInterface {
    protected String yearString, monthString, dayString ;
    public void iso () {
        System.out.println( yearString + "-" +
                            monthString + "-" +
                            dayString );
    }
    public JournalDate (String y, String m, String d) {
        super( Integer.parseInt( y ),
               Integer.parseInt( m ),
               Integer.parseInt( d ) );
        yearString = y;
        monthString = m;
        dayString = d;
    }
}
```

We compile the code in `JournalDate.java`:

```
% javac JournalDate.java
```

`TestDate.java` contains the description of a class, `TestDate`, whose only reason for being is to run its `main` method to exercise the code in `Date.java` and `JournalDate.java`. It's not very fancy; it just creates an instance of

JournalDate and then invokes the iso method on the instance:

```
% cat TestDate.java
import JournalDate;

class TestDate {
    public static void main(String[] args) {
        JournalDate today = new JournalDate ( "2002", "08", "28" );
        today.iso ();
    }
}
```

It has to be compiled, just like all the other classes:

```
% javac TestDate.java
```

Now we list the contents of the directory and notice compiled versions for all of the classes and interfaces:

```
% ls
Date.class                    JournalDate.java
Date.java                     JournalDateInterface.class
DateInterface.class           TestDate.java
JournalDate.class             TestDate.class
```

In order to run the program we just compiled, we use the Java interpreter, called simply java:

```
% java TestDate
2002-08-28
```

Not very interesting output, but at least the iso method defined in the JournalDate class appears to work as advertised.

As another example of using objects in Java code, say that in defining a procedure I declare and instantiate two JournalDate objects as follows:

```
JournalDate today = new JournalDate ( "2002", "08", "28" );
JournalDate yesterday = new JournalDate ( "2002", "08", "27" );
```

Then, later in same procedure, if I were to write today.before(yesterday) and yesterday.before(today), these statements would evaluate to false and true, respectively, thereby exercising the (inherited) methods in the superclass `Date` of the `JournalDate` class.

That probably felt like an awful lot of syntax to wade through for something so simple as comparing a few dates. But libraries, classes, interfaces are the basis for building industrial-strength applications. If you're a company doing anything that has to be dated (contracts, accounts, design documents), then you'd be well advised to use a carefully crafted date library, one that adopts widely accepted standards and can be easily extended to handle new standards as they become available. Industrial-strength applications have to be designed to last, to be easily maintained and upgraded, to scale to handle millions of records or dates, and to be modular so that various pieces can be used for other purposes. Object-oriented programming languages help to achieve these properties, but they can't guarantee them. Perhaps this is why one of the best known and most widely read series of books on computer science and computer programming is Don Knuth's *The Art of Computer Programming*.

The software engineering lessons in this chapter are rather subtle and easy for an inexperienced or stubborn programmer to ignore. These lessons have nothing to do with Java, C++ or any other object-oriented programming language; they have everything to do with developing engineering discipline and protecting against laziness, impatience and hubris. Larry Wall, the creator of Perl, claims that laziness, impatience and hubris are the three cardinal virtues of a truly great programmer.[4] I claim that my statement and Wall's are perfectly consistent with one another, and if you don't believe me, then you should seek out your local Zen master for enlightenment.

So that's about it: inheritance, interfaces, public and private methods; all good stuff from what I hear tell. But remember that a major part of what makes it all work is in your head, the discipline and good sense you bring to designing good code. No amount of fancy syntax, sweet, salty or otherwise, is going to turn you into a good programmer if you don't have discipline and common sense in good measure. Java is a nicely designed language and might well be my favorite language now had it been the first language I did any serious programming in. But it wasn't and it isn't and I'll probably stick to Scheme for most of my mid-size

---

[4] In the online documentation for Perl, you'll find the following line: "The three principal virtues of a programmer are Laziness, Impatience, and Hubris". While I don't necessarily advocate these virtues even in the narrow context of programming, they do provide the impetus to write code to automate tedious tasks, the inclination to produce efficient code and the chutzpah to try something even if everyone tells you it's impossible. All these tendencies and encouragements have to be tempered in good programmers, however, if they are to produce reliable, maintainable and reusable (sharable) software.

programming jobs. There have been times in the past, however, and I expect there are times ahead, when Java and C++ are the right tool for the job and I won't shy away from using them. As I've said before, it's good not to get too wedded to a single idea, if for no other reason than that programming in different languages encourages you to think about computation in new and interesting ways.

CHAPTER EIGHT
You've Got (Junk) Email

The first computers were used primarily to manage information for large companies and perform numerical calculations for the military. Only a few visionaries saw computing as something for everyone or imagined it could become a basic service like the telephone or electric power. This failure of imagination was due in large part to the fact that the people who controlled computing in the early years weren't the ones actually programming computers. If you worked for a large corporation or industrial laboratory, then you might have strictly limited access to a computer, but otherwise you were pretty much out of luck.

In the early years of computing, users submitted their programs to computer operators to be run in batches. You would hand the operator a stack of cards or a roll of paper tape punched full of holes that encoded your program. An operator would schedule your program to be run (possibly in the middle of the night) with a batch of other programs and at some point thereafter you would be handed a printout of the output generated by your program. You didn't interact directly with the computer and if your program crashed and produced no output, you'd have very little idea what had gone wrong.

The people who ran computer facilities were horrified at the idea of having users interact directly with their precious computers. Computers were treated like sacred oracles and the computer operators were the acolytes and high priests who interceded on behalf of the unworthy programmers. But before long the users rebelled against the establishment and demanded access to computers. Indeed, once programmers got a chance to interact with computers they wanted unlimited direct access.

Computers were still very expensive in the 1950s and so the earliest efforts to make computers accessible involved doling out little slices of time to multiple users sitting at consoles connected up to one big computer, technology called time-sharing. Users on time-sharing systems quickly realized that they were connected not only to the computer but to one another. They found that the computer made it very easy to exchange messages with other users, and before long someone had written the first email program.[1]

In the 1960s, the circle of users able to exchange email was still limited to those sharing a particular machine. The 1970s saw the creation of the first continent-spanning computer network and the advent of the personal computer. Led by an eclectic group of visionaries who saw computing as a means of communication and computing devices as a way to augment intelligence, forward-thinking computer scientists were soon visualizing online interactive communities, teleconferencing, computer-aided meetings and electronic documents enhanced with multiple fonts, graphics and hyperlinks.

Email is often called the "killer application" for the Internet, the application that made it obvious that the Internet was here to stay. But it didn't take long for people to see the dark side of email: unsolicited, unwanted and even downright offensive junk email. It's inevitable that a technology for communicating will soon be used for advertising, filibustering, insulting, swindling, proselytizing and every other possible form of human discourse, good or bad.

The combination of computers and communication, however, poses some particularly insidious problems. It's almost as easy to send email to millions of people as to one person. You can even customize a message to thousands of recipients by using simple scripts that insert the recipient's name, address and other personal information, making it appear to come from a friend or business associate.

It takes me just a few seconds each time I read my email to scan the new messages and delete the junk. If you read your email often you hardly notice it. However, if you're away for a few days, you can return to hundreds of email messages, most of them junk. It's annoying to have to filter the deluge, separating the messages you want to read from the advertisements, solicitations and other unwanted and often virus-ridden junk email.

But if you can use computers to automate sending email, you can also use them to automate filtering email. Early advocates of computer-mediated communication anticipated that the new technology would create problems for users

---

[1] Tom Van Vleck, an MIT undergraduate, wrote one of the first email programs for the Compatible Time-Sharing System (CTSS) developed as part of MIT's Project MAC (for "multiple access computer" and "machine-aided cognition"). CTSS was one of the first operating systems that supported multiple users and time sharing. Ray Tomlinson, a computer scientist at Bolt Beranek and Newman (BBN), sent the first email message between two computers. Tomlinson had already written an email program for an early time-sharing system that was running on most machines on the ARPANET (ARPA is the federal government's Advanced Research Projects Agency), which was the precursor to the Internet and the World Wide Web. In 1971, Tomlinson took the next logical step and sent an email message from one machine to another connected by the ARPANET.

unable to cope with huge volumes of information and limited by the relatively slow pace of human thought, and they imagined automated surrogates that would protect us and act on our behalf. Today, such surrogates, sometimes called *agents* or *bots* (a shortening of "robot" or "knowbot" indicating a disembodied software- or knowledge-based robot), are cropping up in all sorts of applications. There are "auction bots" that issue thousands of bids per second in online auctions and "avatars" that provide a computer-enhanced presence for participants in online games and virtual reality environments. The technology driving these agents comes from a variety of disciplines including artificial intelligence.

8.1 ARTIFICIAL INTELLIGENCE

According to John McCarthy, who is generally said to have coined the name, artificial intelligence (AI) is "the science and engineering of making intelligent machines, especially intelligent computer programs." Responding to the obvious next question, McCarthy goes on to say, "it is related to the similar task of using computers to understand human intelligence, but AI does not have to confine itself to methods that are biologically observable." The above characterization leads immediately to the question, "What is intelligence?" and McCarthy admits it has no agreed-upon definition. However, many of us think it reasonable to adopt the stance that we'll recognize intelligence when we see it.

Actually, this stance is complicated by the phenomenon that to many people, as soon as a computer can perform a given task, such as playing chess, that task no longer seems intelligent, or at least intelligent in an interesting way. Many AI researchers prefer to steer clear of this sort of hair-splitting and focus their attention on developing programs that analyze data, make decisions, learn from their mistakes and adapt to a changing environment. Now more than ever, the interesting applications of computer science seem to require such capabilities.

Some of the topics studied in artificial intelligence are rather esoteric and (I gather from experience in broaching them in polite conversation) somewhat dry and academic. Learning or rather machine learning is, however, a good topic for party conversations as long as you don't delve into the theory or get too wrapped up in the philosophical implications. Machine learning is about getting machines to acquire skills, adapt to change and, generally speaking, improve their performance on the basis of experience. Effective machine-learning techniques are already used in a wide range of applications from detecting credit-card fraud to making your car run better.

One of the most thoroughly studied areas of machine learning is *supervised learning*, in which the program doing the learning is given a set of clearly marked training examples. Suppose you're a scientist trying to understand the migration habits of fish and suppose you need to be able to distinguish arctic char from atlantic salmon. The first thing you'd do is observe these fish carefully and probably add various descriptive terms to your vocabulary to capture the differences in coloring, scales, fins and other characteristics useful for making distinctions.

Since initially you can't distinguish between the two kinds of fish, you need an expert to provide a set of training examples: fish clearly marked as char or salmon. You'd probably figure out pretty quickly that some characteristics are shared by both kinds of fish, others are not terribly useful or may even be misleading in trying to make distinctions, but some, called diagnostic characteristics, are perfectly suited to distinguishing one type of fish from the other. After a while, you'll learn to ignore the misleading or useless characteristics and become skilled at using the diagnostic ones.

If you started distinguishing arctic char with orange-red bellies from arctic char with predominantly silver bellies, you'd be wasting your time if what you wanted was to distinguish salmon from char. Humans are good at seeking out diagnostic characteristics for making all sorts of distinctions and we seldom waste time making distinctions that serve no useful purpose. If we find a particularly useful characteristic, such as the different ways in which the lower jaws of the two fish protrude, we often abandon the other characteristics and seize on the particularly diagnostic one. Machine learning is all about turning this process of looking at data and searching for diagnostic characteristics into algorithms that can be used to automate learning.

One common application of machine learning nowadays is distinguishing junk email, or *spam* as it's often called, from non-spam, or *ham* (for "human acceptable mail") as we'll refer to it here.[2] The various approaches to building spam filters, as they have come to be called, all have in common looking at a lot of email messages and learning to separate the spam from the ham. In some approaches the learning is done by humans painstakingly analyzing data and in other cases it is done by computers.

Learning to filter spam is an example of supervised learning not unlike distinguishing arctic char from atlantic salmon. Our scientist learning to distinguish different types of fish needs an expert to provide training examples that clearly distinguish char from salmon. In filtering spam, the user can provide the training

---

[2] SPAM is a registered trademark of the Hormel Foods Corporation. The product from Hormel is marketed as a luncheon meat and has nothing to do with electronic mail.

examples. Since each user's notion of spam is different (you may want to be alerted every time a new album by Destiny's Child is released but I'd just as soon not be bothered), it's important for a spam filter somehow to learn a user's preferences.

The challenge is to create a filter that learns these preferences without requiring too much work of the user, since the whole idea is to save time and avoid aggravation. The user of a spam filter relying on supervised learning might have to mark several thousand messages as spam or ham before the learning program could make distinctions acceptably on its own. A prospective user of such a program might well not want to take the trouble. An alternative to making a single user supply all the training examples is to collect examples from many users with similar preferences and use them to train the spam filter. This is an example of *collaborative filtering*, which identifies patterns in user preferences in order to guide users in finding goods and services and to guide sellers in marketing those goods and services. You see collaborative filtering at work when you visit an online retailer and see something like, "Customers who bought this book (or CD or DVD or video game) also bought:" followed by a list of similar products.

Most email clients keep your email messages in a file typically called an INBOX. There are all sorts of email protocols, for example POP and IMAP, and all sorts of clients and servers that implement these protocols, but sooner or later a spam filter is going to have to grub around in an INBOX file full of messages in some format or possibly in multiple formats. Message formats differ in how they deal with headers (the "To:", "From:" and "Subject:" fields that you see at the top of every message), message content (some email clients allow embedded HTML or other text formatting), and attachments (the different ways that binary files corresponding to images and documents are encoded, compressed and attached to a message). Before we can do any learning, we're going to have to make sense of these formats.

A point about the applications of artificial intelligence is probably in order before we go too much further. AI technologies embedded in applications have been likened to raisins in raisin bread: without the raisins you still have bread, it just ain't raisin bread. The machine-learning algorithms in a spam filter are like the raisins in the raisin bread; they add value to the product but you still need all the dough around them to sell it. A spam filter needs tools to analyze and parse the contents of INBOX files, a user interface to communicate with the user, and an applications programming interface so that the filter can coordinate with the email client. The amount of code involved in machine learning, while important to the product, could be pretty modest. Before examining the raisins more closely, let's take a quick look at some of what is needed in the surrounding dough.

The first thing you might want to do with an INBOX is to identify the pieces of the file that are relevant to your application, spam filtering in this case. A lexical analyzer or *lexer* scans an input stream such as that produced by reading a file one character at a time and applies a collection of rules to convert the stream into a sequence of meaningful *tokens*. Each rule specifies a pattern and an action. If the lexer scanning the input stream sees a group of characters that match the pattern for a given rule, then it performs the action associated with the rule. For example, a set of lexer rules for making sense of an INBOX might include a rule that looks for the sequence of characters "From:" and converts it into a FROM token.

Other tokens might include BEGIN-MESSAGE, END-MESSAGE, ADDRESS, SUBJECT, URL, etc. In some cases, the tokens take the place of pieces of the input stream; for example, the string "From:" is replaced by the token (FROM), as is the string "FROM:" (it's irrelevant whether the characters are upper- or lowercase). In other cases, the tokens are attached to actual pieces of the input stream; for example, tld@cs.brown.edu is replaced by (ADDRESS "tld@cs.brown.edu"). A lexer typically strips away irrelevant information such as spaces, tabs and carriage returns and emphasizes the meaningful content.

Here's an email message I got recently (MIME, for "multipurpose internet mail extensions," is a widely used standard for encoding binary files as email attachments):

```
From: "Sulee Jenerika" <ejls@cs.brown.edu>
To: "Tom Dean" <tld@cs.brown.edu>
Subject: Re: Artemis Brochure

Hi Tom,

We've got a revised draft for the Artemis 2003
Brochure. Take a look and tell us what you think.

Sulee

[MIME-ATTACHMENT ...]
```

A lexical analyzer for a spam filter might turn this message into the following sequence of tokens: (BEGIN-MESSAGE), (BEGIN-HEADER) (FROM), (WORD "Sulee"), (WORD "Jenerika"), (ADDRESS "ejls@cs.brown.edu"), (TO), (WORD "Tom"), (WORD "Dean"), (ADDRESS "tld@cs.brown.edu"), (SUBJECT), (WORD "RE:"), (WORD "Artemis"), (WORD "Brochure"), (END-HEADER), (BEGIN-BODY), (WORD "Hi"), (WORD "Tom"), ..., (BEGIN-MIME-ATTACH), ..., (END-MIME-ATTACH), (END-BODY), (END-MESSAGE).

There's more structure in an INBOX file than is immediately evident in a sequence of tokens. For example, the subsequence (FROM), (WORD "Sulee"), (WORD "Jenerika"), (ADDRESS "ejls@cs.brown.edu") is analogous to a prepositional phrase, indicating that the enclosing message is from (the preposition) someone identified by the supplied words (the proper noun serving as the object of the preposition) and described by the given address (an adjective of sorts further qualifying the object of the prepositional phrase).

The structure in email messages and INBOX files can be described by a grammar with rules not unlike those you may have learned in grade school – for example, a prepositional phrase consists of a preposition and a noun phrase. However, unlike the rules of English grammar, which we're told by grammarians and style mavens alike serve only as guidelines, the grammar of messages and INBOX files is firmly adhered to, making it relatively easy to extract their content. A parser takes the output of a lexical analyzer and applies a set of grammatical rules to transform a sequence of tokens into a structured object capturing the content and structure of the original input stream.

Continuing with our example, the parser turns the token sequence generated by the lexical analyzer into the following structured object:

```
(MESSAGE
 (SENDER (NAME "Sulee Jenerika")
         (ADDRESS "ejls@cs.brown.edu"))
 (RECIPIENT (NAME "Tom Dean")
            (ADDRESS "tld@cs.brown.edu"))
 (SUBJECT "Re: Artemis Brochure")
 (BODY (TEXT ("Hi" "Tom" ...))
       (MIME-ATTACHMENT (FORMAT PDF)
                        (COMPRESSION ZIP)
                        (DOCUMENT ...))
       ...))
```

It may not seem that we gained much, but this format makes it much easier for a program to extract the pieces of an email message relevant for spam filtering. I used a lexical analyzer called lex and a parser called yacc[3] (which stands for "yet another compiler compiler") to convert my INBOX (actually several INBOX files) into a set of structured objects that I could feed into various learning programs written in C, Lisp and Mathematica.

---

[3] The programs lex and yacc are old warhorses: they're still widely used but they're not the latest lexical analyzers and parsers available. If you're interested in playing with such programs, you might want to check out flex and bison, analogous tools available from the GNU Project and the Free Software Foundation.

8.2 MACHINE LEARNING

Let's suppose that we've analyzed and parsed our files of full of email messages, interfaced with the user, interoperated with the email client, prestidigitated the whoozits and whatsits and generally done everything except separate the spam from the ham. The bread is rising and now we need to come up with some nice plump raisins. How do we get our spam filter to tell the difference between spam and ham?

You might imagine there is a general-purpose learning algorithm that can take a raw email message as input and decide on the message's spamishness without our supplying any background knowledge or hints about what's important to attend to and what's not worth worrying about. While learning algorithms exist that are capable of such a feat, they tend to require a large number of training examples in order to perform well. The reason is that they're trying to learn from first principles – they don't have any *a priori* idea of what's important and what's not, and so they have to look at more data and work harder.

It often requires fewer training examples and results in better performance to give a learning algorithm a good idea of what data features are likely to be worth attending to. In trying to distinguish between arctic char and atlantic salmon, an expert might tell a novice to look first at the color of the skin on the underbelly and then at the lower jaw. It's rare in life that we have to learn something entirely new with no outside help, and so it makes sense to give our learning algorithms whatever hints we can manage.

What features might be appropriate for a spam filter? In distinguishing spam from ham, it's often useful to know whether the email came from someone at a company (a "dot com") or a school (a "dot edu"). Other designators, for example organizations (a "dot org") or the government (a "dot gov"), may also prove relevant. If the subject line indicates that someone is replying to an earlier message from you, for example, the subject contains "Re:" or "RE:", that could indicate a legitimate email message – unless a clever spammer is trying to fool you. If the subject line or body of the message includes any of the words "buy", "sell", "winner", "prize", "sale", and the like, then the message may be an advertisement or promotion. Messages with attached images or compressed files with the extension "EXE" are generally, though not always, unwanted.

After you've thought about this for a while, you might think you could write a spam filter yourself. You could specify a bunch of features such as, SENDER-DOT-COM, which is true (#t) if the address of the sender ends with the string "com" or "COM" and false (#f) otherwise. You could process each message to assign values to each of the features you've identified as relevant and then summarize the message as the set of these assignments. For example, our sample message above might look something like this Scheme list:

```
((SENDER-DOT-COM #f)
 (SENDER-DOT-EDU #t)
 (SUBJECT-IS-REPLY #t)
 (SUBJECT-CONTAINS-FREE-WORD #f)
 (BODY-CONTAINS-SALE-WORD #f)
 (BODY-CONTAINS-BUY-WORD #f)
 (BODY-FORMATTED-HTML #f)
 (ATTACHED-PDF-DOC #t)
 (ATTACHED-JPG-IMG #f)
 ...)
```

Given this set of features, your hand-written spam filter might look thus:

```
if SUBJECT-IS-REPLY
    HAM
else if SENDER-DOT-COM
        if BODY-CONTAINS-SALE-WORD
            SPAM
        else if BODY-CONTAINS-BUY-WORD
                SPAM
            else if SUBJECT-CONTAINS-FREE-WORD
                    SPAM
                else HAM
    else if SENDER-DOT-EDU
            if ATTACHED-JPG-IMG
                SPAM
            else HAM
        else if BODY-FORMATTED-HTML
                SPAM
            else HAM
```

So why wouldn't this or something like it work? One reason is that if the program got much larger and more complicated it would be impossible to understand. It's really difficult for a programmer to keep track of all the cases, especially if, as is likely, there are hundreds of possibly relevant features instead of the half dozen or so in our small example. But the biggest problem is that, however good our intuitions about features signifying spam, we'll probably miss some features or combine them in the wrong way and end up with a filter that allows too much spam to pass.

What we need is a learning algorithm that can analyze a lot of data, consider a lot of different features and come up with a high-performance filter. Somehow our learning algorithm must search in the space of possible programs of the sort described above. Think about the set of all such programs using only if-then-else statements and a fixed set of features as variables. Let's say there are n features. How many such programs are there? The answer is lots: there are 2^n possible assignments to the n features and hence 2^n possible email messages that we can distinguish. A spam filter divides the set of messages into two classes, spam and ham, and hence there are as many programs as there are ways of dividing 2^n messages into two classes, which for any reasonably large n is a very big number.

For a given *training set*, the set of examples on which we'll base our spam filter, very likely more than one program will correctly classify all the examples, identifying spam as spam and ham as ham. For example, suppose that spam can be reliably identified by determining that the sender is a dot com and the body of the message contains HTML formatting and an attached JPG image. Here's a filter implementing this characterization of spam:

```
if SENDER-DOT-COM
    if BODY-FORMATTED-HTML
        if ATTACHED-JPG-IMG
            SPAM
        else HAM
    else HAM
else HAM
```

Assuming that our characterization of spam is correct, you could use additional features in implementing a spam filter, such as whether or not there are PDF attachments, but they wouldn't help. Might they hurt? Yes, for a couple of reasons.

One reason is that the extra features might result in a large, slow spam filter. If you use all n features, you would construct a filter of size 2^n, which would certainly be impractical for reasonably large n. A more important reason from the standpoint of learning, however, is that the extra features might be misleading and make it more difficult to generalize beyond the training examples.

Keep in mind that it's this generalizing beyond what you've already seen that you're really after. You've already classified all the training examples as spam or ham, and you're unlikely see these exact messages ever again. You want to classify *future* messages. Suppose all of the messages in your training set containing the word "free" in the subject line just happen to be messages you want to read and so you write the following filter:

```
if SUBJECT-CONTAINS-FREE-WORD
    HAM
else if SENDER-DOT-COM
        if BODY-FORMATTED-HTML
            if ATTACHED-JPG-IMG
                SPAM
            else HAM
        else HAM
    else HAM
```

With this filter, you'll misclassify spam messages that have "free" in the subject line. The first if-then-else statement in the classifier is not only superfluous, it leads to misclassification. In practice, the best classifiers appear to be the simplest, most compact and reliant on the fewest features. This observation is in accord with Occam's razor, a heuristic or rule of thumb harking back to William of Ockham's principle of parsimony: simpler theories are better than more complex ones. There is no fundamental justification for believing that simpler theories are in general better and indeed there are theorems, aptly called no-free-lunch theorems, that suggest there is no best (or universally optimal) method of choosing classifiers. That said, learning algorithms that employ some variant of Occam's razor to choose among classifiers tend to perform well in practice.

How might we design a learning algorithm to select a classifier in accord with Occam's razor? Here's a simple recursive algorithm that is the basis for one of the most widely used and practical methods for machine learning.

The input to our learning algorithm is a set of examples labeled spam or ham. The output is a classifier consisting of nested if-then-else statements. Each if-then-else statement uses one of the n features as its condition or *test*, and the *then* and *else* branches contain either another (nested) if-then-else statement or a classification, spam or ham.

The algorithm, which we'll call `build`, works recursively as follows. `build` takes two arguments: a set of examples that have yet to be classified and a set of features that have yet to be used. If all the examples yet to be classified are spam, then `build` returns SPAM. If all are ham, it returns HAM. If some are spam and some are ham, `build` chooses a feature and constructs an if-then-else statement by inserting the selected feature as the test and computing the then and else branches by calling `build` recursively on the remaining features and the examples split according to those in which the selected feature is true (the then branch) and those in which the selected feature is false (the else branch).

Here's what `build` might look like implemented in Scheme. This code uses the Lisp *quasi-quote* notation ("`"), which is particularly useful in programs that produce other programs as output. We looked at various quoting mechanisms for use in shell scripts in Chapter 2. The Lisp quasi-quote notation is similar to the quoting options available in shells in that it includes mechanisms for both suppressing and forcing evaluation. The quasi-quote mark suppresses evaluation in the expression that immediately follows except when it encounters a comma ("`,`"), which forces the evaluation of the immediately following expression. So, for example, the expression `'(1 ,(+ 1 1) 3)` evaluates to `(1 2 3)`. Here's a somewhat more complicated example a little closer to our present application:

```
> (let ((feature 'SENDER-DOT-COM) (yes 'HAM) (no 'SPAM))
    (if #f
        'HAM
      '(if ,feature ,yes else ,no)))
(if SENDER-DOT-COM HAM else SPAM)
```

Be careful to distinguish the single-quote character or apostrophe, "`'`", from the back-quote character or quasi-quote mark, "`"`; the apostrophe suppresses all evaluation in the expression that immediately follows. Here's the implementation of `build` in Scheme using the quasi-quote mechanism:

```
(define (build examples features)
  (if (all-spam? examples)
      'SPAM
    (if (all-ham? examples)
        'HAM
      (let ((feature (choose-feature examples features)))
        '(if ,feature
             ,(build (true-examples feature examples)
                     (remove feature features))
           else ,(build (false-examples feature examples)
                        (remove feature features)))))))
```

This code should give you a pretty good idea of how `build` produces a classifier, but it doesn't explain how it produces *compact* classifiers that use few features. A key part of this algorithm is in the `choose-feature` function, which considers how each of the remaining features would split the examples into then and else branches and chooses the feature producing the "best" split. I'll give you some examples illustrating how one split might be considered better than another.

Suppose `choose-feature` finds a feature such that the then branch would end up with all spam and the else branch with all ham. That's a great split; you can't do any better than that. Suppose `choose-feature` finds a feature such that the then branch ends up with half spam and half ham and ditto for the else branch. That's a lousy split since it made no useful distinctions among the remaining examples; you can't do any worse.

In general, splits that yield then and else branches in which the remaining examples have more of one type of message than the other are good and those in which the numbers of spam and ham are approximately equal are bad. There are a number of functions ranging from zero (equal proportions of spam and ham) to one (all spam or all ham) that work about equally well for selecting a good split. It's quite amazing that such a simple algorithm is so effective in such a wide range of problems.

Of course, you had to do some of the work: you had to select a set of possibly relevant features. The more features you select, the more likely `build` will find a good set of features with which to implement a classifier. But more features also make `build` work harder, and it's always possible that you'll overlook important features. There's no easy solution to this problem: finding good features is hard and that's why experts capable of making fine distinctions for particular problems are in such demand.

The `build` function implements an instance of what are called *decision-tree algorithms* because the if-then-else structures of the resulting classifiers look like trees whose branches are features that help decide the classification of the input to the classifier. Decision-tree algorithms are among the most common learning algorithms, but there are other algorithms and other approaches to machine learning.

8.3   LEARNING WITH PROBABILITIES

Research in machine learning often looks like a branch of applied mathematics. Ideas from probability and statistics are often used directly in learning algorithms or in analyzing and justifying techniques that at first blush seem to have nothing to do with probability or statistics. We'll take a peek at how to apply this sort of mathematics to spam filtering. This section is a little more technical than earlier ones and you may want to skip it if you don't enjoy playing around with equations and manipulating mathematical symbols.

You probably don't want a primer on probability theory and so I'll go easy on the formalities. Let's say that `Pr(SPAM)` is the fraction of all email messages that are spam; we'll call this the probability of spam. According to this definition, since all messages are either ham or spam, $Pr(HAM) = 1 - Pr(SPAM)$ is the fraction of all email messages that are ham. Let's say that $Pr(COM,HTML)$ is the fraction of all email messages such that the sender is a dot com *and* the body of the message contains HTML. In general, $Pr(X_1, X_2, \ldots, X_k)$ is the fraction of all email messages satisfying X_1 through X_k.[4]

Finally, let's say that $Pr(SPAM|HTML)$ is the fraction of email messages containing HTML that are also spam; this is called the *conditional probability* that a message is spam *given* that it contains HTML (you can read the vertical bar as "given that"). Stated in another way, $Pr(SPAM|HTML)$ is the ratio of $Pr(SPAM,HTML)$ to $Pr(HTML)$: divide the fraction of messages containing HTML by the fraction of messages that are both spam and contain HTML. With these simple definitions, we can do quite a lot of practical mathematics.

To make things simple, suppose our set of features consists of HTML, which is true if a message contains HTML, COM, which is true if the sender's email address is a dot com, and SALE, which is true if the word `sale` appears in the message. We'll put the negation symbol $\neg$ in front of a feature to indicate that that feature is *not* present: thus COM corresponds to (SENDER-DOT-COM #t) and $\neg$COM corresponds to (SENDER-DOT-COM #f). Note that $Pr(HAM) = Pr(\neg SPAM)$ and similarly $Pr(SPAM) = Pr(\neg HAM)$.

Given a message summarized by the assignment (BODY-FORMATTED-HTML #t), (SENDER-DOT-COM #t) and (BODY-CONTAINS-SALE-WORD #f), we're interested in calculating $Pr(SPAM|HTML,COM,\neg SALE)$, the probability that the message (characterized as containing HTML, sent by someone at a dot com, and not containing the word `sale`) is spam. We'd use this quantity in a spam filter by establishing a threshold, say 0.9, such that if $Pr(SPAM|HTML,COM,\neg SALE) > 0.9$, we classify the message as spam and eliminate it from the user's INBOX.

Why the threshold? By using probabilities, we've implicitly given up on distinguishing spam from ham with certainty. Sooner or later we have to choose to treat a message as ham and send it along to the user or treat it as spam and delete it. The threshold determines an important tradeoff. If we set the threshold too high, then nothing is classified as spam and we're likely to send along a lot of it. If we set the threshold too low, then everything looks like spam and we're likely to eliminate some ham. It may make sense to let the user set the threshold; some may prefer

---

[4] Suppose that $X_1 = \frac{1}{2}$ is the probability that a coin lands heads up the first time you flip it, $X_2 = \frac{1}{2}$ is the probability that the same coin lands heads up the second time you flip it, and so on. Assuming that the coin flips are independent of one another in the sense that one flip doesn't influence any other, $Pr(X_1, X_2, \ldots, X_k) = \left(\frac{1}{2}\right)^k = \frac{1}{2^k}$ is the probability that the coin lands heads up all k of the times you flip it. Why do you think many people wrongly believe that a fair coin (not a trick coin from a magic store) that has come up tails many times in a row is likely to come up heads the next time you flip it?

losing an occasional piece of ham to wading through a lot of spam, and others may be willing to accept some annoying spam rather than miss a critical piece of correspondence.

Now we don't know $Pr(SPAM|HTML,COM,\neg SALE)$ and so we'll have to calculate it using the probability calculus, a set of rules for manipulating probabilities. It turns out that while we don't have $Pr(SPAM|HTML,COM,\neg SALE)$ it's pretty easy to calculate reasonable estimates of probabilities such as $Pr(HTML|SPAM)$, $Pr(COM|SPAM)$ and $Pr(\neg SALE|SPAM)$ from looking at a set of training examples. For example, the estimate for $Pr(HTML|SPAM)$ is just the ratio of the number of training examples that contain HTML and are spam to the number of examples that are spam. Using these probabilities and certain assumptions about the probability that features co-occur, we can calculate $Pr(SPAM|HTML,COM,\neg SALE)$ using Bayes' rule, a particularly useful rule of the probability calculus named to recognize the Reverend Thomas Bayes (1701–1761), an English cleric and mathematician. The implications of Bayes' rule are so important that an entire branch of probability and statistics is called Bayesian probability theory.

In medicine, the conditional probability that a patient exhibits a particular symptom given that the patient has a particular disease can often be estimated. This is called causal knowledge since it provides evidence on whether or not the disease causes the symptom. Hospitals keep records to track patients, their diseases and their symptoms. A reasonable estimate of the probability that a patient exhibits a particular symptom given that the patient has a particular disease is just the ratio of the number of patient records showing both the disease and the symptom to the number of patient records showing the disease (whether or not the patient exhibited the symptom).

In treating patients, however, as in identifying spam, we're interested primarily in diagnostic knowledge: the probability that a patient has a particular disease given that the patient exhibits a particular symptom. We could estimate this as the ratio of the number of patient records showing both the disease and the symptom to the total number of patient records showing the symptom, but this estimate tends to be more fragile. If there is an outbreak of the disease, the hospital will suddenly start seeing more patients with the symptom, but until these patients are diagnosed, the physicians won't be able to update their diagnostic knowledge accurately. The causal knowledge, on the other hand, will be unaffected.

Here's the basic formula for Bayes' rule:

$$Pr(A|B) = \frac{Pr(B|A)\ Pr(A)}{Pr(B)}$$

Substitute "symptoms" for B and "disease" for A and you'll see how Bayes' rule applies to medical diagnosis. Substitute "features" for B and "spam" for A and you'll see how Bayes' rule applies to spam filtering. You'll also notice that to get $\Pr(A|B)$ from $\Pr(B|A)$ you need $\Pr(A)$ and $\Pr(B)$. Think about diseases and symptoms and imagine how you'd estimate the probability of a patient exhibiting a given symptom or the probability of a patient having a given disease by using hospital records.

We can derive Bayes' rule using only the definition of conditional probability. The last line (4) of this derivation is the simplest formulation of Bayes' rule.

1.　$\Pr(A|B) = \dfrac{\Pr(A,B)}{\Pr(B)}$　　　– Definition of $\Pr(A|B)$

2.　$\Pr(B|A) = \dfrac{\Pr(A,B)}{\Pr(A)}$　　　– Definition of $\Pr(B|A)$

3.　$\Pr(A,B) = \Pr(A|B)\ \Pr(A)$　　– Algebraic manipulation using (2)

4.　$\Pr(A|B) = \dfrac{\Pr(B|A)\ \Pr(A)}{\Pr(B)}$　　– Substitution using (1) and (3)

In order to use Bayes' rule to calculate $\Pr(\text{SPAM}|\text{HTML},\text{COM},\neg\text{SALE})$, we'll also rely on the rule of probability $\Pr(B) = \Pr(B|A) + \Pr(B|\neg A)$, which we now justify informally. Think about the probability that a message contains HTML. If we know the probability that a message contains HTML given that it's spam (the proportion of spam messages containing HTML) and the probability that a message contains HTML given that it's ham (the proportion of ham messages containing HTML), then, since a message must be either spam or ham, the sum of these two probabilities is the proportion of all messages containing HTML, that is the probability that a message contains HTML.

Finally, we're going to need a way of calculating $\Pr(\text{HTML},\text{COM},\neg\text{SALE}|\text{SPAM})$. If we had enough training examples we could do this directly, but if we have many more features, and we probably will in order to build any really effective spam filter, then we will need far too many training examples to get accurate estimates for all the probabilities of this form. Think about how many probabilities of this form you would actually need; for just three features we'd need

$\Pr(\text{HTML},\text{COM},\text{SALE}|\text{SPAM})$,

$\Pr(\neg\text{HTML},\text{COM},\text{SALE}|\text{SPAM})$,

$\Pr(\text{HTML},\neg\text{COM},\text{SALE}|\text{SPAM})$,

and so on for all eight possible combinations. If you have only ten features (and that's probably not enough) and you need even ten examples to estimate each probability (and that's not nearly enough), then already you'd need at least 10,000 training examples, and there are probably some rare combinations for which you still won't have enough examples.

As an expedient, we'll assume that all our features are mutually independent, given the status of a message as spam or ham. This would mean that the presence of HTML in a document is completely independent of it coming from a dot com. This assumption of independence is unlikely to be true for all pairs of features; for instance, if we see the word `sale` in the subject line of a spam message, it is far more likely to be from a dot com than from a dot edu, so COM and SALE are not independent of one another given spam. Even so, such assumptions are often made on the justification that they won't hurt too much, and practically speaking there aren't many alternatives. If we accept this assumption, then we can calculate $\Pr(\text{HTML},\text{COM},\neg\text{SALE}\,|\,\text{SPAM})$ as the product of $\Pr(\text{HTML}\,|\,\text{SPAM})$, $\Pr(\text{COM}\,|\,\text{SPAM})$ and $\Pr(\neg\text{SALE}\,|\,\text{SPAM})$, all relatively easy to estimate. So, given the above derivations and assumptions, we can calculate the desired probabilities as:

$$\Pr(\text{SPAM}\,|\,\text{HTML},\text{COM},\neg\text{SALE}) = \frac{\Pr(\text{HTML},\text{COM},\neg\text{SALE}\,|\,\text{SPAM})\ \Pr(\text{SPAM})}{\Pr(\text{HTML},\text{COM},\neg\text{SALE})}$$

$$\Pr(\text{HTML},\text{COM},\neg\text{SALE}\,|\,\text{SPAM}) = \Pr(\text{HTML}\,|\,\text{SPAM})\ \Pr(\text{COM}\,|\,\text{SPAM})\ \Pr(\neg\text{SALE}\,|\,\text{SPAM})$$

$$\Pr(\text{HTML},\text{COM},\neg\text{SALE}) = \Pr(\text{HTML},\text{COM},\neg\text{SALE}\,|\,\text{SPAM}) +$$
$$\Pr(\text{HTML},\text{COM},\neg\text{SALE}\,|\,\neg\text{SPAM})$$

$$= \Pr(\text{HTML}\,|\,\text{SPAM})\ \Pr(\text{COM}\,|\,\text{SPAM})\ \Pr(\neg\text{SALE}\,|\,\text{SPAM}) +$$
$$\Pr(\text{HTML}\,|\,\neg\text{SPAM})\ \Pr(\text{COM}\,|\,\neg\text{SPAM})\ \Pr(\neg\text{SALE}\,|\,\neg\text{SPAM})$$

The assumption that all the features are mutually independent given their designation as spam or ham, which is what allows us to compute $\Pr(\text{HTML},\text{COM}\,|\,\text{SPAM})$ as the product of $\Pr(\text{HTML}\,|\,\text{SPAM})$ and $\Pr(\text{COM}\,|\,\text{SPAM})$, is a concession to computational considerations that warrants great care in its application. Other concessions are implicit in the approach described above. In practice, it is likely that for some of the features you decide to use very little data will be available to estimate the required probabilities. You can choose to throw such features out or you can use them with care. Quantifying the consequences of using such questionable features is the province of applied statistics.

Clearly there are complications and problems to overcome in using lessons from probability theory to design a good spam filter. Spam filters already on the market tout their use of Bayesian probability theory. But there are also spam filters using neural networks, decision trees, genetic algorithms and any of a host of other techniques and algorithms studied in artificial intelligence. The engineers and practitioners in the field keep pushing the envelope of what computers can learn. And little bits of machine learning, like raisins in raisin bread, are finding their way into more and more applications. Machine learning may not work in the same way that human learning does, but it's learning nonetheless. Today, computers can play chess, schedule commercial aircraft, identify credit-card fraud and diagnose problems in automobiles better and faster than humans. Tomorrow, who knows what they'll be able to do better than we can?

8.4 LEARNING MORE ABOUT LEARNING

I'm often asked to suggest books to read for a good introduction to artificial intelligence and machine learning in particular. Several years ago I co-authored an introductory artificial intelligence text covering both theory and practice. The text features a brief introduction to programming in a dialect of Lisp called Common Lisp and gives readers the opportunity to connect algorithms to working programs and theory to practice. All the algorithms are specified in both pseudocode and Common Lisp and a supplement available on the web provides all the code described in the book plus examples. The supplement also provides support for translating the Common Lisp code to Scheme. It's still a good beginning textbook but artificial intelligence, like the larger field of computer science, is evolving rapidly.

About the same time as my book came out, Stuart Russell and Peter Norvig published a more comprehensive and detailed textbook. The second edition of their book, which came out in 2003, is even more comprehensive than the first and I've just got to say it is a wonderful text. Extensive supplements include implementations of the algorithms in Common Lisp, Python (which is similar in some respects to Perl but was designed from the bottom up as an object-oriented programming language), Prolog, C++ and Java. It is an excellent introduction to the field accessible to most college students and also containing advanced material of interest to graduate students.

If you're interested primarily in machine learning, Tom Mitchell's *Machine Learning* gives a good basic introduction to machine-learning theory and algorithms. Relevant to the applications covered in this chapter, the web site for the book features code supplements for learning decision trees (written in Common Lisp) and Bayesian learning to classify articles posted to news groups (written in C).

It probably sounds like a typical sort of academic remark, but I can't emphasize enough the advantages of a thorough grounding in basic mathematics including graph theory, linear algebra and, especially if you're interested in machine learning, probability and statistics. For a solid two-semester introduction to probability and statistics, DeGroot's *Probability and Statistics* is my favorite textbook. I consult DeGroot's text and refer my students to it regularly. A third edition is now available.

CHAPTER NINE

Modern Architecture

With all my mumbo-jumbo about conjuring up spirits and casting spells, it's easy to lose track of the fact that computers are real and there is a very precise and concrete connection between the programs and fragments of code you run on your computer and the various electrical devices that make up the hardware of your machine. Interacting with the computer makes the notions of computing and computation very real, but you're still likely to feel shielded from the hardware – as indeed you are – and to be left with the impression that the connection to the hardware is all very difficult to comprehend.

For some of you, grabbing a soldering iron and a handful of logic chips and discrete components is the best path to enlightenment. I used to love tinkering with switching devices scavenged from the local telephone company, probing circuit boards to figure out what they could do and then making them do something other than what they were designed for. Nowadays, it's easier than ever to "interface" sensors and motors to computers, but it still helps to know a little about electronics even if you're mainly interested in the software side of things.

I think it's a good experience for every computer scientist to learn a little about analog circuits (for example, build a simple solid-state switch using a transistor and a couple of resistors) and integrated circuits for memory, logic and timing (build a circuit to add two binary numbers out of primitive logic gates). It's satisfying to understand how the abstract digital logic involving zeros and ones is implemented using analog circuits based on continuously varying voltage levels.

I'm not going to say much about the analog-circuit-to-digital-logic connection. However, I would like to explore the connection between digital logic and a simple model of computation upon which we can base our understanding of software. My goal is to explain how logic components support primitive operations such as adding and multiplying numbers, basic memory management such as fetching (reading) and storing (writing) data and instructions, and simple

140

branching and sequencing as required to execute program instructions stored in memory.

9.1 LOGIC GATES

The traditional starting point in explaining digital computers is the *logic gate* that implements basic Boolean functions like AND, OR and NOT. A *Boolean function* (named after the mathematician George Boole (1815–1864), who is credited with the discovery of the calculus[1] at the foundation of computer logic) is a function that takes 1s and 0s as inputs and provides 1s and 0s as outputs. The abstraction is that each logic gate implements a particular Boolean function whose behavior can be completely specified in a so-called *truth table*. In talking about Boolean functions in computers, we generally replace the traditional truth-value names true and false with the corresponding binary values 1 and 0. Here's the truth table for a two-input AND gate:

INPUT1	INPUT2	OUTPUT
0	0	0
1	0	0
0	1	0
1	1	1

A truth table specifies the output of the logic gate for each possible combination of inputs – one row in the table for each such combination. There are two rows in the table for a gate with only one input, four rows for a gate with two inputs, and 2^n rows for a gate with n inputs. As we'll see, there are also logic gates with multiple outputs, but the number of rows depends only on the number of inputs since the output is completely determined by the input.

A two-input AND is 1 only when both of its inputs are 1. A two-input OR is 1 when either one or both of its inputs are 1; here's the truth table for an OR gate:

INPUT1	INPUT2	OUTPUT
0	0	0
1	0	1
0	1	1
1	1	1

---

[1] A "calculus" is any method of calculation using specialized symbolic notation, not just the invention credited to Newton and Leibniz and referred to in textbooks as differential and integral calculus.

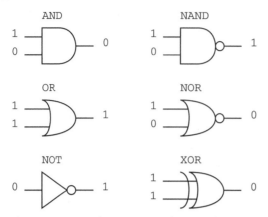

Figure 9.1: Basic logic gates with example inputs and outputs

A three-input AND gate has an output of 1 when all three of its inputs are 1 and 0 otherwise. Here's the truth table for a single-input NOT gate, also called an *inverter* since its output is the opposite of its input.

INPUT	OUTPUT
0	1
1	0

We can construct arbitrarily complex Boolean functions by connecting ("wiring together") the inputs and outputs of logic gates. The resulting digital circuits (also called *logic diagrams*) are drawn using standard symbols to represent the most common logic gates. The left-hand side of Figure 9.1 shows the three basic logic gates whose truth tables I've listed. The logic gates on the right in Figure 9.1 can be defined in terms of those on the left.

One of the gates on the right, however, is particularly interesting. A two-input NOT AND (or NAND) gate can be constructed by feeding the output of an AND gate into the input of a NOT gate. Here's the logic diagram for the NAND gate:

And here's the truth table for the NAND gate:

INPUT1	INPUT2	OUTPUT
0	0	1
1	0	1
0	1	1
1	1	0

NAND gates are particularly versatile: you can construct *any* Boolean function with enough NAND gates. You can use a NAND gate to implement a NOT gate by fixing one input to be 1 and using the other input as the single input to a NOT gate, as in

INPUT1 (fixed)	INPUT2	OUTPUT
1	0	1
1	1	0

or you can simply wire together the two inputs of the NAND gate:

To implement an OR gate using a bunch of NAND gates, feed each input into a NOT (implemented by a NAND) and then wire the outputs of the two NOTs to the inputs of another NAND:

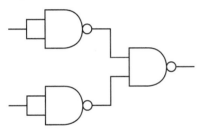

Another very useful logic gate shown in Figure 9.1 is the exclusive OR (XOR) gate defined by this truth table:

INPUT1	INPUT2	OUTPUT
0	0	0
1	0	1
0	1	1
1	1	0

And here's how to build an XOR gate out of NAND gates:

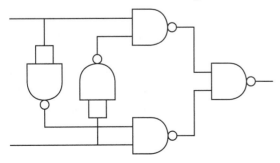

9.2 THE DIGITAL ABSTRACTION

While logic gates and Boolean functions can be a good starting place, you may be curious about how such gates are implemented in more primitive electronic circuits. I'm wary of heading down this path: the danger is that we'll start talking about transistors and resistors, get sidetracked by discussing Kirchoff's current and voltage laws, descend into quantum electrodynamics, and then head off into the stratosphere waving our hands about string theory and beyond. But I think we can avoid a lengthy digression and still say a few words about how logic gates are implemented.

The most basic component in automated computing is a switch. A switch is a device that can be in one of two states, open or closed, and is such that we can change its state by physically manipulating it or sending it an appropriate signal. It's helpful to think about the light switches in your house in considering how to use switches to implement logic gates. Put two switches in series with a light and you have an AND gate:

Put two switches in parallel and you have an OR gate:

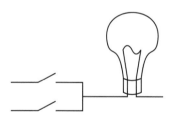

Reverse the labels on a switch ("on" for "off" and "off" for "on") and you have a NOT gate.

Electromechanical relays enable the output of one gate to control the inputs to other gates without someone manually closing a switch. In one of the simplest relays, an electromagnet closes a mechanical switch when the voltage drop across the coil of the electromagnet is sufficient. A small spring keeps the switch open when no current is flowing through the coil. Relays can be wired in any configuration and the switch associated with one relay can be used to control the voltage across the coil of another. Here two relays are implementing an AND gate whose output controls a third relay:

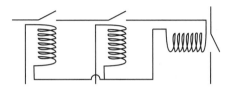

Electromechanical relays work just fine as switches, and you could build a computer entirely from such relays if you had enough of them. Indeed, the first electromechanical digital computers used relays as switches.

This might convince you that it's possible to implement logic gates, but it shouldn't convince you it's possible to build computers of the sort you're probably used to working with. The problem is speed. The switches in modern computers can change from a voltage level corresponding to a binary value of 0 to a voltage level corresponding to a binary value of 1 and back many billions of times a second. Electromechanical relays can change state only a few dozen times per second. The speed of modern computers is made possible by transistors and digital integrated circuits. The transistor-transistor-logic (TTL) family of integrated circuits (ICs) defines binary values in terms of analog values: a binary value of 0 is between 0.0 and 0.8 volts and a binary value of 1 is between 2.0 and 5.0 volts.

Other families of digital ICs, based on other technologies (look up CMOS, NMOS or PMOS on the web), trade speed (how quickly the gates switch and hence how zippily your computer games run) against power (how much current is needed and hence how long my laptop operates before its batteries must be recharged) and heat (how much heat the switching circuits generate and hence how hot my laptop feels on my knees as I type these words). ICs typically package multiple gates implementing several Boolean functions (search the web for information on the venerable 7400 quad NAND, an IC that contains four NAND gates in a single package with 14 pins or places to attach wires, twelve dedicated to the eight inputs and four outputs for the four NANDs and two for power).

There are also high-density circuits with lots of tightly packed transistors called very large scale integrated (VLSI) circuits that implement the logic for an entire computer and combine millions of gates in a single package. Even so, I'll almost guarantee that in another decade, possibly sooner, people will marvel that you and I managed with such a paltry amount of computing power. From gears and cogs to mechanical switches and electromechanical relays, from vacuum tubes to transistors and optical switches, all these technologies have been used to support the digital abstraction.

9.3 ADDITION AND MULTIPLICATION

Once you're comfortable with logic gates, the next step is to figure out how to use them to implement primitive operations of the sort most closely associated with computers, for example, adding, subtracting, multiplying and dividing numbers. Some folks don't think very highly of math (calculators can do it, after all) and would be much more impressed if I were to convince them that they could do something involving symbolic manipulation, say, playing tic-tac-toe, with logic gates. But we'll stick with math for now – tic-tac-toe is trivial after computer arithmetic.

I'll assume you know how to count and do math in different bases. We're used to dealing with decimal or base-10 numbers, but for simplicity computers use binary or base-2 numbers since only two symbols, 0 and 1, are required in base 2, thus making logic gates particularly convenient.

Suppose you want to add 24 and 19 in decimal. You start with the 1s column, add 4 and 9 to get 13, write down the 3 in the 1s column and carry the 1. Then you add 2 and 1 in the 10s column, add in the carry to get 4, and combine the results in the 1s and 10s columns to get the answer 43. Adding two binary numbers is no different except that columns correspond not to powers of ten (1, 10, 100, etc.) but to powers of 2: 1, 2, 4, 8, etc. Adding single-digit binary numbers (called *bits*) is easy because there are only four cases to consider:

INPUT1	INPUT2	OUTPUT	CARRY
0	0	0	0
1	0	1	0
0	1	1	0
1	1	0	1

You might notice that this table without the CARRY column is the same as the table for the exclusive OR gate, and without the OUTPUT column it is the same as the table for an AND gate. The function described by this table, called a *half adder*, can be implemented with an XOR and an AND gate:

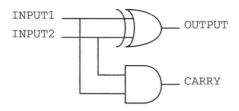

The "half" in the name is because a half adder doesn't allow a carry bit from the next smallest column, so it works for the 1s column but not for any other. A *full adder*, the gate used for the rest of the columns, is described by:

INPUT1	INPUT2	CARRYIN	OUTPUT	CARRYOUT
0	0	0	0	0
1	0	0	1	0
0	1	0	1	0
1	1	0	0	1
0	0	1	1	0
1	0	1	0	1
0	1	1	0	1
1	1	1	1	1

As an exercise, try to implement a full adder with two exclusive ORs, a pair of ANDs and a regular OR.

Now you should be able to string together a half adder and $(m-1)$ full adders to add two m-bit binary numbers. Subtraction is a little trickier and we'll leave it the dedicated reader to figure it out or track it down on the web. (Hint: if you get stuck, search for pages on "two's complement arithmetic.")

One of the most basic components of a computer is a piece of digital circuitry called an *arithmetic and logic unit* (ALU). The ALU performs arithmetic operations like addition and subtraction and logical operations like AND and OR. (Think about what it would mean to AND together two n-bit binary numbers.) The basic ALU takes as input two n-bit binary numbers and another (generally shorter) m-bit binary number that specifies the operation the ALU is supposed to perform – addition, subtraction, logical AND, logical OR. It then provides as output the resulting n-bit number plus some additional bits that tell us such things as whether or not the result is zero and the carry output for additions in which the result is larger than n bits. The primitive operations are mapped onto binary numbers called *opcodes*, so, for example, 000 might be the opcode for addition, 001 for subtraction, 010 for logical AND, and so on.

Multiplication, unlike addition, is not implemented as a primitive operation performed by the ALU. There are a couple of reasons for this. First, representing the result of adding two n-bit numbers requires no more than $n + 1$ bits or one n-bit number and a carry bit, but representing the result of multiplying two n-bit binary numbers could require as many $2n$ bits to represent. And, second, as we'll see, multiplication is considerably more complicated than addition.

Multiplication is facilitated by using circuitry for shifting the bits in a binary number; shifting to the left in binary is equivalent to multiplication. If Z = 0000XXXX is an 8-bit binary number, then Z times binary 00000010 (2^1 in decimal) is 000XXXX0 and Z times binary 00000100 (2^2 in decimal) is 00XXXX00. More concretely, 00001010 in binary is $8 + 2 = 10$ in decimal; to multiply by 2, shift left one bit to obtain 00101000 in binary, which is $16 + 4 = 20$ in decimal, and to multiply by 4, shift left two bits to obtain 00010100 in binary, which is $32 + 8 = 40$ in decimal. Shifting to the right is integer division. Think about what happens to the least significant bits when you shift to the right.

By the way, we're so used to how we write numbers that it's difficult to imagine any other way. Computer engineers, however, are free to represent numbers inside the computer however they like. In most technical writing, we notate numbers by writing the digits from least to most significant starting from the right and working our way to the left. The computer jargon for this notational convention is that the digits (bits in the case of binary numbers) are represented in *big-endian* ("big-end-first"). This is just a convention, and there's no reason why a computer engineer has to follow it in designing the internals of a computer. Indeed, Intel microprocessors represent numbers *little-endian* ("little-end-first"). The binary number 0101 is $2^0 + 2^2 = 5$ big-endian and $2^1 + 2^3 = 10$ little-endian. The notion of big-endian versus little-endian can apply to numbers at the bit level or to larger components of numbers such as bytes, which are components composed of eight bits. We might represent an integer in terms of two eight-bit bytes for a total of 16 bits thus allowing us to represent the integers 0 to 65535 or (using one bit as a *sign bit*) the numbers −32768 to 32767.

But let's get back to multiplying numbers. To multiply two decimal numbers, you have to remember your multiplication tables and you have to shift the intermediate results as you take into account the different columns corresponding to the different powers of ten. But once you've done all the shifting and applied your knowledge of the times tables, the problem reduces to addition:

```
   47
*  23
 ----
  141
 94
 ----
 1081
```

The multiplication tables for binary numbers are pretty simple: 0 times X is 0 and 1 times X is X – that's it! So, all we have to do is figure out how to use binary gates to shift digits and we've got it made:

```
  101 = 1 + 4 = 5 (the multiplicand)
* 101 = 1 + 4 = 5 (the multiplier)
-----
  101    shift 0 columns to the left and multiply by 1
    0    shift 1 column to the left and multiply by 0
101      shift 2 columns to the left and multiply by 1
-----
11001 = 1 + 8 + 16 = 25 (the product)
```

I'll assume that you can imagine some scheme for converting an n-bit binary number of the form 00XXXXXX into 0XXXXXX0. The entire process of multiplying two n-bit binary numbers is a little more complicated than adding two such numbers and involves a procedure, albeit a rather simple one that can be implemented in hardware.

In order to explain how to implement multiplication in hardware, we need to understand how memory is implemented. So far we've imagined that setting the inputs to a logic gate determines the output of the gate. In the analog circuit, we set the input wires by establishing the required voltage levels on the wires and then, after a delay for the transistors to do their thing, the right voltage values are attained on the output wires. There are times (no pun intended) when we want to save the result of a logic gate, perhaps setting it aside while we perform other computations. This is where computer memory comes into play.

9.4 COMPUTER MEMORY

The simplest memory units, called *latches* or *flip-flops*, are used to store a single bit. A very simple latch called a D latch can be implemented with two NOT

OR (NOR) gates:

INPUT1	INPUT2	OUTPUT
0	0	1
1	0	0
0	1	0
1	1	1

Here's the circuit:

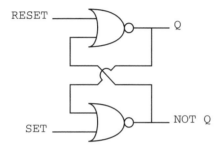

The output from the top NOR gate is fed back into the input of the bottom NOR gate and the output of the bottom NOR is fed into the input of the top NOR. The internal state or value of the D latch is designated as Q and the inverted value as NOT Q.

The D latch is used as follows. Normally, the inputs SET and RESET are at logic level 0. If you want to set the value of the latch to be 0, you make the RESET input go to logic level 1 for a short time. If you want to set the value of the latch to be 1, then you make the SET input go to logic level 1 for a short time.

If the SET and RESET inputs on a D latch are changing between logic levels at the same time, then all bets are off on the final value of the latch. For this reason, other memory units such as the D flip-flop use a clock signal to control when to let the memory unit change its internal state. I won't go into clocked logic except to say that logic gates implemented with analog circuits take time to change between the voltage levels representing binary values; it is important therefore to let the voltage levels "settle out" before making use of them by, say, storing them in memory or using them in subsequent computations.

With a D latch or a flip-flop, we can store a single bit. We use registers to store larger chunks of information. A *register* consists of some number of latches, one for every bit needed. Typically we talk of registers being 16, 32, 64 or more bits wide. We use registers to store *operands*, the inputs to basic operations, to store the results of operations, and to store the results of intermediate calculations. In the case of multiplication, we store the operands, the multiplicand and the multiplier, in appropriately wide registers. For reasons that will soon become apparent, we make sure that the registers for the multiplicand and the product are wide enough to accommodate the product.

Here's a simple procedure for multiplying two *n*-bit numbers. We'll call the three registers the *multiplicand*, *multiplier* and *product* registers. The multiplicand and product registers are 2*n* bits wide and the multiplier register is *n* bits wide. The procedure modifies the contents of the multiplicand and multiplier registers as well as the product register. The additions are handled by the ALU and the shifts right and left are handled by special-purpose shifting registers. The additional logic for counting from 1 to *n* and implementing the conditional (if-then) statement is also handled with special-purpose circuitry. The procedure description uses a C-like or Java-like syntax, but keep in mind that the procedure is implemented in hardware.

```
multiply( multiplicand, multiplier ) {
    multiplicand_register = multiplicand ;
    multiplier_register = multiplier ;
    product_register = 0 ;
    for i = 1 to n {
        if the rightmost bit of the multiplier_register is 1
            then product_register =
                    product_register + multiplicand_register ;
        shift the mutiplicand_register left one bit ;
        shift the mutiplier_register right one bit ;
    }
}
```

Suppose the multiplicand is binary 10 (decimal 2) and the multiplier is binary 11 (decimal 3) and so n = 2. Prior to executing the for loop, the operand and result registers are initialized as:

```
multiplicand_register = 0010
  multiplier_register = 0011
    product_register = 0000
```

After the first (i = 1) iteration of the for loop, we have:

```
multiplicand_register = 0100
  multiplier_register = 0001
    product_register = 0010
```

After the second (`i` = 2) and final iteration of the `for` loop, we have:

```
multiplicand_register = 1000
  multiplier_register = 0000
    product_register = 0110
```

If we allow that primitive operations like adding two numbers or shifting a number one bit either right or left can be performed in one time step, how many time steps are necessary to multiply two *n*-bit numbers? Clearly multiplication is more time-consuming than addition, so it's no surprise that engineers designing computers take considerable pains to devise circuitry for performing multiplication (and division) that runs very fast.

By the way, we needn't restrict ourselves to operations involving only numbers. We could define primitives that operate on letters, symbols, words, sounds, images, or signals corresponding to almost anything you can imagine from brain waves to blood pressure. However, it turns out that numbers will suffice. That is, once we assemble a set of basic primitives that let us manipulate numbers, we can handle all these other forms of input by combining the numerical primitives in programs of varying complexity. There is considerable benefit in sticking with the numerical primitives, since with this minimalist approach it's possible to build compact, inexpensive computing devices that can still perform any computation when given the appropriate software.

What's next? Now we need to encode and execute programs that exercise these basic operations. Registers are our working memory for storing operands and intermediate results, but we need additional memory for storing programs, data and those results we'd like to keep around for a while. We need to be able to load registers with the contents of specified locations in memory, store the contents of registers in specified locations, perform operations on specified registers and store the results in other specified registers. We need to be able to perform certain operations conditionally depending on the outcome of various tests, thereby implementing conditionals and loops. And, finally, we need some way to orchestrate the whole process so that programs execute in accord with the programmer's intuitions of how computations should proceed.

9.5 MACHINE LANGUAGE

The first part of this chapter tried to dispel some of the mystery surrounding computers by convincing you that logic gates can perform basic arithmetical and logical operations. Now I'd like to present a model of computation called the *register-machine model* that lets us string together arithmetical and logical operations to create entire programs. The register-machine model and its many variants are derived from the so-called *von Neumann architecture* whose logical design is the foundation for most modern computers.

A register machine consists of a memory, a *central processing unit* (CPU) – also called the *processor* – and a pathway or *bus* for moving data from memory to the CPU and back. The CPU is constructed from an arithmetic and logic unit (ALU), control logic that implements the basic loop governing program execution and a bunch of registers that keep track of operands, results and other useful information.

We've already seen one type of memory: the registers used temporarily to store operands and results in performing basic operations like addition and multiplication. Registers of this sort play an integral role in the register-machine model, as you may have guessed from the name; however, when we speak about memory in the context of the register-machine model, we're talking about something separate – a place to store lots of stuff for a long time.

In the register-machine model, this sort of longer-term memory is defined in terms of a set of locations in which each location has an address and contents. The addresses are generally assumed to be arranged *consecutively* as the natural numbers 0 through M (of course, we'll represent addresses internally as binary numbers, but that's merely a detail at this level of abstraction). The content of each location is an integer between 0 and N (also represented as a binary number). This model of memory is the *random-access memory* (RAM) model, which assumes that we can access the contents of any location in memory by simply referring to its address. If we have one megabyte of RAM (one megabyte is $2^{10} = 1024$ kilobytes, where a kilobyte is 2^{10} bytes and a byte is eight bits) then M is $2^{20} - 1$ and N is $(2^8 - 1) = 255$. If K is the address of a location in RAM that is greater than or equal to 0 and less than or equal to $(M - 1)$, then $(K + 1)$ is the next consecutive address in RAM.

We'll gloss over lots of details concerning how memory is implemented. For example, static RAM (SRAM) is implemented with the sort of latches and flip-flops we used to construct registers. Dynamic RAM (DRAM) is implemented with fewer transistors by using capacitors to store a charge determining whether a memory cell is interpreted as containing a logical 0 or 1; the charge leaks away, however, and so DRAMs must be periodically refreshed (the dynamic part), complicating their implementation and use. There are also the intricacies of using decoders and multiplexers to address a large RAM; very interesting stuff, but we'll ignore these details. Ditto for the details of implementing the various pathways or buses used for transfers to and from memory. We'll assume that if we have the address of a location in memory, then we can either store a number in that location or read its current contents.

Specifically, if we have the address of a location in RAM in a register of the ALU, then we can store the current contents of the RAM location in some other register in the ALU – this corresponds to reading from memory and is called "loading (the contents of) a register from memory". In addition, if we have the address of a RAM location in a register of the ALU, then we can store the current contents of some other register in the ALU in the location in RAM pointed to by this address – this corresponds to writing to memory and is called "storing (the contents of) a register in memory". That's pretty much it for our model of memory. (We're ignoring other forms of memory such as those involving magnetic and optical disks and tape drives.)

The contents of memory are interpreted differently depending on context. In some circumstances, the CPU interprets the contents of a location in memory as an instruction of one of three types: a primitive arithmetical or logical operation to be performed by the ALU, an instruction to move information between RAM and the registers of the CPU, or a conditional indicating a test and alternative actions. In other cases, the CPU might interpret the contents of a location as an address or part of an address for a location in memory. In still other cases, it might interpret the contents of a location as data to be used as operands for arithmetical or logical operations.

If the registers are large enough, then the CPU may treat their contents as segmented into two or more fields, so that, for example, the first five bits are interpreted as a code for an instruction or basic operation, the next five for an operand or an address, the next five ... well, you get the idea; there are all sorts of strategies for organizing memory. The CPU also includes a special register called the *program counter* (also called the *instruction address register*) that keeps track of where the CPU is in executing a program stored in RAM. We'll assume (without loss of generality, as mathematicians like to say) that when the computer is first started the program counter contains the address of the first location in memory.

The basic loop governing the operation of the CPU is as follows. The CPU interprets the contents of the location in memory pointed to by the address in the program counter as an instruction and does whatever the instruction requires – for example, loading registers from memory, storing the contents of registers in memory, adding the contents of two registers and placing the result in a third register, and so on. There are also important instructions called jump and branch instructions that can modify the contents of the program counter. For example, a jump instruction might specify an address (or a register containing an address) to

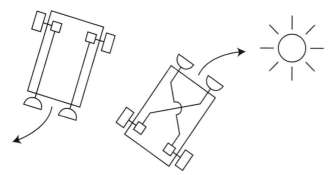

Figure 9.2: Two of Valentino Braitenberg's mobile robots

load into the address counter. A branch instruction typically specifies a test and an address to load into the address counter if the test is positive; the test might be whether or not the number stored in a register is zero. If the contents of the program counter are not changed by a jump or a branch instruction, then the CPU increment the contents of the program counter by one so that it now points to the next location in memory. The jump and branch instructions and the default mode of incrementing the program counter govern the flow of control in programs containing loops, procedure calls, conditionals and much more.

The *machine language* of a particular computer is a language of binary codes that can be directly interpreted by the hardware comprising the CPU. The CPU interprets the bits stored in memory as codes for instructions, memory addresses and registers. Writing in machine language is painful because it's very difficult for us to keep track of what all the bits mean. That said, it's instructive to look at a simple machine-language program to get a better appreciation of what's going on in the CPU.

Let's consider a program for controlling a mobile robot. Figure 9.2 depicts two very simple mobile robots seen from above. Each robot has a rectangular body and two wheels, each attached to a separate motor, and two sensors that respond to light. (The robots are adapted from Valentino Braitenberg's book *Vehicles: Experiments in Synthetic Psychology*.) The sensors are photovoltaic cells: the more light that falls on the sensor, the more current it produces. The sensors are wired directly to the motors and we assume that they generate enough current to drive the motors and turn the wheels. The more the light on the sensor, the greater the current and the faster the motor turns. Depending on how the sensors are wired to the motors, the robots either turn and drive toward the light (the robot on the right) or turn and drive away from the light (the robot on the left). We're going to implement the light-seeking robot on the right.

Instead of wiring the sensors and motors together, we'll assume a small computer mounted on the robot can read the sensors and control the motors. The interface between the computer and the motors and sensors is similar to that used in the Lego Mindstorms Robotics Invention System. As far as the programmer is concerned, the current (double meaning here) value of each sensor is always available in a particular location in memory; external circuitry makes sure this happens. Programs read from the memory locations reserved for sensors but don't write to them. In addition, a memory location is assigned to each motor and its content is interpreted by the external hardware as a measure of how much power to apply to the motor. So our two-motor, two-sensor robot has four locations set aside in memory: one for each sensor that a program reads from and one for each motor that a program writes to in order to control the motor.

A simple program that exhibits the desired light-seeking behavior can be implemented using *bang-bang control*, so called because the devices to be controlled, motors in this case, are either on or off, there's no middle ground. The method may seem a little crude but it's very effective. The program first checks to see which of the sensors is receiving more light. If the left sensor is receiving more, it turns on the right motor and turns off the left; if the right sensor is receiving more, it turns on the left and turns off the right. Then it loops and does the same thing over again until the batteries lose their charge or someone shuts the computer off.

In order to write this program, we need to imagine a simple computer with four registers: the program counter (instruction address register), register 1, register 2 and register 3. We'll use decimal instead of binary numbers to make things a little simpler to understand. Assume we have 100 memory locations with addresses 00 to 99. Suppose that each register and each location in memory is large enough to store a signed (+ or −) four-digit number. Our computer will support the set of instructions described here along with the exact way in which the instructions appear in memory, including any necessary register or address information. Obviously a real computer would have an ADDition instruction as well as SUBtraction instruction, but I'm including only the instructions I need to write this simple program. In each case, the leftmost digit of an instruction codes the type of instruction (opcode) and the remaining digits specify registers and addresses as needed.

1. SUBtract the contents of register i from the contents of register j and store the result in register k; a SUB instruction looks like 1ijk; for example, 1123 subtracts register 1 from register 2 and stores the result in register 3.
2. JUMP to location – change the program counter; an ADD instruction looks like 20mm where mm is a two-digit base-10 number indicating an address; for example, 2099 jumps to location 99.

3. BRANCH – if the number in register *n* is less than or equal to zero, then jump to location *mm*; a BRANCH instruction looks like 3*nmm*; for example, 3199 jumps to location 99 if the contents of register 1 are less than or equal to zero, otherwise the program counter is incremented as usual.

4. LOAD the contents of memory location *mm* into register *n*; a LOAD instruction looks like 4*nmm*.

5. STORE the contents of register *n* in location *mm*; a STORE instruction looks like 5*nmm*.

Now we write the machine code to drive a Braitenberg light-seeking robot. Assume that the right and left sensors write their sensor readings into locations 01 and 02 respectively, and that locations 03 and 04 are read by the right and left motors respectively, thereby determining the power available to the motors. Initially these four locations are zero. I've also stored the value 0000 in memory location 05 and the value 0100 in memory location 06, since it will be convenient to have these constants available to set the power to the right and left motors.

Loading a machine-language program into memory is pretty straightforward. Here's what memory looks like with the program loaded but before the computer starts:

00	01	02	03	04	05	06	07	08	09
2007	0000	0000	0000	0000	0000	0100	4011	4022	1123

10	11	12	13	14	15	16	17	18	19
4105	4206	3316	5203	5104	2007	5204	5103	2007	0000

If this listing seems pretty inscrutable, then you have some idea why hardly anyone programs in machine language anymore. We can improve readability a little by listing the program one instruction to a line followed by some useful commentary. Typically, machine-code programs are listed in files along with a liberal sprinkling of *comments* to help the programmer remember what all the instructions do. Figure 9.3 shows a listing of our machine-code program; the comments follow the sharp (#) sign. A program called a *loader* takes a file containing machine code and loads it into RAM ready to run.

The listing in Figure 9.3 is still pretty difficult to understand. Part of the problem is that in a long program it's hard to remember what all the numbers refer to; comments help but only so much. A reasonable alternative to machine code is to use *assembly language* for writing low-level programs. In assembly language, instructions are given mnemonic (easily remembered) names and we're allowed to use symbolic addresses for memory locations. An *assembler* is a program that converts

```
00    2007    # jump past sensor and constant locations
01    0000    # read right sensor value here
02    0000    # read left sensor value here
03    0000    # write right motor power level here
04    0000    # write left motor power level here
05    0000    # store motor-off constant here
06    0100    # store motor-on constant here
07    4011    # load right sensor value into register 1
08    4022    # load left sensor value into register 2
09    1123    # subtract 1 from 2 and store result in 3
10    4105    # load motor-off constant into register 1
11    4206    # load motor-on constant into register 2
12    3316    # if the left sensor is greater than the
13    5203    # right then turn the right motor on
14    5104    # and turn the left motor off
15    2007    # and then jump to beginning of the loop
16    5204    # else turn the left motor on
17    5103    # and turn the right motor off
18    2007    # and then jump to beginning of the loop
19    0000    # this location is not used by the program
```

Figure 9.3: Machine code for our light-seeking robot

an assembly-language program into machine language. Among other bookkeeping tasks, the assembler figures out the machine addresses for all the symbolic addresses. Once *assembled*, the resulting machine code is loaded into RAM like any machine-code file. Figure 9.4 shows an assembly-code version of the machine code in Figure 9.3.

Here are some tips on understanding the code in Figure 9.4. After the SUB instruction, register 3 contains the contents of register 2 minus the contents of register 1, or LSV − RSV in this case. The contents of register 3 are greater than zero just in case the left sensor value is greater than the right sensor value. If the left sensor value is greater than the right sensor value, that means the light source is off to the left and we want the robot to turn left. We can drive the robot to the left by making the right motor spin faster than the left motor. If register 3 is greater than zero, then according to our specification of the BRANCH instruction, the program counter is incremented normally and the instructions at LFT and LFT + 1 are executed, setting the right motor to ON and the left motor to OFF.[2] If register 3 is less than or equal to zero, then the program counter is set to RGT

---

[2] We'll assume that setting the right motor to ON makes the right wheel turn, thereby moving the right side of the robot forward, and that setting the left motor to ON makes the left wheel turn, thereby moving the left side of the robot forward. Setting a motor to OFF allows the attached wheel to turn freely. We'd have to wire the motors so as to ensure this behavior.

```
START:  JUMP    LOOP        # jump past sensor and constant locations
RSV:    0000                # read right sensor value here
LSV:    0000                # read left sensor value here
RMP:    0000                # write right motor power level here
LMP:    0000                # write left motor power level here
OFF:    0000                # store motor-off constant here
ON:     0100                # store motor-on constant here
LOOP:   LOAD    1     RSV   # load right sensor value into register 1
        LOAD    2     LSV   # load left sensor value into register 2
        SUB     1  2  3     # subtract 1 from 2 and store result in 3
        LOAD    1     OFF   # load motor-off constant into register 1
        LOAD    2     ON    # load motor-on constant into register 2
        BRANCH  3     RGT   # if the left sensor is greater than the
LFT:    STORE   2     RMP   # right then turn the right motor on
        STORE   1     LMP   # and turn the left motor off
        JUMP    LOOP        # and then jump to beginning of the loop
RGT:    STORE   2     LMP   # else turn the left motor on
        STORE   1     RMP   # and turn the right motor off
        JUMP    LOOP        # and then jump to beginning of the loop
```

Figure 9.4: Assembly code for our light-seeking robot

and the instructions at RGT and RGT + 1 are executed, setting the left motor to ON and the right motor to OFF.

The assembly-language program is still hard to read (and write) even for this relatively simple program, but its biggest drawback is that assembly language is specific to a particular machine or family of processors. The advantage of a so-called high-level programming language like C, Java or Scheme is that you can write the code implementing a procedure once and then later use various tools such as compilers and interpreters to convert the high-level specification into the machine code of as many specific computers as you like. A *compiler* is just a program that takes as input a program written in one language and produces as output another program written in a second language (the compiler itself may be written in a third language). A programmer can use one language and one model of computation to think about procedures and processes and rely on the compiler to translate code into machine language that a particular computer can understand directly.

Here is the C-language version of our robot control program. A good C compiler would convert this C code into machine code very much like what we've written but specific to the *target* machine of the compiler. Reviewing and augmenting our piecemeal introduction to C syntax in Chapter 4, let's look at a few hints for deciphering the next code fragment. In C, integer variables and constants are declared with int, assignment is accomplished with =, checking whether one integer is greater than another is handled with >, conditionals look like if (*condition*) { *code* } or if (*condition*) { *code* } else { *code* }, while (*condition*) { *code* } is the syntax for a while loop, and while (1) { *code* } and while (true) { *code* } are two ways to specify a so-called *infinite loop* (1 and true are conditions that are always satisfied).

```
void seek_light() {
  int on = 100 ;
  int off = 0 ;
  while (1) {
    if (left_sensor > right_sensor) {
      right_motor = on ;
      left_motor = off ; }
    else {
      right_motor = off ;
      left_motor = on ; }
  }
}
```

We can specify the same computation as a recursive procedure in Scheme. Again, a good compiler will convert this specification to something that looks pretty much like the machine code described earlier. In a Scheme expression of the form (define (*function arguments*) (define *variable value*) *body*), the inner define introduces a *local* variable that is seen only in the definition of *function*:

```
(define (seek_light)
  (define on 100)
  (define off 0)
  (if (> left_sensor right_sensor)
      (and (set! right_motor on)
           (set! left_motor off))
      (and (set! right_motor off)
           (set! left_motor on)))
  (seek_light))
```

Compilers and interpreters let a programmer specify computations in a language that has some of the convenience and naturalness of human languages but encourages a certain discipline and level of precision that makes the job of the compiler writer easier. The programmer who writes the compiler often has to map one model of computation, for example the substitution model, onto another model, for example the register-machine model.[3]

You can learn about the history of computer architecture by reading about the lives of Alan Turing, John von Neumann, Presper Eckert, John Mauchly and other early computer pioneers. Most of what I know about computer hardware comes from my early training in electrical engineering and then much later from reading *Computer Organization and Design* by John Hennessy and David Patterson. I recommend the Hennessy and Patterson book if you want to go into any of the topics raised in this chapter in greater detail. To learn more about Lego robots, visit the Lego Mindstorms web page or check out Knudsen's *The Unofficial Guide to Lego Mindstorms Robots*. Fred Martin's *Robotic Explorations: A Hands-On Introduction to Engineering* is a more advanced introduction to building and programming small robots.

Learning about computer hardware is both interesting and useful if you program "close to the machine". In robotics, computer networking, embedded control systems for home and automotive applications and even in designing toys containing microprocessors, it's important to know how the hardware works and how to build interfaces to get information into and out of computers. But understanding how computer hardware works is fascinating in its own right, and as a computer programmer you'll also find it useful in understanding all sorts of related concepts in computer science. The next chapter is a perfect example.

---

[3] You could also write a compiler whose input is a program in one high-level language and output is a program in another high-level language, for example, compile Scheme code into Java or C code. In our introductory courses, students write a compiler that translates from Scheme to Java and then another compiler that translates from Java to Scheme. It's a wonderful exercise for learning about programming languages and computing in general.

CHAPTER TEN

Do Robots Sleep?

While writing the previous chapter, I got to thinking about concepts in computer science that connect the microscopic, bit-level world of logic gates and machine language to the macroscopic world of procedures and processes we've been concerned with so far. In listing concepts that might be worth mentioning, I noticed that I was moving from computer architecture, the subdiscipline of computer science concerned with the logical design of computer hardware, to operating systems, the area dealing with the software that mediates between the user and the hardware.

In compiling my list, I was also struck by how many "computerese" terms and phrases have slipped into the vernacular. Interrupt handling (responding to an unexpected event while doing something else) and multitasking (the concurrent performance of several tasks) are prime examples. The common use of these terms concerns not computers but human information processing. I don't know what you'd call the jargon used by psychologists and cognitive scientists to describe how humans think. The word "mentalese" is already taken: the philosopher Jerry Fodor postulates that humans represent the external world in a "language of thought" that is sometimes called "mentalese." Fodor's mentalese is more like machine language for minds. I'm interested in the language we use to describe how we think, how our thought processes work – a metalanguage for talking about thinking.

Much of what I came up with in compiling my list had to do with how multiple computer processes (and mental processes) can operate concurrently and how we manage both computer and mental processes. Have you ever tried to write down your thoughts? It's an interesting exercise. At first, you may find it easy to concentrate on a single thread of thought and the mechanics of writing down the words, but quickly your mind will stray and you'll hear different thoughts competing for attention: "I don't get the point of this exercise", "The word 'attention' doesn't look right to me", and so on.

You may find your thoughts complicated by recursion and self-reference: "I'm thinking about my thinking about my thinking about this silly exercise." You may imagine one part of you listening to another part, critically evaluating a stream of words issuing from some other mysterious thought generator. You may try to push some of your thoughts to the background so as not to be overwhelmed. Soon you are likely to stir up a cacophony of thoughts, whispering, nagging, suggesting, and otherwise vying to be heard. The richness and multitude of our thoughts is amazing even when we're thinking about the most mundane of things.

Computer processes are far less exotic, but they are interesting nonetheless. And, while it's sometimes difficult to harness your own thoughts or quiet the noise in your head when your brain is really buzzing, you can exercise precise control over the processes in your computer.

10.1 STACKS AND SUBROUTINES

Before we get into juggling processes, let's start with the simpler but related problem of what happens when one procedure calls another. The basic issue is to stop doing one thing in order to do another without losing track of whatever you need to keep in mind in order to finish the first thing. More concretely: how does C or Java or Scheme manage passing arguments to a procedure being called by another procedure, returning values produced by the called procedure to the calling procedure, and setting aside the contents of memory locations that are used in the calling procedure prior to the procedure call, that may be overwritten by the called procedure and that will be needed by the calling procedure when the called procedure returns? The trickiest part is doing all of this with a single central processing unit (CPU) that executes one instruction at a time.

The robot program in Chapter 9 written in machine language and then in assembly language was a particularly simple sort of program: it had a loop implemented with a JUMP instruction and a single conditional implemented with a BRANCH instruction. Most interesting programs involve additional structure in the form of *subroutines*. Programmers create subroutines for tasks that are performed often. Procedures and functions are special cases of subroutines, but typically the word "subroutine" is used to refer to blocks of reusable code at the machine- or assembly-code level. The compilers for high-level languages like C, Java and Scheme convert procedures defined in these languages into more readily executed subroutines. The code for a subroutine in a machine- or assembly-language listing, whether written by hand or generated by a compiler, looks similar to other blocks of instructions. The real difference is that the blocks of instructions corresponding to subroutines are ones that get called frequently from other blocks of instructions.

To explain how subroutines are handled, we'll need a method for organizing computer memory called a *stack* or, in other contexts, a *queue*. The idea is that if you're planning to go off and do something other than what you're currently doing, then you place on the stack anything you'll need to remember later when you resume whatever you were doing. The stack is organized so that the items associated with the last (most recently set aside) uncompleted thing you were doing are the items most readily available.

In terms of subroutines, the things you'll want to remember correspond to the contents of registers. The CPU maintains its own stack, which is managed by two machine instructions. The PUSH instruction puts the contents of a specified register on the top of the stack and the POP instruction removes the top item from the stack and loads it into a specified register. Each time you POP something off the stack, it has one less item and each time you PUSH something on the stack, it has one more item. The stack is like a Pez dispenser that you can press candies into or pop them out of. We'll refer to items on the stack as "words" corresponding to binary numbers of the size that fits into a register. Here's what a stack and the PUSH and POP operations might look like in Scheme:

```
(define stack (list))
(define (push word)
  (set! stack (cons word stack)))
(define (pop)
  (let ((word (car stack)))
    (set! stack (cdr stack)) word))
```

The invocation (list) returns an empty list, (cons *item list*) returns a new list whose first element is *item* and whose remaining items are the items in *list*, (car *list*) returns the first item in *list*, and (cdr *list*) returns the list consisting of all the items in *list* except the first. Here are some examples of how PUSH and POP work:

```
> (push "A")
> (push "B")
> (pop)
"B"
> (pop)
"A"
> (push "C")
> (push "D")
```

```
> (pop)
"D"
> (push "E")
> (pop)
"E"
> (pop)
"C"
```

In machine language, PUSH and POP could be implemented by using other machine instructions such as LOAD and STORE to move words to and from memory and ADD and SUB to increment and decrement the address pointing to the top word on the stack. But PUSH and POP are just so useful that it makes sense to make them separate machine instructions.

The next step is to look at a pair of machine instructions that allow the CPU to jump to a subroutine (the JSR or "jump to subroutine" instruction) and then return from it (the RTS or "return from subroutine" instruction). Each time the CPU jumps to (or calls) a subroutine, the JSR instruction pushes the program counter onto the top of the stack; when the subroutine is finished, the RTS instruction pops the top item off the stack and thereby restores the program counter to where the CPU left off before calling the subroutine.

This technique works even if you call one subroutine in the midst of executing another. You can "nest" subroutine calls as deeply as you like (one subroutine calls another subroutine that calls yet another that calls still another ...), or at least as deeply as you've set aside stack space in memory for the necessary register contents. The stack is also used to keep track of the values of arguments and local variables when calling subroutines, or when the operating system must perform some routine task in the midst of running a user program. Here's how the JSR instruction might be described in an assembly-language manual. PC refers to the program counter (or next-instruction-address register) in the CPU.

```
INSTRUCTION NAME
     JSR - Jump to SubRoutine
CALLING PATTERN
     JSR address
FUNCTION
     Pushes the address of the instruction immediately
     following the JSR instruction onto the stack.
     The PC is loaded with the supplied address (the
     only argument to the JSR instruction) and program
     execution continues at the address now in the PC.
```

And here's the relevant information about the RTS instruction:

```
INSTRUCTION NAME
    RTS - ReTurn from Subroutine
CALLING PATTERN
    RTS
FUNCTION
    Pops the word on the top of the stack and loads
    it into the PC. Program execution continues at
    the address now in the PC.
```

Like PUSH and POP, JSR and RTS can be implemented in terms of existing machine instructions, but they are so useful and so often employed that it makes sense to make them specialized instructions.

Of course, when a subroutine call crops up in your code you may be in the midst of doing some very important stuff and perhaps even have some registers full of operands on which you have yet to do some computations. You may even be in the midst of an earlier digression, executing a subroutine call that was called from some other block of code. If the registers contain important stuff, then the programmer writing the code or the compiler generating the code has to take care of it, since JSR doesn't save the contents of any registers except the program counter. Any contents of registers that you're going to need after the subroutine call can be pushed on the stack before the call and popped back off after it.

Imagine how the following fragments of Scheme code might be translated into machine code. The important features of this dummy procedure are, first, that it has information stored in registers that it will need when the factorial procedure returns and, second, that it calls the factorial procedure with an argument that has to be passed to the block of code implementing the factorial procedure.

Here's the Scheme code:

```
(define (dummy)
  (let ((r 0) (n 6))
    ... do some stuff ...
    (set! r (factorial n))
    ... do more stuff ... ))
(define (factorial n)
  ... definition ... )
```

Figure 10.1 sketches the assembly code for the dummy procedure (looking at the machine code would be just too painful). The variables introduced by let are handled by setting aside locations in memory at the beginning of the DUMB subroutine. We're assuming that the missing instructions indicated by "do some

```
DUMB:   JUMP    START       # jump past local variables
R:      0000                # first local variable
N:      0006                # second local variable
START:  ...                 # ... do some stuff ...
        PUSH 1              # push the contents of register 1
        PUSH 2              # push the contents of register 2
        LOAD 1 N            # pass the argument to factorial
        JSR     FACT        # jump to the factorial subroutine
        STORE 2 R           # get the result from factorial
        POP 2               # restore the contents of register 2
        POP 1               # restore the contents of register 1
        ...                 # ... do more stuff ...
        RTS                 # return from the dummy procedure
```

Figure 10.1: Assembly code for the dummy procedure

```
FACT:   MOVE 1 2            # copy register 1 to register 2
LOOP:   BRANCH 1 EXIT       # loop while register 1 is > zero
        DECR 1              # decrement the value in register 1
        MULT 1 2 2          # register 2 = register 1 * register 2
        JUMP LOOP           # continue with the next iteration
EXIT:   RTS                 # the return value is in register 2
```

Figure 10.2: Assembly code for the factorial procedure

stuff" perform calculations and store intermediate results in registers 1 and 2 that will be needed when factorial (implemented by the FACT subroutine) returns and executes the missing instructions indicated by "do more stuff." We use register 1 to pass FACT the value for its single argument and register 2 to obtain the result returned by FACT.

Figure 10.2 shows the assembly code for the factorial procedure.[1] The operation of the MOVE, DECR and MULT assembly-code instructions should be clear from the comments. This implementation of FACT assumes that the value of its single argument is passed to it in register 1 and that the calling procedure knows to look in register 2 for the result. The JSR and RTS instructions implicitly handle pushing addresses on the stack, popping them back off, and assigning the program counter to the appropriate address to ensure that the CPU does the right thing at the right time.

The method of passing results and arguments (or *parameters* as they are called in this context) illustrated in DUMB and FACT is not considered good programming practice. It is generally easier to keep track of all the necessary bookkeeping if

---

[1] This listing simplifies how Scheme handles multiplication. Also, while the FACT subroutine is defined iteratively, the Scheme definition could have been recursive. Conversely, an iterative version of the factorial function in C could end up being compiled into a recursive assembly-code implementation.

you use the stack to pass information to a subroutine or to return information from a subroutine call. Passing parameters and return values on the stack involves allocating space for them on the stack. As an exercise, think about how you'd modify the code in Figures 10.1 and 10.2 in order to pass parameters and values using the stack. (Hint: before executing the JSR instruction, you'll have to allocate extra space on the stack to store the parameters and the return values; then in the subroutine you'll have to dig below the top item on the stack both to retrieve the parameters and to store the returned values.)

If all this sounds messy and potentially error-prone, you're right, it is. Indeed, it's the pain of this sort of nitpicky bookkeeping that discourages many people from programming in machine and assembly language. Modern programming languages and their associated compilers manage this kind of busywork automatically. Juggling registers to orchestrate subroutine calls may seem terribly complicated, but the code for doing it is not all that difficult and once you (or the person who wrote your compiler) have written it you never have to juggle registers again. Compilers do all sorts of tedious mechanical stuff so that we don't have to bother. In the next section we'll see how another complicated juggling act is accomplished.

10.2 MANAGING TASKS

In most computers, processes only appear to be running at the same time: in fact, they are running on the same processor (its CPU to be specific) by switching back and forth very quickly among the processes. I was thinking about this largely because of the robot example in the machine-language program in the previous chapter. A robot often has to perform several tasks at the same time: controlling its motors while looking for a bright light, while avoiding obstacles, while checking its batteries, and so on. How can a single CPU accomplish this juggling feat?

In operating-systems terminology, processes are relatively heavy-duty computations that function independently of one another for the most part. These heavyweight processes are powerful but generally take a fair bit of time and memory to create and maintain. There are also lightweight processes, often called *threads* to distinguish them from their heavyweight counterparts, that are easier to create and maintain but don't have so many bells and whistles.

Processes of all sorts can procreate and commit mayhem. A process can put itself to sleep for a time or it can kill itself.[2] Processes can also create their own

---

[2] If you're running a shell in a window, you can use ps to identify the PID (process identifier) of the process in which the shell is running. You can then kill this process by typing kill -KILL *pid*,

child processes, and, terrible as it sounds, a parent process can kill its children. An application such as a word-processing program is typically implemented as a single heavyweight process with several lightweight threads of control to handle such tasks as spelling and grammar checking, reading keystrokes and mouse movements, and managing text and graphics display.

The CPU can handle only one instruction per *CPU cycle*, and processes vie for those cycles.[3] Every process is assigned a priority that determines what share if any of the CPU's cycles it is allocated. If you're a process with low priority, you have to wait until all processes with higher priority are done before you get your shot at the CPU. If you're one of several processes with the same priority and no processes with a higher priority are ready to run, then you'll get a slice of the CPU equal to that assigned to all the other processes in your cohort. Short intervals of time are doled out to each process; for example, you may be allowed to execute a few hundred or a few thousand instructions before your allotment is up. But the CPU will switch between the processes so quickly that each process will seem to have its own CPU. The part of the operating system responsible for switching between processes is called the *task manager*.[4]

Each process corresponds to a running program. Think about the machine-language program in the previous chapter. To interrupt a program corresponding to one process in order to allow the program corresponding to another process to run, what would we have to do? For a simple program like the light-seeking program in Chapter 9, we'd have to remember where we left off – the address currently in the program counter – and we'd have to remember whatever the program was working on – the current contents of the other registers. Then, the next time the program gets a chance at the CPU, we'd restore the program counter and the other registers and let the program run for another time slice.

The operating system uses a specially designated portion of memory to keep track of this information in much the same way the stack was used for implementing subroutine calls. There are a couple of differences, though. With subroutine calls, the programmer or compiler generating the code is aware of what registers

---

substituting the PID you identified for *pid*. Needless to say, don't try this unless you're sure that you won't lose any work by killing your shell process. When you kill a process you also kill its children, so keep this in mind if your text editor has an open file running in a child process of your shell process.

[3] Actually this isn't generally true: many modern computers have multiple arithmetic and logic units (ALUs) and special circuitry that lets them carry out multiple instructions at the same time. But even so there are generally many more things to be done than there are things to do them on.

[4] The strategy for scheduling processes described here is based strictly on priority. Most modern operating systems use a "throughput-scheduling" strategy in which high-priority processes get a larger fraction of CPU time than low-priority processes but all processes receive some allocation of CPU time on any sequence through all processes.

besides the program counter must be saved to restore state following a subroutine call. When the operating system interrupts a running process, however, it doesn't have the time to figure out which registers are likely to contain useful information, so it's forced to save them all.

Another difference is that a stack organization doesn't work in keeping track of processes. For subroutine calls, you push the relevant register information on the stack and pull it off in last-in-first-out order; this is exactly what you want for nested subroutine calls. But you can't predict in advance exactly the order in which processes will be allocated CPU cycles, so a stack won't work. Information on processes is stored so it can be easily retrieved using indices associated with each process. The process identifier (PID) for a given process serves as the index for that process. You can think of the memory used by the operating system to track processes as being divided into blocks, one block allocated for each process and identified by its process identifier. It should be obvious that each process needs its own separate stack to keep track of subroutine calls.

We'll need some extra hardware to keep track of the short time intervals that the operating system doles out to processes. The processor *clock* serves as a metronome to beat out time for all the other hardware components, in order to synchronize the operations of the CPU and the hardware responsible for reading from and writing to memory. Even more importantly, the clock has a critical role in the digital abstraction by ensuring that the analog signals propagating through logic gates have "settled" before interpreting them as binary values.

The processor clock generates a steady stream of pulses, one pulse per clock cycle. A clock cycle differs from a CPU cycle: indeed, a CPU cycle may require a different number of clock cycles depending on the instruction being executed. If the clock pulses a billion times per second (1 gigahertz), then in order to give each process a time slice of 1 millisecond (an eternity in computer terms), we need a counter that can be set to one million at the beginning of each time slice, decremented by one on each pulse of the clock, and then signal when it reaches zero. This is relatively simple hardware to add to the CPU and most computers have several such counters.

We keep the program counter and other registers of each process not currently running in the portion of memory allocated for storing information about processes. Then we have a strategy for cycling through all of the processes. If all the processes have the same priority, then we just cycle through them. Each time the counter signals it has reached 1 million, we write out to the specially allocated block of memory the contents of the registers of the currently running process, read in the most recently stored contents of the registers for the process next in line, reset the program counter, and restart the process.

This reading out and writing in of register contents is called a *context switch*, a prime example of computerese that has entered the lexicon because of the cachet of computer literacy. Context switching takes time to store the registers of the current running process and restore the registers of the process chosen to run next. The CPU has to be careful not to divide time up too finely, since otherwise it will spend all its time context switching.

The most glaring gap in this explanation involves this "we" I keep referring to. The only entity capable of doing anything inside the computer is the CPU. But the CPU has its hands full executing instructions, a billion or more per second. If we're going to handle multitasking, we'll need some additional hardware to help orchestrate this switching between processes.

We'll need circuitry to implement the counter and a gate that signals when the counter reaches zero. We can add primitive instructions to the computer's machine language to start the timer and specify how many clock cycles it should count off. Then we'd also arrange for circuitry that, whenever the timer reaches zero, resets the program counter to the address of a special program – the program that handles switching between processes. Aside from what it actually does, this program really isn't all that special; it looks pretty much like any other subroutine written in machine code. This program takes care of writing out the contents of the registers used by the current process, choosing what process to run next, reading in the most recently stored contents for the process chosen to run, and resetting the program counter to give the chosen process its chance to run. And that's pretty much it; that's how multitasking is implemented on most computers.

The mechanism whereby the CPU is interrupted by the clock and made to execute a special program is actually quite common. It's called an *interrupt* – the general technical term for stopping the CPU and redirecting the flow of control. There are many types of interrupts and interrupt handlers (the pieces of code run when a particular type of interrupt occurs). Interrupts are used to signal the CPU when some event occurs outside of the computer – a robot's bump sensor is hit, a key on a keyboard is pressed, another computer wants to communicate, or a relatively slow peripheral like a disk drive deposits data in memory. Interrupts are also used to handle unexpected internal events (often called *exceptions*), such as when a program contains gibberish (something other than an instruction that the CPU understands) or tries to write into some forbidden part of memory (in most modern computers, memory is partitioned and protected by the operating system so that a poorly written or malicious program can't overwrite those parts of the operating system required to keep things running smoothly).

10.3 MULTITHREADED ROBOTS

Let's take a somewhat more detailed look at multitasking and lightweight threads in robotics. Chapter 9 featured a simple program to make a little robot seek and drive toward a light. Now we'd like to modify that program so that the robot isn't so single-minded (or single-threaded in this case). Specifically, we'd like the robot to watch out for collisions by detecting when its front bumper switch is depressed by contact with a wall or someone's foot. This requires the robot to do two things at once, like walking and chewing gum at the same time. We're going to consider two different methods for managing this feat, but we'll start with a little more background on the C programming language.

Every C program must have a function called `main` that is called when the program is started. The `main` function is run in a separate process from the one in which it is invoked, and any child processes it spawns are its children. The `execi` function[5] (defined as part of an open-source operating system for the RCX microcomputer that comes with the Lego Mindstorms Robotics Invention System), creates a new process (a lightweight thread) in which it calls the function that appears as its first argument. `execi` returns a reference for the process (think of it as the `PID` for that process) that the parent process can use to kill the process when it's done what it was created for. As usual, squint at the rest of the syntax and ignore the details. The `seek_light` function is exactly as we described it in Chapter 9 except that its formal parameters and return type have been changed to meet the requirements of the `execi` function.

In this first implementation that combines seeking light and watching for collisions, the `main` function works by controlling a thread to seek light, killing it off when a collision is detected and it's time for evasive action and creating it anew when the danger is past:[6]

---

[5] The `execi` function is a convenient means of spawning new processes. It bears only a distant relationship to the `exec` family of routines in Unix for managing processes. The operating system that contains *execi*, called *brickOS* (based on Markus Noga's *legOS*), is described in several online tutorials as well as Baum et al.'s *Extreme Mindstorms: An Advanced Guide to Lego Mindstorms*.

[6] The ellipsis indicated by the . . . in the code for creating the light-seeking thread refers to two additional arguments to `execi` that seem even more distracting than usual. These arguments determine the priority of the newly created thread and the size of the stack allocated to keep track of the subroutine calls invoked while running this thread. In a full specification, unless the programmer is getting really fancy, these arguments are typically assigned to default values provided by the system. For example, the complete call to `execi` might look something like `execi(&seek_light, 0, 0, PRIORITY_NORMAL, DEFAULT_STACK_SIZE)`.

```
int main(int argc, char *argv[]) {
  /* declare a variable of type process identifer */
  pid_t seeker_thread ;
  /* start the light-seeking thread */
  seeker_thread = execi( &seek_light, 0, 0, ... );
  /* loop forever watching for a collision */
  while (1) {
    if ( front_bumper > 1 ) {
      /* if you detect a collision then kill the seeker */
      kill(seeker_thread);
      /* take some appropriate evasive action */
      take_evasive_action() ;
      /* and then resume seeking the light */
      seeker_thread = execi( &seek_light, 0, 0, ... );
    }
    /* otherwise put the parent thread to sleep
       and and let the seeker do its thing */
    else sleep(1) ;
  }
}
```

This is the first code fragment long enough that I thought in-line commentary would help supplement the surrounding text. In documenting large blocks of code, good programmers sprinkle around pieces of prose to explain what the code does and how it is to be used. The prose can precede or follow a code fragment for a procedure or it can be interspersed with the statements comprising a procedure definition. These bits and pieces of prose are called *comments* and the process of annotating code with comments is referred to as *commenting* or *documenting* a program. Since the file containing a program is read by various other programs such as compilers and interpreters, we need some way of distinguishing code from comments. Almost all programming languages have syntactic conventions for indicating comments. In both C and Java, any text between an opening /* and a closing */ is treated as a comment and is ignored by the compiler.

Most of the time, `main` just sleeps, waking up from time to time to check on the front bumper. I haven't bothered to define the `take_evasive_action` function – let's assume it just backs up a random distance, turns a random angle and then sets off in a new direction (performing random actions is quite useful in programming robots).

Here is the `seek_light` function we saw in Chapter 9 modified to accept the arguments and return the type required by the `execi` function:

```
int seek_light(int argc, char *argv[]) {
  int on = 100 ;
  int off = 0 ;
  while (1) {
    if (left_sensor > right_sensor) {
      right_motor = on ;
      left_motor = off ;
    }
    else {
      right_motor = off ;
      left_motor = on ; }
  }
}
```

This implementation works well enough, but creating and destroying processes with such abandon seems somewhat inelegant. In the second implementation, we're going to have the main function spawn two processes, one that seeks light and a second that watches for collisions. But now we have a problem: both the light-seeking and the collision-detection threads want to control the motors (collision detection indirectly by calling take_evasive_action when it senses that the switch attached to the front bumper has been depressed). This is actually quite a common situation in programming: it occurs whenever you have a resource – whether a portion of protected memory or a peripheral device – that only one program at a time can use. Resolving the problem requires some means for asynchronous communicating processes (see Chapter 2) to communicate and coordinate with one another.

To illustrate the problem and one possible solution, we'll turn to a classic example of what can go wrong when independent processes try to use a critical resource at the same time. Whenever you use an automated teller machine (ATM) to make a cash withdrawal, it checks on your current balance and debits your account by the amount of the withdrawal before giving you the cash. Suppose the ATM machine runs this code to perform the checks and debits:

```
if (withdrawal < balance) {
  balance = balance - withdrawal ;
  issue_cash(withdrawal) ;
}
```

Now imagine that you and a confederate each go to separate ATMs and, at exactly the same time, make withdrawals to the tune of $90; let's say your current balance is $100. What if the bank processed the statements for the two threads corresponding to the two separate transactions as follows?

```
ATM 1: (withdrawal < balance) => 90 < 100
ATM 2: (withdrawal < balance) => 90 < 100
ATM 1: balance = balance - withdrawal => balance = 10
ATM 2: balance = balance - withdrawal => balance = -80
```

Voilà, each of you gets $90 in cash. Now, you can't carry out this particular bit of petty larceny because the program that processes transactions wraps the problematic code fragment in a pair of statements: the first requests exclusive control over the location in memory where your balance is stored and the second relinquishes control after the code fragment has conducted its business. If ATM 1 executes its code fragment first, then ATM 2 will find its request denied and will be forced to sleep until ATM 1 has completed its business, at which point ATM 2 will be awakened and allowed to finish. Of course, in this scenario, whichever one of you is at ATM 2 will be disappointed. We'll illustrate this technique for coordinating processes in next version of main by using a global value so that the two threads vying for control of the motors can communicate with each other.

The next version of main starts two threads, one for seeking light and one for detecting collisions. These two threads then run independently. We could just put main in an infinite loop, but this would take up CPU cycles; instead, we put it to sleep for however long we want the robot to seek light and avoid obstacles and then kill off the threads when the time is up and we want to terminate the program. I've rewritten seek_light and put the bump-detection code in a separate function called avoid_bumps. The functions seek_light and avoid_bumps communicate through the global variable evasive_action_in_progress; in particular, seek_light goes to sleep if it sees that evasive_action_in_progress is 1.

```
int main(int argc, char *argv[])
{
  pid_t seeker_thread, bumper_thread ;
  /* start light-seeking and collision-detecting */
  seeker_thread = execi( &seek_light, 0, 0, ... );
  bumper_thread = execi( &avoid_bumps, 0, 0, ...)
  /* then go to sleep for a couple of minutes */
  sleep(120);
  /* finally kill the two threads and halt */
  kill ( seeker_thread );
  kill ( bumper_thread );
  return 0;
}
```

Here we declare the global variable evasive_action_in_progress that will coordinate seek_light and avoid_bumps:

```
int evasive_action_in_progress = 0 ;
```

Notice how the seek_light function now avoids conflicting with the take_evasive_action function:

```
int seek_light(int argc, char *argv[]) {
  int on = 100 ;
  int off = 0 ;
  while (1) {
    /* if evasive action is in progress, sleep */
    if ( evasive_action_in_progress == 1 )
      sleep(1) ;
    /* otherwise seek the light */
    else if ( left_sensor > right_sensor ) {
      right_motor = on ;
      left_motor = off ;
    }
    else {
      right_motor = off ;
      left_motor = on ; }
  }
}
```

The function avoid_bumps signals seek_light using the the global variable evasive_action_in_progress:

```
int avoid_bumps(int argc, char *argv[]) {
  while (1) {
    if (front_bumper == 1) {
      /* if you detect a collision, take over the motors */
      evasive_action_in_progress = 1
      /* make whatever evasive action seems appropriate */
      take_evasive_action() ;
      /* and then relinquish control of the motors */
      evasive_action_in_progress = 0
    }
    /* otherwise sleep and let the seeker do its thing */
    else sleep(1) ;
  }
}
```

This implementation has a bug that is not likely to cause major problems for our robot but is worth pointing out since in other contexts (such as our ATM example) it could be more serious. I'm assuming that the function `take_evasive_action` takes some time to run, perhaps a couple of seconds actually to negotiate its evasive maneuvers. It's possible that `seek_light` could modify the motor control parameters, `left_motor` and `right_motor`, after `take_evasive_action` is called. To see this, think about how the variable `evasive_action_in_progress` is checked (==) in the `seek_light` function and set (=) in the `avoid_bumps` function, and imagine the operating system interleaving the instructions for these two functions as it switches back and forth between the two processes running them.

The C-language *semaphore* library makes it much easier to coordinate access to critical resources required by multiple processes. The semaphores implemented in the C library manage access to resources so that even if several processes request access to a resource at the "same time", only one process is granted access and the others have to wait their turn. After using the shared resource, a process then releases its access and the routines in the semaphore library ensure that all other processes waiting for access get their turn.

There are all sorts of clever solutions to this simple robot problem that involve multiple threads of control, semaphores, interrupt handling, and the ability to make threads go to sleep or alter their priority. Solutions involving lots of threads can be pretty complicated, especially when they're running on tiny little computers with slow clocks and little memory. The RCX microcomputer that comes with the Lego Mindstorms Robot Invention System is based on the Hitachi H8 family of microcontrollers, which have a top clock speed of 16 megahertz (that's 16 million cycles per second). The RCX comes with 32 kilobytes of memory. Compare this with modern PCs that typically have processors rated at 1 gigahertz or more and come with 256 megabytes or more. If you have a slow processor running lots of processes, you'll probably find some of your processes starved for CPU cycles. In general, programs that involve lots of threads can be tricky to manage.

We're already seeing educational and entertainment robots on the market with much faster CPUs and lots more memory; however, there is a tradeoff. It might seem that that you can never have too much memory or too fast a processor. Unfortunately, fast clocks and large memories are expensive both in cost and in the power they require. Even a little Lego robot can wear down its batteries in a matter of minutes if it's running its motors a lot or using its infrared port to communicate with another robot. Some of these robot-implementation problems may seem merely temporary inconveniences; after all, you may say, processors will get faster, batteries will last longer and everything will get cheaper. However, this rosy picture of the future is cold comfort when you're trying to get a robot to do something today. And it's my guess that our aspirations to build better robot programs will continue to outpace hardware technology for some time to come.

10.4   ALLOCATING RESOURCES

In Chapter 2 we introduced the command ps (for "process status") that lets us inspect running processes. Now that we know a little more about how processes are handled by the operating system, we're going to use ps to look at some more interesting processes in terms of allocating system resources. In Chapter 2 we created two processes by running this shell script:

```
% sleep 10 | sleep 20 &
[1] 1453 1454
```

Figure 10.3 shows what's going on in the hardware. Each process is associated with a process identifier, 1453 and 1454 in this case, and with a portion of memory used to keep track of the process and, in particular, the instructions that comprise

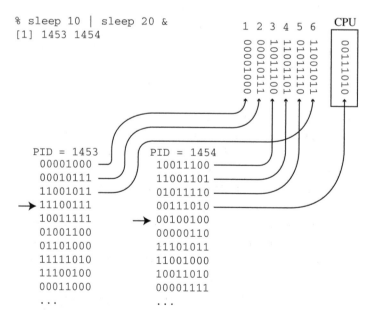

Figure 10.3: The central processing unit interleaving the execution of instructions for two asynchronous processes. The order of execution is noted (1, 2, ..., 6) and the currently executing instruction shown in the box labeled CPU.

the associated program. This portion of memory also maintains a pointer to the next instruction to be executed in running the program. The CPU runs a few instructions from the first process, a few instructions from the second process, back to the first process and so on. The pointer to the next instruction associated with each process identifier makes sure that the CPU won't lose track of where it is in executing each program.

Figure 10.3 is a little misleading in that the "next" instruction is defined by the running program; executing instructions like JUMP and JSR cause the next instruction to jump around in memory. The situation is made more complicated (and more interesting) by the fact that generally a lot of processes need to be run and some of those processes are the very ones that decide which processes to run and when. The entire operating system that is responsible for creating and managing processes is itself just a bunch of programs running as separate asynchronous communicating processes.

The sleep command is not terribly interesting, since the operating system has a simple expedient for handling processes that wish to pause in their execution for a period of time. When the operating system encounters a sleep command, it sets an alarm clock for the required sleep interval, puts the sleeping process aside, and then forgets about it until the alarm goes off, at which point it throws the process back in with the rest of the processes waiting for a chance at the CPU. If we really want to tax the CPU, we'll need to give it a task involving significant computation.

One relatively easy way to get the CPU to work hard is to make it perform a strenuous numerical calculation. The basic calculator command bc comes as standard equipment with many shells and is very handy for numerical calculations. bc has its own special-purpose programming language with a syntax that makes it particularly accessible to C programmers. I'm going to write a little bc program to calculate the sum of the first million integers ($\sum_{i=1}^{10^6} i$) and I'll store the program in a shell variable:

```
% set p = "r = 0 ; for ( i = 1 ; i < 10^6 ; ++i ) r += i"
```

There are more efficient methods[7] of computing $1 + 2 + \ldots + n$. In particular, it can be done almost trivially using the equivalence $\sum_{i=1}^{n} i = (n^2 + n)/2$. However, right now we're trying to make bc do more work, not less, in order to demonstrate how the operating system allocates resources to processes. Even so, it will take bc only a few seconds to do this calculation, just barely enough time for me to invoke

---

[7] The example bc program also requires bc to compute 10^6 every time it evaluates the test, i < 10^6, in the for loop. An alert programmer would correct this inefficiency by assigning a variable to 10^6 outside the loop, say m = 10^6, and then using it in the test, say i < m.

the `ps` command to get some idea what the CPU is doing and how the operating system is allocating resources to different processes.

```
% echo "$p" | bc &
[1] 1981 1982
% ps -o "pid %cpu command"
  PID %CPU COMMAND
  893  0.0 -bin/tcsh
 1982 98.1 bc
```

I used `echo` to pipe the program to `bc` and then, as quickly as I could manage, I asked `ps` to display, for each process, its process identifier (PID), the percentage of time (averaged over some small interval) that the CPU is dedicated to the process (%CPU) and the name of the command associated with the process (COMMAND). `echo $p` did its business so quickly it didn't even appear in the list of processes. Obviously the CPU on my laptop doesn't have a lot of work to do, given that it's dedicating over 98% of its effort to executing the `bc` program (and negligible effort to running the shell I'm working in).

Now watch what happens when we get a couple of processes competing for the CPU:

```
% echo "$p" | bc | echo "$p" | bc &
[6] 1985 1986 1987 1988
% ps -o "pid %cpu command"
  PID %CPU COMMAND
  893  0.0 -bin/tcsh
 1986 56.8 bc
 1988 35.6 bc
```

Again, by the time I typed typed the process status command, the two `echo` processes 1985 and 1987 had already completed. As expected, the two `bc` processes are occupying most of the CPU's time, with the rest allocated to processes associated with the operating system. If we check a few seconds later, the picture has changed somewhat as the operating system tries to balance the work load to be fair to all processes:

```
% ps -o "pid %cpu command"
  PID %CPU COMMAND
  893  0.0 -bin/tcsh
 1986 37.6 bc
 1988 51.6 bc
```

Operating systems have to allocate not only time, as determined by the CPU percentage a process is allowed to use, but also space, as determined by the amount of memory a process is allowed to use. Memory is complicated in modern computers, but most people have heard of two types: magnetic or optical disk storage and RAM. Disk storage is measured in the tens or hundreds of gigabytes while most people count themselves as very fortunate if they have more than one gigabyte of RAM. RAM can be quickly read from or written to, and programs and data have to be in RAM for the CPU to use them. RAM is typically the scarce resource when dealing with computations that require a great deal of space.

Now you might have heard about *virtual memory*, a feature of most modern operating systems that lets you run programs requiring more memory than you have RAM. Virtual memory accomplishes this by using disk storage to simulate a larger RAM memory. If you need to run a program that requires say twice as much memory as you have RAM, you store half of the program and its associated data in RAM and the other half on disk. As long as the CPU is operating on the part that's in RAM, you're in business. If, however, the CPU needs to access the part of the program that's on disk, the operating system has to transfer the part of the program currently in RAM onto the disk before transferring the part of the program that is currently on disk to RAM. There are all sorts of clever ways to make this happen fast, but compared to how fast the CPU can execute instructions that are in RAM, transferring programs and data to and from disk is glacially slow.

All this preliminary discussion is meant to impress on you that memory (and RAM in particular) is a scarce resource, one that the operating system will take pains to allocate carefully. When you start a process, the operating system allocates to it whatever virtual memory it needs; it also allocates an initial portion of RAM to the process. As the process runs, the operating system can choose to allocate it more or less RAM. A process can also request additional virtual memory if it needs more space for its computations.

When you open a large document in a word-processing program, the process in which the word processor is running asks the operating system for more virtual memory to store the document; the process requesting memory will always be granted its request (within reason) but that doesn't mean the process is allocated more RAM. If you're not given enough memory to store your entire document in RAM, then you're likely to experience a delay when you run the spell checker on the entire document or rapidly scan through all its pages. (This characterization of memory management is somewhat cartoonish, especially as concerns word-processing programs, but it conveys the basic idea without bogging us down in hairy details.)

Numerical calculations can be memory hogs. The memory requirements for numerical calculations can quickly grow from a small initial requirement to many times the available RAM. In order to demonstrate the operating system allocating more memory to a process, we'll need a process that uses significant memory. Here I create another make-work task for bc by asking it to build a list (technically it's called an *array* but you can think of it as a list) consisting of $2^{16} - 1$ items such that the ith item in the list is the number i^i:

```
% set p = "for ( i = 1 ; i < 2^16 ; ++i ) a[i] = i^i"
```

I chose $2^{16} - 1$ because that is the maximum array size allowed by the version of bc on my laptop. $2^{16} - 1 = 65535$ is not terribly large for an array; however, the numbers I'm storing in this array are large; they start off small and then quickly, very quickly, become quite large. To illustrate, we can ask bc to tell us how large some of the numbers are. The length function in bc computes the number of significant digits required to represent a given number, giving us a measure of the space required by the computation. bc first computes the number corresponding to, say, $(2^{12})^{(2^{12})}$ and then applies length to determine the number of significant digits required to represent the number. For example, given $(2^3)^{(2^3)} = 16777216$, length((2^3)^(2^3)) returns 8.

```
% echo "length((2^12)^(2^12))" | bc
14797
% echo "length((2^13)^(2^13))" | bc
32059
% echo "length((2^14)^(2^14))" | bc
69050
% echo "length((2^15)^(2^15))" | bc
147963
% echo "length((2^16)^(2^16))" | bc
315653
```

So by the time our little program is only part way through filling in the array, it's storing some pretty large numbers and bc needs a fair bit of memory to store the array and its contents. I'll set bc to running our program.

```
% echo "$p" | bc &
[1] 1995 1996
```

I'm going to check on process 1996 periodically by using ps to display status information for just this process. In addition to looking at the percentage of the CPU (%CPU) as we did earlier, I've also told ps to display the percentage of the total memory (averaged over some small interval of time) that the operating system has allocated to 1996 (%MEM) and the total accumulated CPU usage (TIME):

```
% ps 1996 -o "pid %cpu %mem time command"
  PID  %CPU %MEM      TIME COMMAND
 1996  90.4  0.2   0:08.68 bc
```

As time passes, the average memory allocation is increasing:

```
% ps 1996 -o "pid %cpu %mem time command"
  PID  %CPU %MEM      TIME COMMAND
 1996  95.5  0.6   1:04.41 bc
```

And over time, the memory allocated to this process increases to more than 6% of the total RAM:

```
  PID  %CPU %MEM      TIME COMMAND
 1996  92.9  1.0   2:21.00 bc
 1996  85.6  1.9   6:25.40 bc
 1996  80.2  4.2  22:25.26 bc
 1996  69.6  5.1  29:05.34 bc
 1996  87.7  6.4  40:21.44 bc
```

You might experiment with creating processes and using ps to explore how your operating system responds to various resource requests. See how much memory you can tie up with calculations running in several processes. In these experiments, you're seeing the operating system in action, adapting to the needs of the processes it's responsible for managing. Its adjustments in allocating CPU time and memory constitute a primitive sort of homeostatic system designed to maintain system parameters within allowable limits, much as your body constantly makes adjustments to maintain your internal temperature within a range you can tolerate. As additional processes are created and require increasing amounts of memory, the operating system reallocates its resources so as to run those processes while not sacrificing essential services.

This image of a modern operating system as an animated, self-regulating organism is not too wide of the mark. Indeed, computer scientists are designing self-healing systems that detect and repair problematic software and virus-detection schemes that mimic the human immune system. There are even efforts afoot to build virus-resistant computer systems by simulating evolution and natural selection to create the software equivalent of antibodies. Given the rise of malicious viruses in computer networks, it may not be long before we regularly experience days when our computers are "under the weather" or "recovering from a bout of whatever is going around."

10.5 METAPHORICALLY SPEAKING

The stack of threads in my head is not like the stack of threads the operating system on the computer in front of me uses to support multitasking. My computer will never lose track of a thread (at least assuming the operating system doesn't crash), and eventually even the lowest-priority thread will rise to the top of the heap and be executed. Not so with me. I can sense threads in my head becoming thinner, more tenuous, less emphatic. There is a rough analog in computer systems; a piece of code can "time out" and terminate or "kill" its respective thread of control. But the analogy is very rough, given that my ideas can lie dormant or below the threshold of conscious thought for long periods of time, and they appear to continually evolve and feed off other thoughts.

We pride ourselves on our ability to handle interrupts and switch contexts smoothly. We prioritize everything we have to do and we coordinate and synchronize our activities to try to perform at peak efficiency. And sometimes these attempts to optimize our behavior produce pathological behavior. Imagine the mental equivalents of these computer pathologies: "crosstalk" when two signals destructively interfere with one another, "thrashing" when a CPU has so many processes to run that it spends all of its time context switching (this generally happens when there is limited memory and part of context switching involves moving programs and data from disk to RAM and back again), "deadlock" when two processes find themselves stuck each waiting for something that the other one has, and "segmentation fault" (or "segfault") when a program crashes as a result of trying to write or read in a protected part of memory.

I don't think that my brain operates anything like a modern computer, but I do think that the notions of processes and threads, multitasking and thrashing, deadlocking and segfaulting have some metaphorical value in analyzing human thinking. In *Faster: The Acceleration of Just About Everything*, James Gleick talks about how such notions have influenced how we think about time. If you're interested in models of the mind with a computational flavor, you may enjoy the writings of Marvin Minsky, Allen Newell and Daniel Dennett. And we'll return to some related issues in the philosophy of mind in Chapter 16. David Lodge's novel *Thinks* and Richard Powers' *Galatea 2.2* provide interesting insights into the relationship between human and computer processes. (By the way, the title of this chapter, "Do Robots Sleep?," was inspired by Philip K. Dick's "Do Androids Dream of Electric Sheep?" adapted for the movies by Ridley Scott as "Blade Runner.") To learn more about modern operating systems, I recommend the text by Silberschatz, Galvin and Gagne as a good solid introduction.

CHAPTER ELEVEN

Under the Hood

Have you ever wondered what's going on when you click your mouse on some underlined text in a browser window and suddenly the screen fills with text and graphics that clearly come from some other faraway place? It's as if you've been transported to another location, as if a window has opened up on another world. If you're on a fast cable or DSL ("digital subscriber line", the first of many acronyms in this chapter) connection, the transformation is almost instantaneous; if you're using a slow modem, then updating the screen can take several seconds or even minutes, but in any case the behind-the-scenes machinations making this transformation possible leave little evidence. Occasionally, however, you'll catch fleeting glimpses of the machinery through little cracks in the user interface.

If you use a dial-up connection and modem to connect with your Internet service provider, you may hear an awful squawking as your modem and the service provider's modem initiate two-way communication. Similar noisy exchanges can occur when one fax machine attempts to communicate with a second. In both cases, computer programs at each end of a telephone connection are validating, handshaking, synchronizing and otherwise handling the transmission of information. As smarter modems and fax machines replace older technology, these noisy accompaniments are being silenced, since a human need no longer overhear them to check that things are proceeding as desired.

In surfing the web, however, we still often see the underlying machinery of the Internet peeking through. Many browsers display a line of text along the top or bottom of the browser window that shows the address of the web page you're currently looking at and in some cases lets you edit the line in order to jump to another address. If you were looking at my web page, for example, you'd see some variant of `http://www.cs.brown.edu/people/tld/`. HTTP is the acronym for a *protocol* that the browser uses to communicate with a program running on a distant computer to fetch the web page contents.

11.1 CLIENT-SERVER MODEL

A communication protocol specifies, among other things, how to request that information be transmitted, how to respond when information is requested, how to package information for transmission, and how to signal that you've received the information you requested. HTTP is one of several protocols that are necessary for you to surf the web. Protocols are just specifications, and in order to be useful they have to be implemented as parts of programs. The programs that implement protocols such as HTTP are often characterized as *clients* or *servers* or some combination of the two. In the *client-server* model of computing, server programs provide ("serve up") services to client programs that request them. The services can be web pages in the case of a web server or answers to queries in the case of a database server. Communication protocols must run on both the client and server to conduct the transfer of information among running programs.

The word "server" has several computer-related meanings that are relevant to understanding what happens when you click on a link in a web page. A program that provides particular services or implements a particular protocol is sometimes referred to as *server software*. Once the program is running, the on-going computation managed by the operating system can be called a *server process*. Such a process often involves many separate threads of computation for such operations as processing database transactions and checking for clients requesting services. Finally, the computer on which such a process is running is often called a *server*. Such a server is usually a relatively powerful computer, with redundant power supplies, lots of disk storage and multiple processors to make sure it won't crash, run out of memory, or bog down when many clients request services at the same time. Companies conducting business on the web rely on their web and database servers being available 24 hours a day, seven days a week, 365 days a year.

In order to request services, a client program needs to know the address of the server (the machine on which the server process is running), and to provide services, the server needs to know the address of the client machine. Different protocols are assigned specific *ports* on servers so that the server process implementing a particular protocol knows where to look for client requests.[1] The operating system

---

[1] A port was originally a piece of circuitry used to transfer data into and out of a computer, but modern systems blur the boundaries between hardware and software and nowadays a port is simply a source of digital data that the operating system can be made to attend to using interrupts (interrupts are described in Chapter 10). The operating system can choose to ignore such data or can send it along to other programs waiting to process it. Ports have numbers – HTTP uses port number 80 – that give the operating system a hint about what program might be appropriate for processing the data.

assists by routing incoming requests to the right ports. If the program implementing a given service crashes or was never started, then a client requesting this service won't get a response. Similarly, if some part of the network linking the client to the server isn't working, then no requests or services are communicated.

A computer connected to a network is said to *host* web pages if that computer runs a server process implementing the HTTP protocol that responds to requests for these web pages by transferring the relevant content and dealing with related chores such as handling forms and processing the data that such forms produce. When you click on a link in your web browser window, your browser (an HTTP client) figures out the address of the machine hosting the web page associated with the link and sends a request to the HTTP port on the host machine. The server looks for the page and if possible sends the relevant data (HTTP stands for "hypertext transfer protocol") back to the client, which formats the data and displays it on your monitor.

Millions of computers are connected to the Internet and many of these computers provide services by implementing various protocols. In addition to HTTP, FTP ("file transfer protocol") servers enable users to transfer files from remote machines, SMTP ("simple mail transfer protocol") makes it possible to send email messages from one computer to another, and TELNET[2] lets users log on to remote computers and lets system administrators administer machines all over the world without leaving their offices. I won't dwell on the negative aspects of such services, but the ports that traffic in the various protocols also offer targets for malicious hackers who try to find ways of redirecting these protocols to access protected data or coopt the servers for their own purposes.

Nowadays most users consider protocols like FTP and TELNET hopelessly low-level. Modern client applications implementing these protocols hide their details behind fancy user interfaces. Most programmers, however, know how to use simple programs that implement protocols like FTP or TELNET just in case the fancy clients or the display routines and graphical interfaces they rely on don't work. In the following exchange, I type `ftp 192.168.1.101` to invoke a text-based FTP client in a shell and connect to an FTP server running on a remote machine identified by network address `192.168.1.101`. The FTP client tells me that I successfully logged on to the specified machine, and the next few commands I type at the `ftp>` prompt are interpreted by the client and then relayed to the server running on the remote machine. I use this indirect means to look around in the file system on the remote machine, using the `cd` (change directory) and `ls` (list directory)

---

[2] TELNET originally stood for "teletypewriter network" but now refers to the "network virtual terminal" protocol – which accounts for all the letters if not their order.

commands that my FTP client relays to the remote machine for processing by the server. The numbered statements, for instance, `226 Transfer complete`, are diagnostic messages printed by the client that give me some idea what's happening on the server side. Having found the file I was looking for, I download it with the `get` command and type `exit` to end the session.

```
% ftp 192.168.1.101
Connected to 192.168.1.101.
Name: tld
331 Password required for tld.
Password:
230 User tld logged in.
ftp> cd email/code/
250 CWD command successful.
ftp> pwd
257 "/u/tld/email/code/" is the current directory.
ftp> ls
150 Opening ASCII mode data connection for '/bin/ls'.
total 1
-rw-r--r--  1 tld   staff   11151 Nov 18 12:17 soup.txt
-rw-r--r--  1 tld   staff   37708 Nov 18 11:47 nuts.txt
226 Transfer complete.
ftp> get soup.txt
150 Opening BINARY mode data connection for 'soup.txt'.
226 Transfer complete.
11151 bytes received in 00:00 (26.35 KB/s)
ftp> exit
```

The FTP protocol is implemented in both the FTP client and server programs, thus providing the software equivalent of the winking, nodding and handshaking necessary to ensure that information is reliably passed back and forth between client and server and that both programs are aware of what has happened – for example, the protocol requires each program to acknowledge the receipt of any information passed to it by the other.

As low-level as HTTP, SMTP, FTP and TELNET may seem, they are just the tip of the iceberg; these protocols reside in one layer of a complex set of layered communication services. You probably don't want to know all the details, but it's useful (or at least interesting) to have some idea of what's going on in the guts of the Internet. To that end, let's delve a little deeper.

11.2 ACRONYM CITY

We'll begin our descent into the lower realms of communications software pur-gatory with the layer immediately below HTTP, SMTP, FTP and TELNET. Protocols such as HTTP exist in what's called the *application layer*, though you might con-sider the primitive clients implementing these protocols too low-level to be con-sidered applications. Just remember that HTTP and FTP implementations are part of your web browser and that your email application relies on an implementation of SMTP to send messages (and on implementations of other application-layer pro-tocols such as POP for "post office protocol" and IMAP for "interactive mail access protocol", to fetch messages).

Immediately below the application layer is the *transport layer*. Protocols in the application layer rely on sending messages from one machine to another. These protocols don't want to worry about how their messages are packaged or how they're transported. They simply want their messages to get to their intended des-tinations, in one piece and without error – just do it and spare me the details. You might think that the application-layer protocols would also require some guar-antees of security – for instance, don't let anyone read my love letters. But these services are typically handled at the application layer by using encryption meth-ods to render messages unreadable should they find their way into other hands. In presenting itself to a protocol in the transport layer, an application-layer protocol provides a destination address and a stream of bits and expects the bits to be de-livered quickly and in their original order, or if necessary to be told that this can't be done.

The most commonly used protocols at the transport layer are TCP ("transmis-sion control protocol") and UDP ("user datagram protocol"). UDP is often used to exchange data over a network where high speed is important and occasional transmission failures are acceptable – for example, in a teleconferencing applica-tion where you're willing to lose a few frames of a video signal. TCP, the workhorse of the Internet, is the transport-layer protocol responsible for transmitting the data used by HTTP clients and servers to support web surfing.

Given the address of a destination machine and a message, TCP begins by repackaging the message into a sequence of fixed-size packages. If a message is smaller than the fixed-size packages, that's fine: it'll rattle around in its package, but it still ends up in a one-size-fits-all container. This repackaging enables the next-lower-layer protocols to avoid worrying about large messages. Just as parcel delivery services limit the size of the packages they'll ship to make sure they'll fit on their trucks, so the protocol that TCP relies on places limits on package size.

Digital data is great because it can always be broken up into smaller pieces that can be shipped individually and then reassembled at the other end. In fact, that's pretty much TCP's job: TCP repackages arbitrary-sized messages into one or more fixed-sized packages, labels the individual packages, sends them separately to the destination address, if necessary resends packages that have taken too long and are presumed lost in transit, and then, when all the packages have arrived, uses the labels to assemble them in the proper order and delivers the reconstituted message to the intended recipient.

To get its work done, TCP needs to be able to send relatively small fixed-size packages from one machine to another. This is the job of the *network layer* and TCP relies on IP ("internet protocol") at this layer to handle such transmissions. The problem faced by IP is that there isn't a wire connecting every possible pair of computers. Instead, there are a lot of computers out there, only some of which happen to be connected to one another. For its part, IP doesn't want to worry about the individual connections – they could be implemented using smoke signals for all it cares. IP relies on the next lower layer of protocols to worry about transmissions between connected pairs of computers.

IP views the network as a system of roads linking towns: the towns are computers and the roads are data connections along which packages can be sent. IP's job is to find a sequence of roads that starts at the town corresponding to the machine originating the request and ends at the town corresponding to the destination machine. Each package has a label that specifies its final destination. Since at any instant some roads are busier than others, IP uses frequently updated routing tables to select a route that's likely to be congestion free. IP doesn't plan out a route for each package in advance; rather, it relies on the other towns – other computers also running IP – to accept packages sent to them and then, using the information in the routing tables, to forward the packages to the next town.

Except for computing the routing tables (which is actually done by a separate protocol), IP operates in a completely decentralized fashion: individual computers running IP accept packages of data and forward them to the next computer along the route. Things can get complicated when, for example, individual computers get bogged down with lots of packages to forward or the networks connecting pairs of computers become less reliable. If a package doesn't arrive at its intended destination within a specified time limit, TCP gives it up for lost and tells IP to resend it.

TCP relies entirely on IP to deliver packages to network addresses. It's for this reason that the two protocols are typically referred to by the collective name TCP/IP. IP, however, has to depend on a variety of protocols at the next lower or *data-link* layer. The data-link layer has more acronyms than you can shake a stick at and IP has to deal with all of them. From Ethernet-based LANs ("local area networks" – most computers come equipped to communicate on a LAN using Ethernet technology and its related family of protocols) to ISDN ("integrated services digital network") networks realized by digital phone connections and ATM ("asynchronous transfer mode") networks based on a different switching technology, IP has to figure out the right data-link-layer protocol to invoke to forward a package to the next computer in its multi-stage journey.

Below the data-link layer is the *physical* layer consisting of fiber-optic cables, twisted pairs of copper wires, coaxial cables and radio frequencies, but I suspect you're layered out. If all these acronyms, layers and protocols are confusing, don't worry, it's not just you. Modern computer networks are mind-bogglingly complex and my brief overview barely skims the surface. The remarkable thing is that programmers generally concern themselves with only one or two levels and don't worry about the rest: the abstractions at one level shelter them from the complexity at lower levels. And these abstractions do more than simply hide detail; they also describe services and qualities of service at one level that are not available at lower levels. For example, TCP supports reliable communication by using an unreliable protocol, namely IP. It does so by using IP as subroutine in a more complicated protocol, invoking IP services, monitoring IP performance, and terminating or re-invoking IP services as needed to ensure reliability.

Whether you're a professional, occasional or recreational programmer, you're not likely to invoke TCP, UDP or any other communication protocol directly. Programmers generally exploit libraries that package protocols for different purposes. Whether you're implementing a distributed game in Java, remotely controlling a robot over a wireless network using C, or building a web server in Scheme, you'll very likely find a library in your favorite programming language that suits your purposes.

If you'd like to learn more about the history of computer networking and the Internet in particular, you might enjoy M. Mitchell Waldrop's *The Dream Machine: J. C. R. Licklider and the Revolution That Made Computing Personal* and Steven Segaller's *Nerds 2.0.1: A Brief History of the Internet*. To learn more about the technical details behind networking software, I recommend Andrew Tanenbaum's *Computer Networks*.

11.3 ALPHABET SOUP

As long as we're talking about the protocols and programs that power the World Wide Web, I might as well point out some other highlights of the acronym-laden vocabulary for web pages and the services they offer. As I mentioned earlier, HTTP stands for "hypertext transfer protocol" and the most common Hypertext languages in use today are HTML ("hypertext markup language") and XHTML ("extended hypertext markup language"). Hypertext languages are used for formatting and displaying text and images, with GIF (Graphics Interchange Format) and JPEG (Joint Photographic Experts Group) being the most common formats for encoding image data.

Hypertext languages also allow the embedding of *hyperlinks*, without which the World Wide Web wouldn't be a web. Hyperlinks are essentially pointers to web pages called URLs ("universal resource locators") that tell your browser how to request a web page from the web server hosting that web page and presumably implementing the HTTP protocol. We've already talked about that aspect of surfing the web, but there are lots of other goodies embedded in web pages worth knowing about.

You may have heard that web pages can have *dynamic content*, and even if you haven't, you've probably experienced them: web pages with pop-up advertisements, animations, images that change as you move your cursor over them, menus that seem to anticipate your choices, and text windows that beckon you to type something. This sort of dynamic content is powered in a variety of ways that illustrate new programming models.

One of the oldest but still quite common ways to create dynamic content uses various server-side scripting languages. It used to be that if you could program in Perl you could get a job for the summer writing CGI ("common gateway interface") scripts. Here a "script" is a program written in a scripting language, and since Perl programs can be invoked from many scripting languages, many of these scripts were just Perl programs. CGI scripts are run on a web server (hence the designation as a "server-side" scripting language) when someone requests a page containing such a script. The script can create custom content and thus generate brand new, never-before-seen hypertext that's sent back to the browser requesting the page. Many early online businesses displayed their catalogs and filled customer orders using CGI scripts.

Today there are several alternatives for server-side computations. ASP ("active server page") is part of a much larger collection of languages and tools provided by Microsoft and known as .NET (pronounced "dot net"). JSP ("java server pages") from Sun Microsystems provides similar services. PHP ("PHP hypertext preprocessor"[3]) is another popular scripting language used for delivering dynamic content.

---

[3] PHP is called a recursive acronym. One of the most famous recursive acronyms in computing is GNU, which stands for "GNU's not Unix" and is most closely associated with the Free Software Foundation and its collection of extraordinarily useful pieces of high-quality software.

All these server-side languages can create new HTML or XHTML content. They're often used to generate SQL ("structured query language") queries and submit them to database servers to add new information or access existing data. Nowadays when you click on a link in your browser, all sorts of computations can take place on the web server before it spits back a page of hypertext on your screen. And usually all this takes place in the blink of an eye.

Sometimes, however, it makes sense for some computations to occur not on the web server, which could get bogged down running scripts and dynamically producing content, but on the client side. When you're just sitting there browsing the web, your computer usually doesn't have a lot to do. So, Internet content providers figure, why not put those spare computing cycles to good use to power all those cute little animations that make your screen jump and sparkle like a cinema marquee? Java and JavaScript are the languages of choice for embedding in web pages and running on your computer. For client-side computations, when you request a web page containing Java or JavaScript, the code or, in the case of Java, a platform-dependent compiled version of the code called *bytecodes* is downloaded along with the rest of the web page. Many browsers can directly interpret JavaScript programs, while Java requires a special program called the Java Virtual Machine (JVM). Small Java programs called *applets* are often used to add effects and interactive components to dynamic web pages.

So when you click on a link in your browser you trigger a complicated sequence of computations. Your browser implements an HTTP client that uses TCP to send messages to a web server. The bits making up these messages are shuttled across the Internet in small packages using IP. Server-side scripting languages make computations happen on the web server and these computations can initiate exchanges with database servers or other remotely running programs. The web server uses TCP/IP to reply to your browser by sending back content as hypertext, graphics and embedded Java and JavaScript destined to run on your computer and provide a dynamic, interactive experience. All that just find out if it's going to rain tomorrow.

11.4   SMART MILK CARTONS

I can't leave the subject of the web without a nod to the many people responsible for establishing, refining, adopting and then sticking to the standards without which no computer could talk to any other computer and the web would be impossible. Standards are everywhere in world of programming. Standards organizations like ANSI ("American National Standards Institute"), IEEE ("Institute of Electrical and Electronic Engineers") and ISO ("International Organization for Standardization") have established standards for programming languages (e.g., ANSI C), communication protocols (e.g., IEEE 802), date and time notation (e.g., ISO 8601), and even character sets (e.g., ISO 10646).

I'll bet you didn't even realize that character sets need standards. Characters codes are definitely the nuts and bolts of the computer world. And, just as engineers need standards for the pitch of threads so the nuts manufactured by one company will screw on the bolts of another, so software companies need standards for how to encode to the characters that appear on your keyboard and are displayed on your computer screen. For a long time, programmers got by with the 7-bit ASCII character code (ASCII stands for "American standard code for information interchange"), published in 1968 as ANSI X3.4. But a good portion of the world doesn't want to be limited to what's available on most keyboards, and so an 8-bit standard called ISO 8859 was developed in the 1980s. ISO 8859 defines several multilingual character sets including Cyrillic, Arabic, Greek and Hebrew and more are on the way (talk about alphabet soup!). A more ambitious standard called Unicode (ISO 10646) promises to provide a unique code for every character no matter what language you're using.

When it makes sense to standardize so computers can talk with one another and programmers can understand one another's code, then the standards organizations get the interested parties to sit down at the table and hash out a standard. There are times when economic interests and just plain stubbornness stick us with ungainly compromises. But more often than not, reason and good design win out over other interests and we get something we can live with. The fact of the matter is that we couldn't have a World Wide Web were it not for standards.

Standards are making possible a host of new technologies that promise to free us from wires and cables while at the same time connecting us to everything imaginable. IEEE 802.11 is a standard for wireless LANs that lets people move from home to office to classroom to conference room, and even to suitably equipped cafes, restaurants and airport waiting lounges, without missing an email message. Bluetooth, another wireless technology, combines several standards and protocols and is used for short-range (a few meters) wireless communication. Bluetooth will allow digital cameras to exchange data with laptops, audio headsets and microphones to communicate with cell phones, and cellphones to talk with hand-held organizers, all without wires. A number of companies are scrambling to figure out which applications are likely to become commercially viable. Imagine that a carton of milk in your refrigerator senses it's nearly empty or will soon pass its expiration date and then tells your hand-held organizer to add milk to your grocery list. Such applications are now technically possible with the new standards; it remains to be seen whether people will want or be willing to pay for them.

While these standards may make our lives a little simpler and less cluttered, the consequences for computing are even more striking. When I think about computation, I think of dynamic processes, evolving threads of control that sense and adapt to their environment. With the advent of networked computers, computations were no longer confined to individual computers and the network became the computer. With the advent of wireless LANs and Bluetooth-enabled devices, computations will literally take flight, freed from the constraints of wires. Scientists imagine tiny solar-powered sensors equipped with even smaller computers and wireless transceivers that could be sprinkled from aircraft to gather weather data, aid in searching for lost hikers, or gather military intelligence. Once you enable the most mundane of objects to perform computations and share information, the possibilities are extraordinary.

CHAPTER TWELVE

Analyze This

Most physicists believe that the speed of light is a fundamental limit on how quickly we can move through space. This claim is based on the predictions of mathematical theories and the results of experiments that appear to support them. According to theory, it doesn't matter whether you move through space with a pogo stick or an anti-matter drive, you're still subject to the rules governing all matter in the universe and thus unable to exceed the speed of light.

What if there are limits on what you can compute? Pharmaceutical companies simulate interactions at the atomic level in searching for molecules to cure diseases. There could be viruses for which it will take years to find a vaccine – there is simply no way to speed up the necessary computations. Software developers who write the programs that keep airplanes flying and emergency rooms functioning would like to prove that their code won't malfunction and put lives at risk. But maybe it's impossible to provide such assurances.

In some cases, computational limitations can work to our advantage. Some programs exploit the difficulty of computing answers to particular problems; for example, the most popular encryption schemes for transferring information securely on the World Wide Web rely on the difficulty of computing the prime factors of large composite integers. Of course, if someone figures out how to factor large numbers efficiently, our privacy will be seriously threatened. It would be nice if we could guarantee the security of our encryption schemes.

Many computer scientists believe that there are fundamental limits to computation. Specifically, they believe that some problems are so hard it would take an impractically long time to compute their answers and that other problems simply can't be solved. Theoretical computer scientists try to resolve fundamental questions about the limitations of computing as well as shed light on the performance of programs that we depend on every day.

Computer science as a discipline behaves at times like a physical science – computation is, after all, a fundamental determiner of change in the universe – and at times like a kind of engineering – modern software systems are among the most complicated artifacts ever created so it's not surprising that computer science has its own theoretical foundations and a large body of engineering knowledge.

In this chapter we're going to look at how computer scientists analyze problems. We'll consider various mathematical models that provide general techniques for describing computations and quantifying their performance. And, finally, we'll talk about theories concerning fundamental questions about what can and cannot be computed.

12.1 ANALYZING ALGORITHMS

We started off Chapter 4 by distinguishing between specifications and implementations and in so doing we introduced two components of specifications, algorithms and data structures. An *algorithm* is a step-by-step recipe for how to carry out a given computation; the factorial procedure we looked at in Chapter 5 is such a recipe. A *data structure* is a strategy for organizing and manipulating data; lists and stacks together with their associated operations are examples of data structures. The relevant subfield of theoretical computer science is often called the "design and analysis of algorithms and data structures" or just "algorithms."

A specification describes a computation independent of any programming language or computer hardware with which we might implement that computation. In theoretical computer science, algorithms and data structures are typically specified in terms of a pseudo-language that doesn't correspond to any particular programming language used in practice. Doing this levels the playing field: anyone can understand such specifications and easily translate them into one or another programming language for implementation.

But while the algorithms and data structures that comprise a specification are language- and machine-independent, they must nonetheless connect to some model of computation in order to be comprehensible to us as computations. We've seen several models of computation, for example, the substitution model in Chapter 5 and the register-machine model in Chapter 9, that would be appropriate for this purpose. For a detailed analysis, we'd have to expand and be more precise about these models, but when we talk about an underlying model of computation for a given analysis you can safely think about one of these two.

Indeed, theoretical computer science abounds with interesting formal computational models. Every such model provides a mathematical framework in which one can talk about how information is represented and how computations proceed. These abstract models let theorists investigate what can be computed and how hard (how much time and memory they require) such computations are likely to be.

Not all computational models are equal, however, and so you can ask if one model of computation is more expressive than another in the sense that there are computations that you can specify in one but not in the other: One question often asked about a given model is whether or not you can tell if a computation specified in that model will halt. Sounds like a simple thing to require of a computational model, but many models turn out to be expressive enough that you can't answer this question for all computations they can express.

Can you think of reasons why you'd want to adopt a less expressive, more restrictive model of computation? With some less expressive models you can get some nice properties, like the ability to check whether a computation will halt or a guarantee that every computation takes only a relatively short amount of time. Models with such properties might cramp your style somewhat, but they also might let you produce software with very desirable attributes.

We're not going to worry about the more esoteric models, however. For our purposes, it suffices for you to think about computations in the register-machine model. For a generic programming language, we'll use a variant of ALGOL ("algorithmic language"), which looks a bit like C. Here's how to specify the `square` function in ALGOL:

```
integer procedure square(n)
    integer n;
    begin
        square := n * n
    end;
```

Squint at the notation as usual, but note that the `integer` statements are "type declarations" (these would be `int` in C) and can safely be ignored, `:=` indicates assignment[1] (x `:=` 2 assigns to the variable x the value of 2) and, internal to the procedure definition, assigning the procedure name to a value (`square := n * n`) is the way to specify the return value for the procedure. You could then translate this ALGOL specification into Scheme as

```
(define (square n) (* n n))
```

---

[1] A lone equal sign = (`:=` without the `:`) indicates an equality test; x `=` 2 evaluates to true if x is equal to 2 and to false otherwise.

or into C as

```
int square(int n) { return n * n ; }
```

The touted advantage of using an agreed-upon standard like ALGOL is that everybody knows ALGOL (not true!) and that it doesn't favor any particular language (well, O.K., ignoring dialects of ALGOL itself, in a way this is true, but it does favor languages with syntax similar to ALGOL). But this is one of the least interesting observations about the design and analysis of algorithms. You write algorithms in a general specification language to be clear about what they mean, to make it easy to implement them in a variety of languages, and to enable computer scientists to analyze their characteristics independent of the particular language in which they are written.

To illustrate how a computer scientist analyzes algorithms, we'll look at a relatively simple mathematical algorithm: computing the nth term in the *Fibonacci sequence*. The Fibonacci sequence is 0, 1, 1, 2, 3, 5, 8, 13, 21, ... so that the nth term for n greater than 1 is the sum of the $n - 2$ and $n - 1$ terms in the sequence. These so-called Fibonacci numbers may seem a bit academic but they have broad application, from a popular stock-trading strategy to the multiplication of rabbits.[2] Here's how we might compute the nth term in the Fibonacci sequence in Scheme:

```
> (define (fibonacci n)
    (if (= n 1) 0
        (if (= n 2) 1
            (+ (fibonacci (- n 2))
               (fibonacci (- n 1))))))
> (fibonacci 8)
13
```

And here is the same algorithm written in ALGOL, which doesn't look too different from the Scheme implementation:

```
integer procedure fibonacci(n);
  integer n;
  if n = 1
    then fibonacci := 0
    else if n = 2
            then fibonacci := 1
```

---

[2] Leonardo Pisano, or Fibonacci as he called himself, was a mathematician born in Pisa around 1175. He investigated the sequence bearing his name as a means of describing how quickly rabbits would multiply under ideal breeding circumstances.

```
   else fibonacci := fibonacci(n - 1) +
                     fibonacci(n - 2);
```

Think about how many times the function `fibonacci` is called in order to compute the *n*th term in the Fibonacci sequence. It is called once in computing the first and second terms, three times in computing the third term, five times for the fourth term, and so on. Extending this sequence out a bit further, we get a new sequence: 1, 1, 3, 5, 9, 15, 25, 41, 67, 109, 177, 287, 465, ..., well, you can see the pattern; the *n*th term in this sequence is 1 plus the sum of the $(n-2)$ and $(n-1)$ terms. This sequence is upsetting to a theoretical computer scientist because it says that the work required to compute the *n*th term of the Fibonacci sequence approximately doubles each time *n* increases by 1; such a sequence is said to grow *exponentially* in *n* (think about 2^n in which *n* is the exponent or power to which the base, 2 in this case, is raised).

In order to compute the 100th term of the Fibonacci sequence using this procedure, we would have to call the `fibonacci` function approximately 2^{100} or 1,267,650,600,228,229,401,496,703,205,376 times.[3] How long would this take? To keep our analysis simple, let's focus solely on the arithmetic operations and let's suppose that each addition (application of the + operator) takes on the order of a millionth of a second. I know it's going to take a long time to perform the calculation, so let's measure the time in years. How many seconds are there in a year?

```
> (* 60 60 24 365)
31536000
```

or around 32 million, ignoring leap years and such. And about how many seconds will our calculation take? (The `expt` or exponent function raises its first argument to the power specified by its second argument: (`expt` *k* *n*) returns k^n.)

```
> (* (expt 2 100) (/ 1 (expt 10 6)))
1980704062856608439838598758458584/15625
```

Oops, this version of Scheme is trying to be clever by returning the answer I requested as a rational number. It does this so it doesn't have to give me an

---

[3] The function 2^n isn't a particularly good approximation for the work done by our algorithm in computing the *n*th term in the Fibonacci sequence. Indeed, the size of the error in this approximation increases exponentially in *n* (convince yourself that $a^n - b^n$ is an exponentially increasing function for all $a > b > 1.0$). Is there a base *b* such that b^n is a better approximation? It turns out that the *golden mean* ($\phi = (\sqrt{5} - 1)/2$) is closely related to the Fibonacci sequence and $(1 + \phi)^n/\sqrt{5}$ is a good approximation of the *n*th element of the Fibonacci sequence. See if you can use this fact to get a better estimate of the work done by our algorithm.

approximation of what I asked for. (How would you print out 1/3 as a "real" number? 0.33 or perhaps 0.3333333? Both of these answers are approximations to 1/3.) If I include a "real" number in the calculation, then Scheme tries to print the result as a real. Let's try again:

```
> (* (expt 2 100) (/ 1.0 (expt 10 6)))
1.2676506002282293e+24
```

Well, I guess that's progress! Now Scheme is offering me an approximation, but it displays it in scientific notation with a lot more precision (the digits to the right of the decimal point before e+24) than I can use. Let's just say $1.27 * 10^{24}$, which is a pretty big number. Since 31536000 is 3.1536000e+7 in scientific notation or approximately $3.15 * 10^7$, we can estimate that it would take $4 * 10^{16}$ years.

That's an incomprehensibly long time and that's just to compute fibonacci(100). Remember that things get exponentially worse as *n* gets larger, so fibonacci(101) takes *twice* as long as fibonacci(100):

```
> (/ (* (expt 2 101) (/ 1.0 (expt 10 6)))
     (* 60 60 24 365))
8.039387368266294e+16
```

But when you think about it, this sort of performance just isn't necessary. If you compute the sequence in order, remembering all the earlier terms (or at least the two most recent ones, the ultimate and the penultimate terms in the sequence seen so far), then computing the next term requires simply adding together the previous two terms. The only trick is to remember the previous two terms. Here's an algorithm that exploits this idea:

```
integer procedure fibonacci(n);
  integer n;
  if n = 1
    then fibonacci := 0
    else if n = 2
            then fibonacci := 1
            else begin
                    integer penultimate;
                    penultimate := 0;
                    integer ultimate;
                    ultimate := 1;
                    integer temporary;
                    for i = 3 step 1 until n do
```

```
          begin
               temporary := penultimate +
                                penultimate;
               penultimate := ultimate;
               ultimate := temporary;
          end ;
     fibonacci := ultimate
end
```

In analyzing these two algorithms, a computer scientist would say that the first scales exponentially in n while the second scales linearly in n. Assuming that each addition takes on the order of a millionth of a second and ignoring all other aspects of the computation, computing `fibonacci(100)` with the second algorithm would take considerably less than a second ($10^2/10^6 = 1/10^4$ seconds). That's quite a difference – and we got the improvement just by thinking about the solution in a different way.

My fooling around with Scheme to calculate how many times the `fibonacci` function is called wasn't entirely gratuitous. Don't believe anyone who tells you that computer arithmetic is simple; what goes on behind the scenes when you multiply and divide numbers in a calculator or general-purpose computer is fascinating and comprises an important subfield of computer science called numerical analysis. In analyzing some algorithms, it's not enough simply to count the number of arithmetic operations; it can be necessary to look more carefully at how those operations are implemented. The numbers in the Fibonacci sequence quickly get very large thereby affecting the running time of the algorithm.

To represent a number n in binary you need around the log to the base 2 of n bits, which is typically written as $\log_2 n$. You may recall from high-school algebra that raising a number to a power (exponentiation) and taking logarithms are inverse operations, so that $\log_2 2^n = 2^{\log_2 n} = n$. The binary representation of a number requires one plus as many bits as the exponent of the largest power of 2 that the number can contain. So for example, $25 = 2^4 + 2^3 + 2^0$ is 11001 in binary, requiring $1 + \log_2 2^4 = 5$ bits. To perform operations on numbers you must at least read them and that means scanning every bit, so even something as seemingly simple as adding two numbers has to be thought about carefully. If you return to the discussion in Chapter 9 concerning computer arithmetic, you can figure out how many primitive operations are required to add and multiply integers.

Algorithms can scale in other ways than linearly or exponentially. For example, suppose you have a list of the birthdays of all your friends and you want to check to see if any of them have the same birthday. One algorithm for this check would be to consider each possible pair of friends and explicitly compare their birthdays.

This algorithm is said to scale polynomially in n (the number of friends you have) because there are n^2 possible pairs, and hence the algorithm would have to perform n^2 comparisons (n^2 is said to be a polynomial of degree 2).

This isn't a great algorithm for this problem, however. Here's a better one. Sort the birthdays by date to produce a new list in chronological order and then scan this list to see if any consecutive items in the list are identical. Aside from the sorting part, this algorithm requires n comparisons to check for possible identical consecutive items. The sorting requires $n \log_2 n$ comparisons. The total number of comparisons is therefore $n + n \log_2 n$, which is less than polynomial of degree 2 but more than linear. If $n = 2^{10} = 1024$, the n^2 algorithm does 1,048,576 comparisons while the $n + n \log_2 n$ algorithm needs only 11264 comparisons.

Here's a quick and dirty implementation using a shell script and the `sort` and `uniq` commands (the `-d` option to `uniq` displays duplicates only – it does not output lines that are not repeated in the input):

```
% cat dates.txt
12.01
08.08
02.28
07.31
08.08
% cat dates.txt | sort | uniq -d
08.08
```

Could we manage with fewer than $n + n \log_2 n$ comparisons? How did I know that sorting a list of n items takes $n \log_2 n$ comparisons? You'll discover the answer to these and many other interesting questions if you take a course on algorithms or consult a good book on the subject. The text by Cormen, Leiserson, Rivest and Stein is a little daunting in both size (it's over 1000 pages) and mathematical detail, but it does provide a comprehensive introduction to algorithms and their analysis. David Harel's book *Algorithmics* provides a somewhat less demanding and very entertaining introduction to the field.

In case it's not already obvious, this branch of computer science uses a lot of mathematics. In analyzing algorithms, as in other highly mathematical areas of science and engineering, "getting it right" is important. Earlier I said that our first algorithm for finding a pair of friends with the same birthday scaled polynomially in n because there are n^2 possible pairs in a list of n distinct friends and hence the algorithm would have to perform n^2 comparisons. Actually, there are $n(n-1)/2$ possible pairs. The algorithm is still said to scale polynomially in n, since $n(n-1)/2 = 1/2(n^2 - n)$ is a polynomial of degree 2, but I was careless about the details.

Figuring out such details is the subject matter of an area of mathematics called *combinatorics*, which is the source of many important tools for analyzing algorithms. I'll give you a little taste of combinatorics by proving that there are $n(n-1)/2$ possible pairs of distinct items in a list of n items.

Let's enumerate the possibilities one item at a time. Consider the first item in the list. There are $n-1$ items we can choose to pair with this first item since it can't pair with itself. The resulting $n-1$ pairs account for all pairs that include the first item, so we can leave this item out in considering the remaining possibilities. Now consider the second item. There are $n-2$ ways of pairing this item with the remaining items and now we can ignore the second item. Continuing in this manner, we see that the total number of pairs is $(n-1) + (n-2) + \ldots + 1 + 0 = \sum_{i=1}^{n}(n-i)$ or $\sum_{i=1}^{n-1} i$.

Well, that's wonderful to know, but it doesn't prove what we set out to prove. However, you might recall from Chapter 2 that $\sum_{i=1}^{n} i = n(n+1)/2$. Using this equality, we see that $\sum_{i=1}^{n-1} i$ simplifies to $n(n-1)/2$. Unfortunately, we didn't offer any proofs in Chapter 2 and so we're not much better off than we were before. To make sure that we don't leave any loose ends, we have to prove that $\sum_{i=1}^{n} i = n(n+1)/2$. We'll begin by assuming that n is an even number. Watch carefully to see where we use this assumption.

$$\sum_{i=1}^{n} i = n + (n-1) + \ldots + 1$$

$$= \left[n + (n-1) + \ldots + \left(n - \frac{n}{2} - 1 \right) \right] + \left[\left(n - \frac{n}{2} \right) + \ldots + 1 \right]$$

$$= \left[n + (n-1) + \ldots + \left(n - \frac{n}{2} - 1 \right) \right] + \left[\frac{n}{2} + \ldots + 1 \right]$$

$$= \left[\sum_{i=0}^{\frac{n}{2}-1} (n-i) \right] + \left[\sum_{i=1}^{\frac{n}{2}} i \right]$$

$$= \left[\sum_{i=1}^{\frac{n}{2}} (n+1-i) \right] + \left[\sum_{i=1}^{\frac{n}{2}} i \right]$$

$$= \sum_{i=1}^{\frac{n}{2}} (n+1+i-i)$$

$$= \sum_{i=1}^{\frac{n}{2}} (n+1)$$

$$= \frac{n(n+1)}{2}$$

By assuming that n is even we were able to divide the list into two smaller lists, each consisting of $n/2$ items. Now suppose that n is odd and let's take advantage of the fact that $n-1$ is even. Again, watch carefully for where we exploit this assumption to make use of the case we just proved.

$$\sum_{i=1}^{n} i = n + \sum_{i=1}^{n-1} i$$
$$= n + \frac{(n-1)(n+1-1)}{2}$$
$$= n + \frac{(n-1)n}{2}$$
$$= 2\frac{n}{2} + (n-1)\frac{n}{2}$$
$$= \frac{(n+1)(n)}{2}$$

That should do it. If you followed all the steps, you should be convinced that there are $n(n-1)/2$ pairs of distinct items in a list of n items. And if you like this sort of thing then you'll probably like combinatorics and analysis of algorithms. This kind of thinking is obviously quite useful if you want to write code that runs fast; it's also a lot of fun if you like logic, puzzles and mathematics.

We're giving data structures rather short shrift in this chapter, but the design and use of good data structures is integral to designing good algorithms and we'll take a close look at some of the most useful data structures in Chapter 13. First, though, let's look at some things that computers either can't do very well or can't do at all.

12.2 COMPUTATIONAL LIMITATIONS

On October 14, 1947, Chuck Yeager, flying an experimental jet aircraft, was the first human to fly faster than the speed of sound. I know this random factoid because I recently watched "The Right Stuff", a movie about test pilots and the NASA Mercury 7 astronauts based on the book by Tom Wolfe. Yeager broke what at the time was called the *sound barrier*, believed by some engineers to prevent aircraft from ever flying faster than sound. The sound barrier turned out not to be a fundamental limit, and eventually engineers found a way to overcome the increase in drag and loss of control produced by the shock waves of compressed air an aircraft creates as it approaches the speed of sound. Fundamental limitations do exist, however, and the history of science and engineering is as much about understanding real limitations and circumventing them as it is about debunking myths and crashing through imaginary barriers. Theoretical computer science and the theory of *computational complexity* in particular are about understanding and overcoming fundamental computational limitations.

A story in the first chapter of Garey and Johnson's *Computers and Intractability* concerns a programmer who tells his boss that he can't make his program run any faster because the problem he's trying to solve is in the class of *NP-complete problems*. The class of NP-complete problems is a class of computational problems with the interesting property that, if you could solve any one of them easily, then you could solve all the others easily as well. It is conjectured that the problems in this class are intractable in the sense that any algorithm solving one of them will require an amount of time that scales exponentially in the size of the problem.

Unfortunately, the programmer couldn't say to his boss that it was *impossible* to write an efficient algorithm (one that, say, scales linearly or polynomially in the problem size), but only that no one has done it *yet* and that a lot of computer scientists believe it can't be done. Proving whether or not the class of NP-complete problems is composed of intractable problems is one of the most interesting open problems in the theory of computation. Is NP-completeness a fundamental limitation or simply a limitation of current technology, like the sound barrier in 1947? Before I try to answer this question, I'd like to look at a few other questions concerning the fundamental limitations of computers that have been resolved over the years.

In 1930, Kurt Gödel showed that any system sufficiently expressive to capture formally the machinery of arithmetic, the rules and definitions that describe numbers and how they must behave, must be *incomplete* in the sense that it contains assertions that can neither be proved nor disproved. The realization that the tools of mathematics were not up to the task of discovering the whole truth about mathematics was a profound shock to many mathematicians of the time, but Gödel's proof has broader implications that were yet to be understood.

Gödel's proof left open the possibility that there is a mechanical procedure, an algorithm, to let us determine whether a given assertion is *decidable*, whether it can be proved or not. Alan Turing was able to show in 1936 that no such mechanical procedure exists (the problem of determining whether an assertion is provable or not is *undecidable*) and moreover that, since we can represent in a suitably expressive language assertions of the form "this computer program will halt", there is no mechanical procedure, no computer program, that given any computer program can determine whether or not it will halt. This is the so-called *halting problem*. In a formal sense, Turing showed that there are some problems that cannot be solved by any algorithm running on any computer.

Turing also was able to demonstrate the existence of a general-purpose or *universal computer* that can solve any problem solvable by a special-purpose computer. Indeed, the idea of a universal computer is not all that difficult for us to comprehend, given our familiarity with modern-day computers. The abstract computer that underlies the von Neumann architecture discussed in Chapter 9 is a universal computer but for one problem: it lacks a memory of infinite capacity. Turing's universal computer required a tape on which to read and write bits and, in order to be able to carry out any computation, that tape had to be infinite in length. Modern-day computers, no matter how much memory (RAM and disk storage) they might have, are not universal computers as defined by Turing.

The word complexity is the the source of much confusion on the part of computer science professionals and dilettantes alike. Its standard dictionary definitions provide little hint of its technical meaning (or meanings). What makes one computer problem more complex than another? One measure of complexity of interest to computer scientists concerns how long a computer takes to solve a particular problem; a related measure concerns how much memory or space is required to solve a particular problem.

Theoretical computer scientists aren't interested in how fast a program runs on a 1.5 gigahertz Pentium III running Microsoft Windows versus a 1.2 gigahertz PowerPC G4 running Apple OS X. Or in how much time on the clock, or megabytes of RAM, an algorithm takes to complete a task. Like any good mathematician, a theoretical computer scientist abstracts away the irrelevant details to get at the heart of the matter. Time is measured in terms of the number of basic operations required to complete a computation. In comparing various algorithms for computing the nth term in the Fibonacci sequence, we used the number of additions as a function of n as our measure of complexity. Space is measured by how many bits are required to represent a computation's intermediate and final products. The algorithms for computing the nth term in the Fibonacci sequence used only integers for their intermediate and final results, but other algorithms use more complicated data structures that require significant space overhead.

Computing the nth term in the Fibonacci sequence is an easy problem as computational problems go. I presented an algorithm that runs in time linear in n.[4] Other problems require time that scales polynomially in the size of the input,

---

[4] Well, the algorithm was linear in the number of additions, but adding two n-bit numbers takes time linear in n. So, strictly speaking, the running time of our second version of `fibonacci` is n^2 or polynomial in n.

which we designate as *n* in what follows. Polynomial scaling, often called polynomial time, is obviously worse than linear scaling, but for low-order polynomials (polynomials whose biggest exponent, 3 in the polynomial ($4n^3 + 2n^2 + 1$), is relatively small), polynomial time is seldom a practical concern. Are there problems for which the fastest algorithms scale exponentially in *n*? The answer is yes. But a more interesting question is: are there problems *that we care about* for which the fastest algorithms scale exponentially in *n*? The answer to this question lies at the heart of the theory of NP-completeness.

Let P be the class of problems that can be computed in polynomial time and NP be the class of problems that can be computed in *nondeterministic polynomial time*. NP problems have the property that you can check whether or not a proposed answer to one of these problems is correct in polynomial time: therefore you could solve the problem by *nondeterministically* choosing a possible solution and then checking it. If you were always lucky and chose a correct answer, then you would be able to solve the problem in polynomial time. The class of NP-complete problems is a particular class of problems that are in the class NP but are not known to have polynomial-time solutions; indeed, every known algorithm for these problems runs in time that scales exponentially[5] in *n*.

In addition to the fact that the best-known algorithms for NP-complete problems take exponential time, this problem class is interesting for three reasons. First, if you could solve one problem in this class in polynomial time, then you could solve them all in polynomial time. Second, this is about the easiest class one could imagine that is still not known to be in P. And, third, the class of NP-complete problems contains a bunch of problems that we really care about.

One of the most famous NP-complete problems concerns a traveling salesman trying to minimize his travel in calling on his customers. The problem can be described in terms of a set of *n* cities representing customers' locations and a table like a bus or train schedule that lists the routes between pairs of these cities and their distances. The problem is to find a *tour* (a sequence of cities that begins and ends with the same city and visits each city exactly once) whose length (the sum of distances traveled) is minimal.[6] This problem is important in a wide range of practical situations from scheduling commercial aircraft to routing garbage trucks in large metropolitan areas. Other NP-complete problems are important in genetic

---

[5] Strictly speaking, I should say super-polynomially rather than exponentially so as to include functions such as $n^{\log n}$, which is super-polynomial but not exponential, and n^n, which is super-exponential.

[6] Technically, all of the problems in the class of NP-complete problems are *decision problems*, which means they must have yes-or-no answers. In order to turn our *traveling salesman problem* into a decision problem, we would have to phrase it as follows: Does there exist a tour whose length is less than *k* for some fixed threshold *k*? Think of the problem faced by a salesman on a strict budget.

and pharmaceutical research and a host of otherwise unrelated problems from packing furniture to making computers run faster.

The mathematics involved in defining and characterizing the class of NP-complete problems is an extraordinary achievement attributable in no small measure to Stephen Cook, Leonid Levin and Richard Karp, among other pioneering theoretical computer scientists. Since the basic formulation, computer scientists have erected a hierarchy of classes of problems of increasing complexity and studied the complexity not only of problems for which we require exact answers but also problems for which we'll accept approximations. There remain many open questions but one in particular looms above all the others: is P = NP? If someone can find a polynomial-time solution to one problem in the class of NP-complete problems, then all problems in the class will have been shown to have polynomial-time solutions.

Many computer scientists believe that P $\neq$ NP: the classes are distinct and eventually someone will prove it. (By the way, it's not unusual for a mathematical problem to remain unanswered for years, decades or even centuries after first being posed. The celebrated "Last Theorem" of Pierre de Fermat (1601–1665) remained unproven for over three centuries until Andrew Wiles, aided by the accumulated wisdom of many mathematicians, produced in 1994 a formal proof that stood up to careful scrutiny.) A proof that P $\neq$ NP will make it easier for the programmer we talked about earlier to convince his boss that he shouldn't keep working on a polynomial-time algorithm for an NP-complete problem.

If it is determined that P = NP, the repercussions will be very interesting. Not only will NP collapse into P, but there will be additional collapses and compression within the complexity hierarchy. And if P = NP, have we then been missing something fundamental in our understanding of algorithms and computing machinery? Why haven't the best hackers in the world been able to find polynomial-time solutions to any of the problems in the eminently practical and exhaustively studied class of NP-complete problems? Well, perhaps "exhaustively studied" is a bit of an exaggeration; we've only been at this for a little over 50 years. The field is young. Perhaps you'll be the one to prove that P $\neq$ NP or to turn the field topsy-turvy by demonstrating a polynomial-time algorithm for the traveling salesman problem.

Popular accounts of computing have frequently focused on the theory of computing and the scientists who pioneered it. Douglas Hofstadter's *Gödel, Escher, Bach* is a very readable introduction to Gödel's work and its implications. *Alan Turing: The Enigma* by Andrew Hodges is a wonderful introduction to Turing's life and work. Martin Davis wrote an interesting and entertaining book about universal computers and the logicians and mathematicians from Leibniz to Turing who provided the theoretical foundations for modern computer science. Martin Gardner's essay on the traveling salesman problem in *Gardner's Whys and Wherefores* is a nice introduction to the ins and outs of this problem. Shasha and Lazere's *Out of Their Minds* contains a number of interesting biographies of computer scientists, including Steven Cook and Leonid Levin mentioned in this chapter, Donald Knuth, who is responsible for several fundamental algorithms as well as one of today's most powerful typesetting systems, John McCarthy, who coined the term "artificial intelligence" and invented Lisp, and Alan Kay, who developed Smalltalk, one of the first object-oriented programming languages. David Harel's book on the limitations of computers is an excellent introduction to the theory of NP-completeness. For an in-depth technical discussion of the broader field of computational complexity suitable for graduate-level study, I recommend the text by Christos Papadimitriou.

12.3 THEORY THAT MATTERS

Students often ask about the significance of NP-completeness results for practicing software engineers. One response is that the results on computational limitations provide general guidance in how to approach problems much as results on the speed of light guide engineers in building faster computers – you're unlikely to be able to make information flow faster between the components in a circuit, so think harder about how to make the components smaller and closer together. Algorithm designers faced with a hard problem typically look for approximations rather than wasting their time on exact solutions.

The most important point is that there are problems we actually care about, lots of them in fact, that are likely to remain beyond us for a considerable time to come. We can't compute solutions to these problems even though we know how, in the procedural sense, because they require too much time or space. The computational requirements for these problems increase so rapidly that they will probably outpace anything we can build for longer than we care to wait. Here's an example.

Suppose you're trying to design an efficient algorithm to find patterns in human DNA as part of a diagnostic test for a new cancer treatment. And suppose that the best-known algorithm for this pattern-finding problem runs in exponential time. For patterns of size 10, this algorithm currently takes several hours.

For the diagnostic test to be useful in a clinical setting, you need to be able to solve the problem for patterns of size 100 in a matter of minutes. Even if you could rely on the speed of computers doubling – improving exponentially – every year for the foreseeable future, you'd still have to wait 90 years before your diagnostic test will run quickly enough to help patients.

It should be clear from this example that the fact a problem is NP-complete doesn't mean that we stop working on it; the programmer's excuses to his boss were misleading in this regard. You often hear programmers say that everything interesting or useful that's not trivial is NP-complete or worse. Their advice is to stop complaining about NP-completeness and get on with it.

From their perspective, if P = NP, then they're no worse off than they were before, since they never had the luxury of telling their boss that there are no better algorithms. These programmers have to invent heuristics and uncover hidden structure in special classes of problems in order to solve or approximate the problems they're stuck with. And, if P ≠ NP, their heuristics may end up being the best we can hope for.

Either way, they have to pound their heads against hard, seemingly intractable problems and come up with solutions. In the case of our hypothetical diagnostic test for the cancer treatment, if the treatment appears to help patients, then programmers will do their best to find an approximate solution to the pattern-finding problem so that the diagnostic test will run in some reasonable time with acceptable error.

Beginning students and experienced practitioners alike often fail to distinguish between problems and *instances* of problems, and between problems and algorithms or programs for solving those problems. A particular instance of the traveling salesman problem involving, say, ten cities is of little interest to a theoretical computer scientist: it may be hard to find an answer to it, but once you do, then you're done; the problem is solved.

The traveling salesman problem is really an infinite set of instances with an infinite number of instances involving ten cities, an infinite number of instances involving eleven cities, and so on. It's this infinite set of instances, whose sizes are measured in terms of the numbers of cities and the tables used to represent the distances between cities that constitutes the traveling salesman problem. And while a particular algorithm or program implementing an algorithm may scale linearly, polynomially or exponentially in the size of the problem instances, complexity results are about problems, not particular algorithms.

Such results, called asymptotic worst-case complexity results, seek to characterize the best we can expect of any algorithm under the worst possible circumstances: that is, how the best algorithm scales as a function of the size of the hardest possible problem instances. If there were only a finite number of instances it would be possible to solve each of them in finite time, and hence the most efficient algorithm would solve them before being asked and then simply trot out the answer when asked for the solution to a particular instance.

We don't know for sure that NP-complete problems require exponential time for their solution, only that a fair number of well-respected computer scientists believe that NP-complete problems require exponential time. The problem is still open; the class NP could collapse into P, and therein lies the mystery and the challenge, a mystery whose resolution will probably have a much greater practical impact than the incompleteness results of Gödel or the undecidability results of Turing.

CHAPTER THIRTEEN

Forest for the Trees

Often when you're trying to solve a problem, you pull out a pen or pencil and grab a handy piece of paper to write down a column of numbers, draw a diagram, or make a list. In solving the problem, you might sum the numbers, trace lines in the diagram, or match items of the list with items of a second list. These auxiliary scribblings are used to organize information – as with the list or column of numbers – or represent objects so they can be easily manipulated – as with the diagram. Data structures are the algorithmic analog of these handy pieces of paper.

In Chapter 11 we saw that browsers and web servers in a computer network exchange information by bouncing small packages of data from one computer to another until they arrive at their final destination. How can we represent a computer network so that an algorithm can figure out what sequence of computers to use in transferring a data package? For that matter, how do we represent airline schedules, circuit diagrams, computer file systems, road maps and medical records so that they can be manipulated algorithmically?

Many algorithms use special data structures to represent their inputs and outputs or to perform intermediate calculations. In Chapter 7 we used lists and vectors to keep track of journal entries. In Chapter 10 we learned how to use a stack to keep track of the contents of registers in nested subroutine calls. We've also seen even more basic data structures: strings and integers are among the simplest of "primitive data types". Other primitive data types include characters, other varieties of numbers (single and double floating-point numbers, rationals, short integers and long integers), and pointers that let you directly address locations in memory.

But when computer people talk about data structures, they're usually referring to *composite* data types that let you organize multiple instances of the same data type or combine instances of several primitive (or composite) data types. All the obvious organizing strategies are generally available, including *bags* (which assume no particular order), *lists* (which assume a linear ordering and are often called *arrays*), and *tables* (in which items are arranged vertically and horizontally in a grid and which are often called *two-dimensional matrices*). There are also more specialized composites like *association lists* (which, like telephone books, store information, like telephone numbers, under various keys, like individuals' names) and the *records* and *relational tables* that we saw in Chapter 3.

But no discussion of data structures is complete without some mention of *graphs* and their various important subclasses, including *directed graphs, directed acyclic graphs* and, perhaps the most important and useful class of graphs of all, *trees*. Graphs are everywhere in computer science; indeed, while we didn't make a fuss over them, you've already seen several examples of graphs in earlier chapters.

13.1 GRAPH THEORY

Graph theory is a subarea of discrete mathematics (that's the part of mathematics that deals with discrete, separable and often countable objects rather than, say, the continuous variables of calculus and real analysis) that is particularly relevant to computer science. The mathematics can be pretty abstract but the applications are everywhere and very concrete. A computer network, a web site, the entire World Wide Web, and a hierarchical file system containing directories and files can all be thought of as graphs.

Mathematically, a graph is a set of *nodes* (also called *vertices*) and a set of *links* (also called *edges*). A link is specified by a pair of nodes and can be either one-way (unidirectional) or two-way (bidirectional). The distinction between one-way and two-way links can be used to model the difference between connections that allow information to flow in both directions or in only one direction. Graphs are usually drawn by depicting the nodes as circles and the links as lines (bidirectional) or arrows (unidirectional). Sometimes the nodes are labeled, as in these three examples:

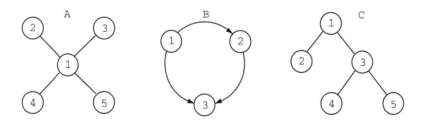

Graph theorists and computer scientists like to talk about the *topology* of a graph: A is a graph with a star topology, B (ignoring the arrows) has a ring topology and C has a tree topology.

Think about how we might represent a network of computers as a graph. Simplifying somewhat, computers are connected via cables to various pieces of equipment including other computers and specialized connection boxes variously called switches, hubs, routers and bridges (you'd need a short course in computer networks – or a browser, a search engine and patience – to understand the differences among these). Some of the "cables" can be a little complicated – for example, a serial cable from a computer to a modem that via a phone line communicates with a second modem connected by another serial cable to a second computer. But the basic idea is that there is some way of sending information back and forth along the cable between the devices attached to either end.

Computers in the same building are often connected via hubs and switches to form a local-area network (LAN). LANs are typically organized in graphs with star or ring topologies. Large computer networks are configured (hierarchically) at multiple levels so that whole chunks of the network at one level correspond to the simplest atomic components at the next higher level. Computers within a company can be arranged as a wide-area network (WAN) containing one or more LANs. In some cases, it makes sense to think of a WAN as a graph whose nodes consist of LANs. Then there are metropolitan-area networks (MANs) and global-area networks, some of whose connections might be via satellite or cables laid along ocean beds. The graphs corresponding to these larger, continent-spanning networks can be thought of as having WANs and MANs for nodes.

Generally, all the links in a particular graph are either one-way or two-way, and we refer to a graph with all one-way links as *directed* and a graph with all two-way links as *undirected*. It usually makes sense to represent computer networks as undirected graphs since communication is bidirectional. Assuming that only one link connects any two nodes, we can unambiguously specify any link as an ordered pair of nodes in which the "arrow" points from the first node in the pair to the second in the case of directed graphs or as an unordered (the order doesn't matter) pair in the case of undirected graphs. Example A is an undirected graph that we can represent as a set of five nodes {1,2,3,4,5} and a set of four links {{1,2},{1,3},{1,4},{1,5}}. Similarly, we can represent the directed graph B as a set of three nodes {1,2,3} and a set of three (directed) links {{1,2},{2,3},{1,3}}.

Graph theory is full of terms and definitions that turn out to be useful in describing physical systems; I'll give you a little taste. A *path* from one node to a second node in a graph is a sequence of nodes and links of the form $node_1$ (read "node sub one"), $link_1$, $node_2$, $link_2$, ..., $link_{n-1}$, $node_n$, where $node_1$ is the beginning of the path and $node_n$ is the end of the path. In graph A, there is an undirected path from the node labeled 2 to the node labeled 4 defined by {2,{1,2},1,{1,4},4}. In graph B, there is a directed path from the node labeled 1 to the node labeled 3 defined by {1,{1,2},2,{2,3},3}. There is also an undirected path from 4 to 2 in A defined by {4,{1,4},1,{1,2},2}, but there is not a directed path from 3 to 1 in graph B. We might imagine an undirected version of B, call it B', in which all the one-way links are replaced by two-way links, so that there is an undirected path in B' from 3 to 1.

A graph is said to be *connected* if there is a path between all pairs of nodes in the undirected version of the graph. A *circuit* is an undirected path that begins and ends at the same node and has at least one link.[1] A `tree` is an undirected graph that is both connected and circuit free. A and C are trees but B' is not because it contains a circuit {1,{1,2},2,{2,3},3 {1,3},1}.

A *cycle* in a directed graph is a directed path that begins and ends at the same node and has at least one link. A directed graph that doesn't contain any cycles is called a directed acyclic graph or DAG; B is a DAG.

There's also a directed version of trees. A directed graph is said to have a *root* node r if there is directed path from r to every other node in the graph. The node labeled 1 is a root of B. A directed graph is called a directed tree if it has at least one root and its underlying undirected graph is a tree. B is not a directed tree, but imagine a directed version of C, call it C', with all its links pointing down (toward the bottom of the page). C' is a directed tree and the node labeled 1 is its only root.

In a directed graph, the *parents* of a node are all those nodes that have links pointing to the node, and the *children* of a node are all those nodes that have links pointed to starting from that node. A node can have 0, 1, 2 or more parents and any number of children, including none at all. In C', node 1 has no parents and two children, 2 and 3, while node 5 has one parent, 3, and no children.

A *subgraph* is part of a graph. The graph consisting of nodes {3,4,5} and links {{3,4},{3,5}} is a subgraph of C; indeed, it's a *subtree* of C.

Mathematicians like graph theory because both the mathematics and the graphs themselves are beautiful. Computer scientists like graph theory for the same reasons and also because they can use it to analyze algorithms that operate on graphs, or things like computer networks that can be represented as graphs. For example, there's an algorithm due to Edsger Dijkstra that finds the shortest path between any two nodes in a graph using a number of primitive operations that scales polynomially in the number of nodes and links in the graph. This result is important because it tells us that packages of data in computer networks can be routed relatively efficiently.

So how would you actually go about representing a graph in a form (data structure) that a computer could use? We can use the mathematical notation introduced

---

[1] For simplicity, we'll assume there are no self-loops, links connecting a node to itself.

earlier almost directly. Indeed, Mathematica would be quite happy representing graph B as a pair

```
{{1,2,3},{{1,2},{1,3},{2,3}}},
```

in which the first element of the pair is the list of nodes and the second element is the list of links. And Lisp (or Scheme) would have no trouble using its list notation to represent graph B, with the curly brackets replaced by parentheses (what else!) and commas replaced by spaces:

```
((1 2 3) ((1 2) (1 3) (2 3)))
```

Another convenient representation is as a list of pairs, one for each node, in which the first element of each pair is the node (or the label for the node) and the second element is a list of nodes (possibly empty) the node is linked to. This is called the *adjacency-list* representation since it includes a list of the nodes that are adjacent to each node in the graph. Here is graph B in Mathematica using this representation:

```
{{{1,{2,3}},{2,{3}},{3,{}}}}
```

or in Lisp:

```
((1 (2 3)) (2 (3)) (3 ()))
```

In an adjacency list, we no longer need keep around a separate list of all the nodes, since each node is represented as a pair consisting of the label of the node along with a list of the labels of all of its adjacent nodes.

13.2 GRAPH ALGORITHMS

Now that we can encode graphs in a programming language, let's see what we can do with them. Graph algorithms, that is, algorithms that operate on graphs, are a particularly important subarea of algorithms. Their applications include routing delivery vehicles, designing cellular networks and laying out digital circuits, as well as a host of problems involving computer and communication networks.

It's often useful to determine whether or not there is a path from one node in a graph to another, and algorithms that find such paths are called graph-searching algorithms. Let's take a look at a Scheme version of one the most basic (and important) such algorithms; it's called `dfs_path?` because it tells you whether or not a path exists using *depth-first search* (DFS), a strategy for searching graphs that we'll explain shortly.

```
(define (dfs_path? graph queue goal max_steps)
  (if (or (empty_queue? queue)
          (= max_steps 0))
      "no"
      (if (= (first_node queue) goal)
          "yes"
          (dfs_path? graph
                     (append (get_links (first_node queue)
                                        graph)
                             (remaining_nodes queue))
                     goal
                     (- max_steps 1)))))
```

We'll also need some auxiliary functions whose definitions (with one exception) I hope you won't worry about too much, since they're not critical for understanding how depth-first search works. Just interpret the function names as you would English; for example, (`first_node` *queue*) means return the first (`car`) node off the *queue*, (`remaining_nodes` *queue*) means return the rest (`cdr`) of the nodes on the *queue* (minus the first), (`empty_queue?` *queue*) returns the Scheme equivalent of true if the *queue* is empty and false otherwise, and (`initialize_queue` *node*) returns a list consisting of a single item, *node*.

```
(define (first_node queue) (car queue))
(define (remaining_nodes queue) (cdr queue))
(define (empty_queue? queue) (null? queue))
(define (initialize_queue node) (list node))
```

The function `get_links` is a little more complicated:

```
(define (get_links node graph) (cadr (assoc node graph)))
```

The `get_links` function uses the *association-list* data structure, which is often useful in designing algorithms.[2] Here's how `assoc`, a Scheme function for extracting information from association lists, is used to extract the list of links associated with a node in a graph represented in adjacency-list format:

```
> (define G '((1 (2 3)) (2 (3 4)) (3 ()) (4 ())))
> (assoc 2 G)
(2 (3 4))
```

---

[2] Association lists are called *hashes* in Perl for the way in which they are implemented in Perl, namely, with yet another very useful data structure called a *hash table*. It's common to use one data structure, say, a list, to build another data structure, a tree for example.

The single quote "'" in the define statement tells Scheme to treat as literal the expression immediately following (delimited by the opposite balancing parenthesis), and, in particular, not to treat it as an attempt to call a function. The function `cadr` returns the second element in a list ((`cadr` '(1 2 3)) returns 2), and so (`get_links` 2 G) returns the list (3 4).

Back to depth-first search. Here's a paraphrase of what the function `dfs_path?` does. The function is called with four arguments: a graph in adjacency-list format, a queue of nodes to explore next (which initially contains only the starting node), a destination (or goal) node, and an integer indicating the maximum number of steps to take before calling it quits; `dfs_path?` returns "yes" if it finds a path from the starting node to the goal and "no" if it doesn't.

If the queue is empty or you've used up your allowance of steps, then you're done and `dfs_path?` returns "no". Otherwise, if the first node on the queue is the goal node, then you're also done and it returns "yes". If neither of these conditions holds, then `max_steps` must be greater than zero and there's at least one more item on the queue. So in this case call `dfs_path?` recursively with the same graph, a new queue that we'll describe presently, the same goal, and `max_steps` less one. The new queue contains all the nodes reachable by following a link starting at the first node on the queue appended[3] to the list of all nodes remaining on the queue minus the first (since we've now determined it isn't the goal).

Now let's see if it works. First, we use the single-quote mechanism to load the adjacency-list representations for the example graphs A, B and C:

```
(define A '((1 (2 3 4 5)) (2 (1)) (3 (1)) (4 (1)) (5 (1))))
(define B '((1 (2 3)) (2 (3)) (3 ())))
(define C '((1 (2 3)) (2 (1)) (3 (1 4 5)) (4 (3)) (5 (3))))
```

Is there a path from 1 to 3 in graph B? Let's give `dfs_path?` a maximum of 10 steps to find an answer, where each step corresponds to traversing a link in the graph:

```
> (dfs_path? B (initialize_queue 1) 3 10)
"yes"
```

Sure enough. What about from 3 to 1?

```
> (dfs_path? B (initialize_queue 3) 1 10)
"no"
```

---

[3] The append function takes two lists and returns a new list consisting of all the items on the first list followed by all the items on the second list; so, for example, (`append` '(1 2 3) '(4 5 6)) returns the list (1 2 3 4 5 6).

Right again. What about from 1 to 5 in graph C?

```
> (dfs_path? C (initialize_queue 5) 1 10)
"yes"
```

We're on a roll. DFS is mighty useful and you'll find it cropping up as a subroutine in all sorts of algorithms. But DFS has some drawbacks and it isn't the method of choice for searching all graphs. Time to draw another bunch of graphs:

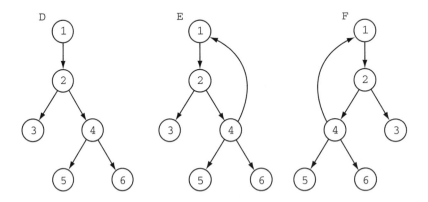

Graph D is a tree and would be described as a list of nodes and links as

```
{{1,2,3,4,5,6},{{1,2},{2,3},{2,4},{4,5},{4,6}}}
```

and in adjacency-list format as

```
{{1,{2}},{2,{3,4}},{3,{}},{4,{5,6},{5,{}},{6,{}}}} .
```

E is just like D except that a cycle was introduced by adding a link from 4 to 1:

```
{{1,2,3,4,5,6},{{1,2},{2,3},{2,4},{4,1},{4,5},{4,6}}}
```

It's a pretty common sort of graph, though not a tree nor a DAG (directed acyclic graph). In adjacency-list format, it looks like

```
{{1,{2}},{2,{3,4}},{3,{}},{4,{1,5,6}},{5,{}},{6,{}}}}
```

Finally, F is really the same as E: it's the mirror image of E. Here's the adjacency-list format:

```
{{1,{2}},{2,{4,3}},{3,{}},{4,{1,5,6}},{5,{}},{6,{}}}}
```

I've thus reversed the order in which 3 and 4 appear in the lists of nodes adjacent to 2; as we'll see, this turns out to make a crucial difference to DFS. We define these graphs in Scheme as:

```
(define D '((1 (2)) (2 (3 4)) (3 ()) (4 (5 6)) (5 ()) (6 ())))
(define E '((1 (2)) (2 (3 4)) (3 ()) (4 (1 5 6)) (5 ()) (6 ())))
(define F '((1 (2)) (2 (4 3)) (3 ()) (4 (1 5 6)) (5 ()) (6 ())))
```

Let's see if there is a path from 1 to 4 in D:

```
> (dfs_path? D (initialize_queue 1) 4 10)
"yes"
```

Yep. How about in E?

```
> (dfs_path? E (initialize_queue 1) 5 10)
"no"
```

That can't be right! E has all of D's links plus one. If there's a path from 1 to 5 in D there has to be a path in E.

We can modify `dfs_path?` just slightly so that it detects the path in E. The following function, called `bfs_path?` for *breadth-first search* (BFS), is defined just as `dfs_path?` with the exception of the order of the arguments in the call to append. This small change makes BFS explore the graph by traversing links in the order in which they are loaded onto the front of the queue. BFS looks at all nodes reached by paths of length n before it looks at any of the nodes that can be reached only by a path of length greater than n. DFS searches by plunging deeper and deeper into the graph – hence the name depth-first search.

```
(define (bfs_path? graph queue goal max_steps)
  (if (or (empty_queue? queue)
          (= max_steps 0))
      "no"
      (if (= (first_node queue) goal)
          "yes"
          (bfs_path? graph
                     (append (remaining_nodes queue)
                             (get_links (first_node queue)
                                        graph))
                     goal
                     (- max_steps 1)))))
```

With `bfs_path?` we get the answer we expected earlier:

```
> (bfs_path? E (initialize_queue 1) 5 10)
"yes"
```

Neither `dfs_path?` nor `bfs_path?` can tell when they've previously visited a node in the graph, and so, starting from node 1, both algorithms may return to 1, having followed the path {1,{1,2},2,{2,4},{4,1},1} and then again having followed {1,{1,2},2,{2,4},{4,1},1,{1,2},2,{2,4},{4,1},1}, and so ad nauseam. We could fix this by having both algorithms remember where they've been.

If we were to remove the link from 4 to 1 in F and ask to check for a path from 1 to 6, DFS would traverse the graph in depth-first order, 1, 2, 4, 5, 6, 3, and BFS would traverse the graph in breadth-first order, 1, 2, 4, 3, 5, 6. Try to think of cases in which DFS is the better choice (hint: consider graphs without cycles in which the goal is some considerable distance from the starting node) and cases in which BFS is the better choice (hint: consider very large graphs in which the goal is not far from the starting node and each node has few children). Graphs are easy to sketch on paper and such sketches help a lot in testing your intuitions.

Often, in addition to knowing whether or not a path exists, you'd like to see the path, perhaps multiple paths if there are several. We could modify `dfs_path?` and `bfs_path?` to return paths, but instead I'm going to show you an alternative way to write a search algorithm that illustrates another model of computation touched on in Chapter 1.

In `dfs_path?` and `bfs_path?`, the recursive call picks out one node to follow from the queue, and passes on the rest of the nodes as an argument to the recursive call. Suppose we could generate a separate recursive call for each possible new link to follow; then we could generate a recursive call with a new starting node and include the path information as an additional argument. We wouldn't even need to keep a queue around, since we'd immediately spin off a recursive call for each possible link out of the current node.

Scheme provides a nice way of spinning off such recursive calls or, more generally, applying a procedure multiple times to different sets of arguments. It involves what are called *mapping* operators and is part of a more general approach to programming called *functional programming*. Mapping operators have appeared in many different programming languages over the years and once you start using them it's hard to stop.

The special operator `map` takes a procedure that has some number of formal parameters n and a set of n lists each of length m for some arbitrary m. You can think of map as applying the procedure not to each list of arguments but to what's called a *cross section* of all the lists. The first cross section consists of the first item in the first list, the first item of the second list, and so on. The procedure is applied to this first cross section and then to the second cross section consisting of the second item in the first list, the second item in the second list, ..., and so on until the procedure has been applied to all *m* cross sections. In the expression (map + '(1 2 3) '(1 2 3)), the procedure + is applied to (+ 1 1), (+ 2 2), and (+ 3 3), and the results are returned as a list:

```
> (map + '(1 2 3) '(1 2 3))
(2 4 6)
```

The map operator accepts any procedure including the kind with no name that we can specify using lambda, as we saw in Chapter 6:

```
> (map (lambda (x y z) (- (* x y) z))
       '(2 3)
       '(3 4)
       '(1 2))
(5 10)
```

Here's the definition of our procedure to search for and report as many paths as possible. We can no longer count all the steps taken in all the recursive calls, but we can do something that in many cases is even better: we can put a limit on how deep (the number of links traversed) we want any recursive call to search. This procedure explores the graph in breadth-first search and so inherits both the advantages and disadvantages of that method.

```
(define (find_all_paths graph begin end path max_depth)
  (if (= begin end)
      (display_path (extend_path end path))
      (if (> max_depth 0)
          (map (lambda (new_begin)
                 (find_all_paths graph
                                 new_begin
                                 end
                                 (extend_path begin path)
                                 (- max_depth 1)))
               (get_links begin graph))))
  "done")
```

In order to understand how `find_all_paths` works, we also need some auxiliary functions that hide details you don't need to know:

```
(define (display_path path) (printf "Path: ~A~N" (reverse path)))
(define (initialize_path) (list))
(define (extend_path node path) (cons node path))
```

Let's give it a whirl on graph B:

```
> (find_all_paths B 1 3 (initialize_path) 10)
Path: (1 2 3)
Path: (1 3)
"done"
```

It doesn't do any better than `dfs_path?` or `bfs_path?` on graphs with cycles; in fact, it can be downright distracting:

```
> (find_all_paths E 1 3 (initialize_path) 24)
Path: (1 2 3)
Path: (1 2 4 1 2 3)
Path: (1 2 4 1 2 4 1 2 3)
Path: (1 2 4 1 2 4 1 2 4 1 2 3)
Path: (1 2 4 1 2 4 1 2 4 1 2 4 1 2 3)
Path: (1 2 4 1 2 4 1 2 4 1 2 4 1 2 4 1 2 3)
Path: (1 2 4 1 2 4 1 2 4 1 2 4 1 2 4 1 2 4 1 2 3)
Path: (1 2 4 1 2 4 1 2 4 1 2 4 1 2 4 1 2 4 1 2 4 1 2 3)
"done"
```

But again we could fix this by keeping an extra argument to remember all the places we've visited before.

When I started writing about the adjacency-list format, I resolved to say something about another handy representation for graphs called *adjacency matrices*. But before we can represent an adjacency matrix, it might be a good idea to learn how to represent a regular old matrix. An n by m matrix[4] is a table consisting of $(n * m)$ numbers arranged in n rows and m columns; typically we represent such a matrix as n lists each of length m, so that a 2 by 3 matrix all of whose entries are 1 would look like $\{\{1,1,1\},\{1,1,1\}\}$.

To represent a graph with n nodes as an adjacency matrix, you associate the nodes in the graph with the integers 1 through n and construct an n by n matrix such that the entry in the jth column of the ith row is 1 if there is a directed link in

---

[4] We'll confine our attention to two-dimensional matrices, even though matrices can be of any dimension.

the graph from the ith node to the jth node and is 0 otherwise. Using the labels of the nodes of graph B {{1,2,3},{{1,2},{1,3},{2,3}}} as the associated integers, the adjacency matrix for B would be

```
{{0,1,1},
 {0,0,1},
 {0,0,0}}
```

Adjacency matrices are useful for representing small graphs and larger graphs that have lots of links. A graph with n nodes can have as many as n^2 links (since any pair of nodes could have two directional links linking them together), and an adjacency matrix for a graph with n nodes has exactly n^2 entries.

Mathematica likes graphs represented as adjacency matrices, just the way I entered the matrix for B. Mathematica even has nifty functions for displaying matrices so they are easy to decipher:

```
In[1]:= TableForm[ {{0,1,1},{0,0,1},{0,0,0}} ]

Out[1]= TableForm= 0   1   1

                   0   0   1

                   0   0   0
```

Mathematica also has very convenient operators for combining matrices and vectors (one-dimensional matrices) that are very useful in *linear algebra*, another branch of mathematics important in computer science, especially in graphics and robotics. I can use Mathematica's facility with symbolic operations to show you what it means to add two 2 by 2 matrices together:

```
In[2]:= TableForm[ {{a,b},{c,d}} + {{e,f},{g,h}} ]

Out[2]= TableForm= a + e   b + f

                   c + g   d + h
```

and to take their *inner product* (also called the *dot* product):

```
In[3]:= TableForm[ {{a,b},{c,d}} . {{e,f},{g,h}} ]

Out[3]= TableForm= a e + b g   a f + b h

                   c e + d g   c f + d h
```

You'll need a larger example to generalize, so I'll throw in the dot product of two 3 by 3 matrices:

```
In[4]:= TableForm[ {{a,b,c},{d,e,f},{g,h,i}} .
                   {{j,k,l},{m,n,o},{p,q,r}} ]

Out[4]= TableForm=
          a j + b m + c p    a k + b n + c q    a l + b o + c r

          d j + e m + f p    d k + e n + f q    d l + e o + f r

          g j + h m + i p    g k + h n + i q    g l + h o + i r
```

If we take the dot product of an adjacency matrix with itself,

```
In[5]:= TableForm[ {{a,b},{c,d}} . {{a,b},{c,d}} ]

Out[5]= TableForm=  a a + b c    a b + b d

                    a c + c d    b c + d d
```

the entry in the jth column and ith row of the resulting matrix tells us if it's possible to get from i to j by traversing a path consisting of exactly one link. In general, if M^n is the matrix we obtain by taking the dot product of an adjacency matrix with itself n times (for example, $M^3 = M.M.M$), then the entry in its jth column and ith row tells us if it's possible to get from node i to node j by traversing a path consisting of exactly n links. If you add together all of the matrices M^1, M^2, ..., M^n you get a matrix in which the entry in the jth column and ith row tells us how many different paths connect node i to node j by traversing n or fewer links.

Here's the adjacency matrix for graph F:

```
In[6]:= F = {{0,1,0,0,0,0},
             {0,0,1,1,0,0},
             {0,0,0,0,0,0},
             {1,0,0,0,1,1},
             {0,0,0,0,0,0},
             {0,0,0,0,0,0}}
```

Here's the same matrix displayed in a somewhat easier-to-read format:

```
In[7]:= TableForm[ F ]
```

```
Out[7]= TableForm= 0   1   0   0   0   0

                    0   0   1   1   0   0

                    0   0   0   0   0   0

                    1   0   0   0   1   1

                    0   0   0   0   0   0

                    0   0   0   0   0   0
```

And now we compute a new matrix in which the entry in the jth column and ith row indicates how many different paths of length four or less connect node i to node j:

```
In[8]:= TableForm[ F . F +
                   F . F . F +
                   F . F . F . F +
                   F . F . F . F . F ]
```

```
Out[8]= TableForm= 1   1   2   2   1   1

                    2   1   1   1   2   2

                    0   0   0   0   0   0

                    1   2   1   1   1   1

                    0   0   0   0   0   0

                    0   0   0   0   0   0
```

We're actually searching this graph by performing matrix operations; the resulting matrix tells us whether there is a path connecting any pair of nodes and if so how many. This isn't the method of choice for most graph-searching problems, but a variant of it will turn out to be useful when we consider searching the World Wide Web in Chapter 14. First, let's consider some other applications that involve graphs.

13.3 FILE SYSTEMS AS GRAPHS

The directories in most file systems in most operating systems are arranged as trees. Using a command-line-oriented interface such as a shell or, more typically nowadays, some sort of a graphical interface, you can create (make) new directories using `mkdir`, remove an existing directory with `rmdir`, change your current working directory using `chdir` or list the contents of a directory using `ls`.

I have an alias (think of it as a little program) called `cd`[5] that I use instead of `chdir` and that, in addition to allowing me to change my current working directory, changes my prompt to help me keep track of where I am in the file system (it's really easy to get lost). This program first initializes the `prompt` shell variable, which determines what the shell prints at the beginning of a line. It then defines (`alias` is a little like `define` in Scheme) `cd` as a program that first calls `chdir` and then resets the prompt by referring to the `cwd` shell variable that the system uses to keep track of my current working directory:

```
set prompt = "$cwd % "
alias cd 'chdir \!* ; set prompt = "$cwd % "'
```

The expression `\!*` appearing in an `alias` refers to the arguments of the command being defined, `cd` in this case, when the command is read by the shell; thus, for example, my typing `cd /u/tld/` is transformed into `chdir /u/tld/ ; set prompt = "$cwd % "`. This little program resides in a file (named `.cshrc` in my top-level directory) with a lot of other useful little programs that are evaluated every time I start up a shell. I use it many times a day and hardly ever thought about it until in working on this chapter I wondered how it would handle graphs with cycles – yes, you can create cycles in file systems.

---

[5] The change directory command is built into most shells. On some systems, both `cd` and `chdir` refer to this command, with `cd` being the name used by most Unix aficionados. I also prefer the shorter `cd` but I'm not satisfied with its default behavior, and so I've used `alias` to redefine `cd` to suit my preferences. I didn't need to define `cd` in terms of `chdir`; the invocation `alias cd 'cd \!* ; set prompt = "$cwd % "'` works just fine, and you may want to check your online documentation to learn why.

I'm going to invoke `mkdir` and create a tree just like graph D in the previous section:

```
/u/tld % mkdir one
/u/tld % cd one
/u/tld/one % mkdir two
/u/tld/one % cd two
/u/tld/one/two % mkdir three four
/u/tld/one/two % cd four
/u/tld/one/two/four % mkdir five six
/u/tld/one/two/four % ls
five   six
/u/tld/one/two/four % cd ..
/u/tld/one/two/ % ls
four three
/u/tld/one/two/ % cd four
/u/tld/one/two/four % ls
five   six
```

In the shell "`. .`" always means the parent directory of the directory you're currently in. With the exception of symbolic links (which we'll get to in a moment), each directory has a unique parent directory.

Each time I invoked `cd` it correctly redisplayed the prompt showing my location in the directory structure. Now I'm going to create a *symbolic link* using the link command `ln` with the symbolic (`-s`) option.[6] The link command takes as arguments the path to the destination directory (the destination of the link) and a name for the link (considered to symbolically represent the destination). We'll set the name to be the same as the name of the destination directory:

```
/u/tld/one/two/four % ln -s /u/tld/one one
/u/tld/one/two/four % ls
five   one   six
```

Now we have a graph with a cycle in it that is exactly the same as graph E above (and graph F, since E and F are really just different drawings of the same

---

[6] A symbolic link is how you link one directory to another. When linking a directory to a file in another directory, you can also create a "hard" link so that the file is indistinguishable when accessed from either directory. Symbolic links have the advantage that they can span file systems on different computers.

graph). But now watch what happens as we walk around on the graph traversing links:

```
/u/tld/one/two/four % cd one
/u/tld/one/two/four/one % cd two
/u/tld/one/two/four/one/two % cd four
/u/tld/one/two/four/one/two/four % cd one
/u/tld/one/two/four/one/two/four/one % cd two
/u/tld/one/two/four/one/two/four/one/two % cd four
/u/tld/one/two/four/one/two/four/one/two/four/ %
```

Just as `find_all_paths` was fooled by cycles in graph E, so my little `cd` program has become confused, thereby confusing me as well with its prompt that encodes my entire cyclic traversal. Luckily, another program called `pwd` provides a more reasonable and cycle-free report of my working directory as the shortest path from the root, "/", to my working directory. It turns out that "u" was another symbolic link that I'd completely forgotten about.

```
/u/tld/one/two/four/one/two/four/one/two/four/ % pwd
/home/tld/one/two/four
```

The fact that you can create trees and graphs using directories means that you can create data structures for storing your stuff right on top of your computer's file system. For example, in Chapter 1 I described a tree-like structure of files and directories that I used to organize my journal entries. I expect you can think of similar ways to keep track of old email messages, digital photos or music files.

13.4 THE WEB GRAPH

This notion of file systems (and hence graphs) as efficient ways of organizing information is pretty useful, and before we leave the subject, I'd like to say a few words about the mother of all file systems, the World Wide Web. The World Wide Web, perhaps the largest artifact ever, can be modeled quite naturally as a graph with the web pages as nodes and the hyperlinks as links. We talked at length in Chapter 11 about the technology that makes the World Wide Web possible and we'll visit the web again in Chapter 14, but for now I just want you to think about it as a graph.

The *web graph*, as it is now called, has billions of nodes. That's such a big graph that in searching for information in it, you might as well think of it as infinitely large.[7] Assessing the size of the web is complicated by the fact that lots of it is virtual – many of its pages, such as those showing merchandise at online stores, don't exist until someone wants to see them; they're created on the fly and often personalized in content and format for a particular customer.

Strictly speaking, the web graph is a directed graph with cycles; hyperlinks tell you how to go from the page you're on to the page they point to, but you have to do more work – search the graph exhaustively or nearly so – in order to find out what other pages point to a given page. However, we can uncover interesting structure in the web graph just by looking at how web pages are connected to one another, without even looking at their contents. We'll need a couple of technical terms and definitions to talk about this structure more precisely.

A *strongly connected graph* is a directed graph that has a directed path from each node to every other node. A *strongly connected component*, C, is a strongly connected subgraph of a directed graph, G, such that no node in G can be added to C and it still be strongly connected. A *sink* in a graph is a set of nodes that have no links to nodes outside the set. The web graph has sinks corresponding to connected components that have incoming hyperlinks but no outgoing links: once you enter a sink, you can't exit simply by following hyperlinks. It also has large connected components without incoming links, so once you leave you can't get back in by traversing hyperlinks (of course, you can always just connect to a URL if you remember it). Here are the big connected components of the web graph as depicted in Broder et al. (1999):

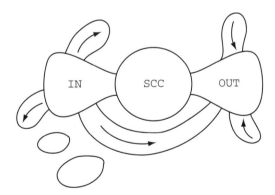

This so-called *bow-tie* diagram is based on a *snapshot* of the web taken in May, 1999. The circle in the middle (the knot of the bow tie) is labeled SCC because it's

---

[7] Of course, search-engine companies like AltaVista, Google and Lycos have ample computational resources to search the entire web.

the largest strongly connected component of the web graph, consisting of some 56 million nodes. The left side of the bow, labeled IN, is the set of nodes not in the SCC but connected to a page in the SCC by some path; it contains about 44 million pages. The right side of the bow, OUT, is a set of pages with the following property: any node in OUT can be reached by following hyperlinks starting from any page in SCC, but no page in the SCC can be reached by following hyperlinks starting from a page in OUT.

Other interesting pieces of the web graph appear in the bow-tie diagram: tendrils that lead out to "nowhere" starting from IN or start at "nowhere" and lead into OUT, or that tunnel from IN to OUT without hitting SCC. There are also completely disconnected pieces (the separate blobs). Since someone adding a hyperlink to a page expresses interest in that page, one can infer that pages that aren't pointed to either don't interest anyone or haven't yet been discovered. Pages in SCC exist in a complex tangled web of references. The IN pages are interested in the SCC but no one in the SCC is interested in them; just the opposite for OUT pages.

And, of course, the bow-tie diagram is based on a snapshot at a particular moment in time; the web is evolving quickly to reflect the changing interests of people all over the world. It used to be that people created most of the pages on the web by writing HTML. Today more pages on the web are created by programs than are written by humans, but even so many of the most interesting and most visited web pages have human authors. More than ever the web is a human creation reflecting human wants, needs, hopes and dreams; it's as hard to predict what it will become as to predict what we will become.

13.5 PIANOS AND ROBOTS

But we've strayed beyond graphs and graphs algorithms and, as I mentioned, we'll return in Chapter 14 to investigate the technology (and, to some extent, the psychology) that makes the World Wide Web possible. Before we leave the subject, I want to look at one more application involving graphs.

One summer day while I working on this chapter and looking for some interesting examples of applications involving graphs and graph algorithms, I had to interrupt my work to meet someone from the Neuroscience Department and go pick up a robot arm they were letting us use. I had asked a student by the name of Albert, an undergraduate working at Brown for the summer, to help me move the arm from Neuroscience to the Computer Science Department. The arm was a very nice multi-jointed arm with an industrial-quality controller and a force-torque sensor for the wrist joint that had never been installed (the force-torque sensor lets the arm detect when it hits something or sense the weight of an object held by its gripper). This arm was described as having *six degrees of freedom*, meaning that it had six different joints, each capable of turning independently of all the others.

The arm weighed around 40 kilograms (that's around 88 pounds for the metrically challenged) and the controller about half that. In addition, we had to move the heavy table that the robot was mounted on and a bunch of crates and miscellaneous boxes. It was a good hour's sweaty work but made interesting by having to figure out how to use the ancient (and woefully undersized by modern standards) freight elevator in the Neuroscience building and maneuver heavy and ungainly objects through doors and corridors.

I explained to Albert that our task was an instance of the general *piano-movers problem*, a problem in computational geometry that involves moving an object, represented in terms of a set of coordinates and surfaces in three-dimensional space, from an initial location to a final destination in an environment containing other objects also represented in terms of points and surfaces. The objective is to find a path from the initial to the final location such that the object to be moved doesn't intersect (collide) with the objects in the environment. Some human beings (piano movers in particular) are pretty good at this. This sort of thing is also important in robotics; think of planning a path for a mobile robot through a crowded room or for an assembly-line robot reaching into a partially assembled automobile to drill a hole or attach a part.

One elegant method of solving such problems involves reformulating them in a higher-dimensional space with one dimension for each degree of freedom. In general, a degree of freedom corresponds to the ability to move in a particular direction, for example, back and forth along some axis (also called a translational degree of freedom) or circularly around some axis (a rotational degree of freedom). Using an idea generally attributed to Tomás Lozano-Pérez, you can "shrink" the object to be moved and "grow" the objects to be avoided to obtain an equivalent problem in which the object to be moved is a point. The resulting formulation, called a *configuration space*, can then be "discretized" by carving up the space into a bunch of smaller regions.

A simple example will help visualize this. Suppose you have a mobile robot that looks like a trash can (remember R2D2 in "Star Wars"?). This shape is convenient, since we'll assume that the robot can move in any direction in the horizontal plan and looks the same (a circle) from any angle when viewed from above. Let's say this robot is supposed to go into your room, find your trash can and empty it. The first thing it has to do is plan a path from the door of your room to the trash can. To simplify things, we won't worry about the z-axis (the height of the robot) but only the x- and y-axes (the floor of your room). The robot has two degrees of freedom, translation in the x and y directions. Suppose that you have a drawing of your bedroom showing your bed, desk, chairs, etc. – everything that might be an obstacle to a robot trying to maneuver there. Here's a picture of the room with our robot standing just outside the door.

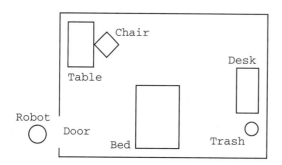

Now we grow the all of the obstacles, including the walls, by the radius of the trash-can-shaped robot, so that we can shrink the robot to a point. The next picture shows the result. The area enclosed by the curved line is called "free space" and indicates that portion of the room in which the robot can move without bumping into things.

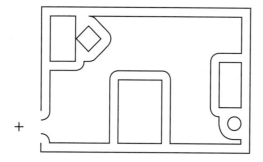

In the next drawing I've penciled in a grid over the room sketch. This is the first step in discretizing the problem. Next, I filled in the little square cells of the grid with gray if the area covered by a grid cell is more than 90% free space, and otherwise left it white. I've also marked the starting and target locations for the robot by coloring the corresponding cells black.

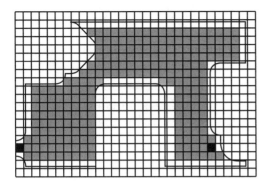

By laying down the grid over the continuous lines of the original drawing, I transformed a geometric problem to a problem involving graphs that I can solve with a path-finding algorithm. Where's the graph? Nodes correspond to the cells designated as free space in the drawing above and links are defined as adjacency in the grid: there's a link from one cell to another if the two cells are adjacent in the grid in any of the four compass directions or in any of the four diagonal directions. This last drawing, showing only the cells in free space, depicts a path (in gray) from the starting location to the target location that can easily be found using breadth-first search.

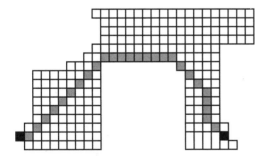

This same idea works for all kinds of robot shapes (not just trash-can shapes), in three dimensions of physical space as well as two, and with robots having many degrees of freedom, though the problems are harder computationally with many degrees of freedom. The computational effort also depends on how finely your grid divides up the space. The graph produced using this method is said to be of size exponential in the number of degrees of freedom. If you slice up the space using, say, 1000 lines along each dimensional axis, which is not uncommon, and you want to plan paths for a robot like the one Albert and I moved, then you'll have a graph with $(10^3)^6$ or 10^{18} (1,000,000,000,000,000,000) nodes. Solving problems of this size requires more sophisticated algorithms and data structures than we've considered so far, but you can bet that trees and graphs play an important role.

You'll encounter graph algorithms in every branch of computer science and the basic algorithms should be in the repertoire of every programmer. For a nice balance of theoretical analysis and practical algorithms I recommend Shimon Even's *Graph Algorithms*. Most general algorithms textbooks, for example Cormen, Leiserson, Rivest and Stein's *Introduction to Algorithms*, include substantial sections devoted to graph algorithms.

CHAPTER FOURTEEN

Searching the Wild Web

The technology supporting the World Wide Web enables computations and data to be distributed over networks of computers, and this lets you use programs that you don't have to install or maintain and gain access to information that you don't have store or worry about backing up. The World Wide Web is essentially a global computer with a world-wide file system.

Many of the documents in this huge file system are accessible to anyone with a browser and a network connection. Indeed, their authors really want you to take a look at what they have to offer in the terms of advice, information, merchandise and services. Some of these documents, we tell ourselves, contain exactly what we're looking for, but it isn't always easy to find them.

It's difficult enough to search through files full of your own personal stuff – now there are billions of files generated by millions of authors. Some of those authors are likely to be somewhat misleading in promoting whatever they're offering, others may be downright devious, and some will just be clueless, ignorant about whatever they're talking about. How can we sift through this morass of data and find what we're looking for?

14.1   SPIDERS IN THE WEB

Billions of files are stored on web servers all over the world and you don't need a browser to access them. Programmers typically use libraries implementing the HTTP and FTP protocols to grab files off the web. We'll continue to use a shell for our investigations and, not surprisingly, there are all sorts of programs for exploring the web that can be easily invoked from a shell. `curl` is a popular utility program supporting several protocols to transfer files specified as URLs. Here I use `curl` to grab an HTML file sitting in the directory on the Brown web server that stores my web pages:

```
% curl www.cs.brown.edu/people/tld/file.html
<HTML>
<HEAD>
<TITLE>Simple HTML File</TITLE>
</HEAD>
<BODY>
<H1>Section Heading</H1>
<P>
Here is a file containing HTML formatting
commands that has a body consisting of
one section heading and a single paragraph.
</P>
</BODY>
</HTML>
```

Perhaps you've seen files containing HTML commands before. This file is very simple HTML code and I expect you can figure out the basic idea. Sometimes the HTML formatting can be useful in searching files on the web, but for our purposes it'll just get in the way. I could pipe the output of curl into an HTML-to-text converter, but I can't find a converter on this machine and I'm lazy so I'm going to take a shortcut. Your web browser interprets (or *parses*) HTML formatting commands and then displays the results in a graphics window using all sorts of pretty fonts and images. I'm going to use a text-based (no graphics, no fancy on-screen formatting) browser called lynx to parse HTML files and strip away all the formatting commands so I can manipulate the raw text. lynx is a very useful tool to add to your bag of tricks: you can use it to surf the web, but I use it here just to dump the text – minus the HTML formatting – to a shell or to a file with the -dump option and the -nolist option, which suppresses any information about hyperlinks found in the HTML file:

```
% lynx -dump -nolist www.cs.brown.edu/people/tld/file.html

   Section Heading

   Here is a file containing HTML formatting
   commands that has a body consisting of
   one section heading and a single paragraph.
```

There is still a bit of formatting (spaces and line breaks) in the text-based output, but I can filter that out by removing the extraneous white space. The important point is that I can now treat the web as a huge repository of text files. These files aren't stored in a single hierarchical directory like my personal files; they are located on machines all over the world. But even if I had the time and the storage space, how could I ever download all the files on the web? And why would I ever want to?

The answer to the second question is easy. You can't know for sure whether a file contains what you're looking for unless you, or your computer-animated proxy, at least look at it, and, in order to look at a file, you have to download it to your machine. As for how you'd download all the files on the web – at least in principle, you'd do so by following hyperlinks. While the details can get pretty complicated, the basic algorithm is simple.

Start with one or more URLs. For each URL, use `curl` or some other HTTP-savvy program to download the file and store it in an appropriately named file (in theory, URLs are unique, so a file name based on the URL is a good starting point; in practice, you have to work harder to find a unique name). Next use an HTML parser like the one in `lynx` to extract all the URLs corresponding to hyperlinks in the file and add these to your set of URLs to download. (Be sure to eliminate any URLs you've already downloaded, otherwise you may get into an *infinite loop*, loading the same files over and over again.[1]) Now just settle down and wait for your algorithm to terminate.

As they say, "don't try this at home." It would take you a very long time to traverse the entire web, and even if you were to strip off all the JPEG and GIF image files and all the MP3 music files and just store the raw text, you'd still end up with a lot more data than you could possibly handle. But that's not to say it isn't done. Companies that provide content searches on the web (so-called *search-engine* companies) like Google, AltaVista, Lycos, and others employ thousands of computers arranged in huge *server farms* to constantly scour the web in order to maintain as accurate an account of the files on the web as is technologically feasible. These server farms together with the software that runs on them, variously called crawlers, trawlers, bots and spiders, reduce searching the web to searching through a set of files, albeit a very large set of files.

So why can't we just use `grep` again? Part of the problem is that a simple keyword search, like looking for all files containing the words Java and Scheme, is

---

[1] Remember that the web can be thought of as a huge graph, a directed graph with cycles and billions of nodes. You can search such a graph using depth-first or breadth-first search, but you do have to be wary of cycles, otherwise you'll waste a lot of time repeatedly visiting the same nodes.

likely to include lots of irrelevant files. In addition to finding files that only casually mention Java and Scheme, you're likely to find files concerned with decorating plans involving shades of brown, coffee cultivation strategies and Indonesian politics. We could pay a lot of people to read the files and then index them and even rank their relevance (indeed, some search-engine companies do exactly that). But we're lazy (and impatient), and besides it's a losing battle with thousands if not millions of new web pages being produced every day. How can we automate finding relevant files and ranking their importance? How do we find the really good stuff?

14.2 MEASURING SIMILARITY

We don't yet have programs that can read and understand prose, but the field of *information retrieval* has discovered some useful tricks for searching large archives (called *corpora*) of text documents. As far as our linguistically challenged programs are concerned, a file is just a bag full of words with some formatting that may or may not be relevant. Some of the words are probably meaningful, such as those that appear in few files, and others aren't particularly useful, such as words like "a", "the" and "of" that appear frequently in almost every file. If the word appears in only a few files, then the number of times it appears in a file may provide additional information; files containing information about Java will probably include several occurrences of the word "Java."

Let's take a look at some actual data. Here are the URLs of nine web pages, including three pages concerned with the Java programming language, three about HTML and the World Wide Web and three that have something to do with Scheme (the terms on the right will be used to refer to the URLs in tables and graphs):

java.sun.com	Sun Microsystems Java	java
www.javalobby.org	Java Discussion Forums	lobby
www.javaworld.com	Java News and Information	world
www.w3.org	World Wide Web Consortium	www
www.hwg.org	The HTML Writers Guild	guild
www.htmlgoodies.com	HTML Tools and Resources	html
www.scheme.org	Information about Scheme	scheme
www.drscheme.org	An Implementation of Scheme	doctor
www.schemers.com	Scheme Educational Software	edsoft

I want to look at the frequency of the words in some of these files. A *word histogram* for a file gives each word in the file along with the total number of times the word appears. The following interaction with the shell lists a short Perl program[2] that counts the number of occurrences of each word in a file and then prints out the file's histogram.

```
% cat tf.pl
#!/usr/bin/perl
while ($_ = <ARGV>) {
    tr/A-Z/a-z/;
    @words = split(/\W+/, $_);
    foreach $word (@words) {
        $wordcount{$word}++;
    }
}
sub bycount {
    $wordcount{$a} <=> $wordcount{$b};
}
foreach $word (sort bycount keys ( %wordcount )) {
    printf "%10s %d\n", $word, $wordcount{$word};
}
```

You can get the gist without understanding every particular, but it helps to know that `tr` converts characters to lower case, `split` breaks a line of text into a list of the words appearing in the line, and `wordcount` is a list of pairs each consisting of a key (a word in this case) and an integer that keeps a running count of the number of occurrences of each word. In the terminology of Chapter 13, `wordcount` is an association list and `$wordcount{$word}` returns the value associated with

---

[2] I couldn't find a generally available Unix command to produce a word histogram for a file, but in the spirit of Perl's "There's more than one way to do it", here's a shell script that does the trick and more or less fits on a single line: `cat file.txt | tr -dc "a-zA-Z' \n" | tr " " "\n" | sort | uniq -c | sort -k1,1nr -k2`. Its main drawback, a common problem with short programs, is that it takes much longer to explain than to write down. You may recall the trick of using `sort` followed by `uniq` from Chapter 12. It's a useful exercise to figure out how this script works and then experiment with variations on the basic theme. Here's how the pieces play together: `tr` translates characters; the first invocation, `tr -dc "a-zA-Z' \n"`, deletes (the d in -dc) the complement (the c in -dc) of the characters specified in its first and only argument (all alphabetic characters plus the apostrophe, space and new-line characters (\n) characters), and the second invocation, `tr " " "\n"`, translates all spaces to new-line characters, thereby ensuring that each line contains at most one word. `sort` sorts lines; its first invocation makes sure that lines containing the same word appear consecutively in the output, thus paving the way for `uniq`, which filters out consecutive identical lines in a file; the -c option directs `uniq` to precede each line with the number of times the line appears in the input. The final invocation of `sort` uses some tricky directives to sort the output of `uniq` so that the most frequently occurring words appear first and those occurring the same number of times appear alphabetically.

the word corresponding to $word, the count of the number of occurrences of the word. $wordcount{$word}++ is convenient shorthand syntax for incrementing the count associated with the word corresponding to $word.

We'll use this little program to display part of the word histogram for the JavaWorld web page:

```
% lynx -dump -nolist www.javaworld.com | perl tf.pl | tail
 javaworld 9
      from 9
       for 9
       net 10
        of 10
         a 12
        to 13
       and 19
       the 23
      java 28
```

I used `tail` to list only the ten (the default value for `tail`) most frequently appearing words in the file. Using simple variations on this script, I determined that the JavaWorld file contains 605 words of which 339 are distinct. Commonly used words (called *stop words* in information-retrieval parlance) and topic-related words appear the most often in the text. The only way to distinguish stop words from topic-related words is to have some idea of the frequency with which the words appear in all files.

Let's take a look at the HTML Writers Guild web page:

```
% lynx -dump -nolist www.hwg.org | perl tf.pl | tail
    online 5
    member 5
      html 7
       for 7
       web 9
        to 10
        in 10
       and 11
     guild 13
       the 25
```

The word "java" doesn't appear (at least in the top 10) but the words "html", "web" and "guild" do. In this case there are only 345 words of which 200 are unique. So, what information can we easily extract from the text file that our programs see as a bag of words? There is the set of words, their respective word counts and the total number of words. In addition, by looking at the entire collection of files (the corpus), we can determine the frequency with which a word appears in any file, thereby obtaining some insight on how common it is. We want to summarize each file by stripping off the information we can't use and emphasizing the information that we can. As a first step, I'll run a little shell script that reads each test file and then prints summaries to a data file `tf.dat`. This shell script is written in the scripting language for the C shell (`csh`), which looks a lot like Perl or C. Here's how to parse it.

The first line, `#!/bin/csh`, indicates that this script should be run using the C shell program, `csh`. The statement `if ( -r tf.dat ) /bin/rm tf.dat` removes (using the `rm` command) the old file `tf.dat` if one is present in the current directory. The `touch tf.dat` line creates a new empty file of the same name. The variable `urls` is assigned to be the list of all the URLs for the web pages we want to process. Finally, the `foreach` statement processes each URL and appends the resulting information to the file `tf.dat` using the `>>` redirection operator.

```
% cat tf.csh
#!/bin/csh
if ( -r tf.dat ) /bin/rm tf.dat
touch tf.dat
set urls=(java.sun.com\
          www.javaworld.com\
          www.javalobby.org\
          www.scheme.org\
          www.schemers.com\
          www.drscheme.org\
          www.w3.org\
          www.htmlgoodies.com\
          www.hwg.org)
foreach url ( $urls )
        printf "(%s" $url >> tf.dat
        lynx -dump -nolist $url | perl tf.pl >> tf.dat
        printf ")" >> tf.dat
        end
% csh tf.csh
```

In brief, this script specifies a list of URLs and then uses a little loop to invoke `lynx` and the word-histogram Perl script on each URL. The result of executing this script is a file, `tf.dat`, comprised of lists (note the `printf` statements that bracket each call to `lynx`) consisting of a URL followed by word/count pairs.

Why did I do this? I wanted to convert the URLs to summaries of the information in their respective files and I wanted the summaries in a format that I could easily use in a Scheme program to manipulate the data further. Shell and Perl scripts are wonderful tools for managing files but I prefer languages like C, Java and Scheme for more complicated computations, partly from habit and partly because high-level languages like Java and Scheme in particular are designed to encourage good programming habits. The summaries in `tf.dat` are now in a form that I can easily read from Scheme. I'm not going to list the entire Scheme program (you can download it from www.cs.brown.edu/people/tld/talk/ if you're interested in looking at it, running it or modifying it for your own purposes). Here's what my Scheme program does with the summaries.

First, it scans all the summaries and creates a list of all the words in any file[3]. There are 1492 distinct words appearing in the nine files. The program assigns to each word an integer between 1 and 1492 called its *index*. Then for each file corresponding to a URL, the program creates a list (called a *vector*) in which the ith item is the number of times the word with index i appears in the file. Many items in the vector for a given file are likely to be 0 since many of the 1492 words appear in only one file. If the indices for the words "and", "the" and "java" are 1, 2 and 3, respectively, then the vector for JavaWorld is (19 23 28 ...) and the vector for the HTML Writers Guild is (11 25 0 ...). These vectors, with their consistent method of using indices referring to word counts, will replace the original summaries.

How might we analyze two such vectors to determine if the corresponding two files are similar? Information-retrieval experts use mathematical tools from linear algebra and probability theory to measure similarity, but there are simpler expedients that do a pretty good job. Most methods operate by combining differences at the word level. For example, take the sum of the absolute values of the differences of the word counts: then the similarity of the JavaWorld and HTML

---

[3] Most information-retrieval systems preprocess the data much more extensively than I have. In addition to converting all the text to lower-case letters and eliminating punctuation, most systems remove common stop words like "a", "an" and "to" that add little information to a document summary. Many systems also use various *stemming* algorithms to map words to a common root – for example, the words "sink", "sinks" and "sinking" would all be mapped to "sink." Stemming conflates words, which sometimes you want and sometimes causes confusion: for example, "universe", "universal" and "university" are all mapped to the root "univers". Sophisticated stemmers use a combination of morphological analysis – remove all "ing" endings – and lexical analysis – check to see if the words mapped to the same root have similar meanings. Not surprisingly, the methods used to preprocess a list of words prior to analysis can make a huge difference in performance.

Writers Guild web pages would be measured by (+ (abs (- 19 11)) (abs (- 23 25)) (abs (- 28 0)) ...), or (+ 8 2 28 ...). You could take the square of the difference of the word counts and you'd get a measure related to Euclidean distance, albeit in a geometry of 1492 dimensions instead of the usual three.[4] With a few optimizations, variations on these basic ideas turn out to work well in practice.

My little Scheme program uses some standard tricks from information retrieval. Instead of the raw word counts, my program uses the *term frequency* for each word, defined as the number of times the word appears in the file divided by the total number of words in the file. By using (19/605 23/605 28/605 ...) and (11/345 25/345 0/345 ...) instead of (19 23 28 ...) and (11 25 0 ...) for the JavaWorld and HTML Writers Guild vectors, we adjust the word counts to reflect different file sizes – (- 19/605 11/345) is tiny compared to (- 19 11). The term frequencies are further adjusted by weighting them by some function of the *inverse document frequency*, the total number of files divided by the number of files in which the word appears. This adjustment deemphasizes differences based on commonly occurring words.

Finally, instead of using a sum of absolute differences, my program treats each vector as a line through the origin of a 1492-dimensional vector space (linear algebra jargon) and computes the cosine of the angle between the vectors as the measure of similarity. Suffice it to say that this cosine method is easy to compute, makes perfect sense to someone who is comfortable maneuvering in super-high-dimensional vector spaces and yields a measure that ranges from 1, very similar, to 0, not similar at all. When I load my Scheme code it automatically reads in the data in tf.dat and computes the vectors for the nine test files:

```
% scheme
> (load "tf.scm")
```

The file tf.scm contains about a hundred or so lines of code, most of which handles cleaning up the data and creating and comparing vectors. In particular, this file defines a Scheme function that takes a string specifying a URL and uses the cosine method to compare the vector for the corresponding file with the vectors for the other files. It then prints out each of the nine test URLs preceded by the

---

[4] The location of a point in three-dimensional (Euclidean) space is specified by its x, y and z coordinates. The Euclidean distance between two points (x_1, y_1, z_1) and (x_2, y_2, z_2) is the length of the path connecting them and is calculated as the square root of the sum of the squares of the differences of their respective coordinates $\sqrt{(x_1 - x_2)^2 + (y_1 - y_2)^2 + (z_1 - z_2)^2}$.

	java	lobby	world	www	guild	html	scheme	doctor	edsoft
java	1.000	0.087	0.087	0.070	0.046	0.085	0.015	0.051	0.044
lobby	0.087	1.000	0.086	0.063	0.058	0.088	0.019	0.033	0.040
world	0.087	0.086	1.000	0.053	0.042	0.069	0.011	0.016	0.027
www	0.070	0.063	0.053	1.000	0.098	0.075	0.017	0.013	0.045
guild	0.046	0.058	0.042	0.098	1.000	0.070	0.008	0.007	0.040
html	0.085	0.088	0.069	0.075	0.070	1.000	0.021	0.026	0.043
scheme	0.015	0.019	0.011	0.017	0.008	0.021	1.000	0.058	0.043
doctor	0.051	0.033	0.016	0.013	0.007	0.026	0.058	1.000	0.034
edsoft	0.044	0.040	0.027	0.045	0.040	0.043	0.043	0.034	1.000

Figure 14.1: Similarity matrix based on term-frequency analysis

result computed with the cosine method:

```
> (compare "www.w3.org")
1.000 www.w3.org
0.098 www.hwg.org
0.075 www.htmlgoodies.com
0.070 java.sun.com
0.063 www.javalobby.org
0.053 www.javaworld.com
0.045 www.schemers.com
0.017 www.scheme.org
0.013 www.drscheme.org
```

Not surprisingly, the URL of the World Wide Web Consortium matches best with itself and then next with URLs relating to HTML. All the Java-related URLs come next, presumably because Java is one of the main tools for creating web pages with dynamic content. Figure 14.1 shows the result of all pairwise comparisons involving the nine URLs identified by the abbreviations introduced earlier.

This method does a pretty good job of determining if two files are similar. You could also perform a query-based search by treating the list of keywords in a query as a short file. Here's what happens when we do this for the keywords "scheme" and "java":

```
> (query '(scheme java))
0.170 www.scheme.org
0.077 www.schemers.com
0.050 www.drscheme.org
```

```
0.043 java.sun.com
0.035 www.javaworld.com
0.021 www.javalobby.org
0.015 www.htmlgoodies.com
0.000 www.hwg.org
0.000 www.w3.org
```

Not much better than using `grep`. A more effective method would be to start with a query, let the user identify one or more of the top-ranked files that actually come close to satisfying the query, and then use these files to find more of the same. The only problem is that most of us are too impatient or lazy to provide such feedback, and so we seldom do. An alternative is to perform a lot of comparisons ahead of time, group files according to similarity and then work backwards to the keywords that are most likely to call forth such similar files. The keywords for a group of files might be identified by a human or through various machine-learning techniques. Groups of similar files would then be indexed under the assigned keywords so that they can be called up quickly when a query containing them is issued.

Search engines depend on networks of computers crawling the web to find web pages, summarizing their content (using a variety of methods based on term-frequency statistics), indexing the content and answering queries. A lot of very interesting algorithms and data structures are required to perform these tasks efficiently. It's hard to say exactly how any particular search engine works, since their methods are typically corporate secrets, but most of them use some variant of the methods described here as part of their overall strategy.

And all search engines have to work around the problems associated with these methods. One problem is that you can fool a naive search engine just by adding words to your web page whether or not they make any sense in context. If I wanted my home page to come up whenever anyone typed a query containing "Java", I could just append a hundred instances of the word "Java" to the end of my home page. There are more subtle variations on this basic idea, and programmers at search-engine companies are constantly modifying their indexing algorithms to counter tricks used by web-page builders to get their pages to display prominently in response to common queries.

Another problem is that some web pages contain all the right words for talking about a given topic but there's no reason to believe that the author is making any sense. I don't want to take medical advice from a quack or financial advice from a crook. How would I know – or, more to the point, how would a stupid program know – whether a given page was written by an authority on its subject matter? For an answer to this question, we take a closer look at the hyperlinks that tie the web together, borrow from a method used by scientists and scholars to establish credentials, and exploit some ideas from graph theory.

14.3 MEASURING AUTHORITY

When a scientist or a scholar writes a paper that other scientists and scholars think is important, they tend to mention or *cite* it in their papers. Sometimes papers are cited because they're controversial or because they contain errors, but the most frequently cited papers tend to be ones worth reading. If you're looking for an authoritative account of some subject, it's worth checking out the papers on that subject that have received the most citations.

Of course, this is just a general rule of thumb and you'd be wise to sample some of the citations to make sure they're authoritative; it could be that the paper is liked by a small group of prolific bozos who cite only one another's papers. So, being cited a lot isn't enough to establish authority; you have to be cited in a lot of authoritative papers or be one of the few papers cited in one or two very authoritative papers. Authority is defined recursively: authoritative papers confer authority on the papers they cite.

The analogous notion of authority for the web is pretty obvious: you cite a web page by including a hyperlink to it. Measuring authority is a little harder, given its recursive definition and the presence of cycles in the web graph, but a little common sense combined with a little math gives us a nice solution.

Figure 14.2 is a fictional web-graph fragment based very loosely on the URLs we looked at earlier. We'll say that page p cites page q if p contains a hyperlink to q. Figure 14.2 is arranged in an inner and an outer ring with java, www and scheme in the inner ring and the rest in the outer ring. Java, www and scheme have three citations each, including one each from another page in the inner ring. All the other pages have one citation each. In Figure 14.2, java, www and scheme appear to be the authoritative pages. How might we confirm this, and indeed how might we compute some measure of their authoritativeness?

In reading papers on a given topic, scientists and scholars follow citations to learn what the papers cited add to the discussion. Usually cited papers are just skimmed – perhaps the abstract is read along with a quick look at the introduction and conclusions. However, if you keep returning to the same paper by following different chains of citations, then you might just take the time to read that paper more carefully. For the web, the analog is of a web surfer choosing at random from the hyperlinks emanating from whatever pages he is visiting. In a program, we can't simulate a scholar skimming papers and selectively following

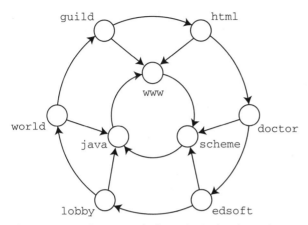

Figure 14.2: A fragment of a hypothetical web graph

	java	lobby	world	www	guild	html	scheme	doctor	edsoft
java	0	0	0	1	0	0	0	0	0
lobby	1/2	0	1/2	0	0	0	0	0	0
world	1/2	0	0	0	1/2	0	0	0	0
www	0	0	0	0	0	0	1	0	0
guild	0	0	0	1/2	0	1/2	0	0	0
html	0	0	0	1/2	0	0	0	1/2	0
scheme	1	0	0	0	0	0	0	0	0
doctor	0	0	0	0	0	0	1/2	0	1/2
edsoft	0	1/2	0	0	0	0	1/2	0	0

Figure 14.3: Transition matrix for web-graph fragment

citations, so we very roughly approximate this behavior by selecting hyperlinks at random.

Figure 14.3 shows a table called the *transition matrix* for the graph in Figure 14.2 in which, for example, the number in the row labeled world and the column labeled java is the probability that our surfer will jump to the java page given he is in the world page. Instead of measuring how often the surfer returns to a page – which depends on how long he surfs – we'll measure the probability that the surfer returns to a page – which settles down (it's said to *converge*) to a fixed number as the surfer continues to search the web. To show this convergence and demonstrate how to compute measures of authority, we'll use the mathematics-savvy program Mathematica to apply some basic ideas from the theory of graphs and stochastic processes.

Mapping the row and column names in Figure 14.3 to the integers 1 through 9, we can represent the matrix in Figure 14.3 in Mathematica as (in Mathematica, semicolons distinguish separate statements or commands, much as in the C programming language; when typed at the end of a line submitted to the Mathematica interpreter, a semicolon suppresses any display of output):

```
In[1]:= A = {{0.0, 0.0, 0.0, 1.0, 0.0, 0.0, 0.0, 0.0, 0.0},
             {0.5, 0.0, 0.5, 0.0, 0.0, 0.0, 0.0, 0.0, 0.0},
             {0.5, 0.0, 0.0, 0.0, 0.5, 0.0, 0.0, 0.0, 0.0},
             {0.0, 0.0, 0.0, 0.0, 0.0, 0.0, 1.0, 0.0, 0.0},
             {0.0, 0.0, 0.0, 0.5, 0.0, 0.5, 0.0, 0.0, 0.0},
             {0.0, 0.0, 0.0, 0.5, 0.0, 0.0, 0.0, 0.5, 0.0},
             {1.0, 0.0, 0.0, 0.0, 0.0, 0.0, 0.0, 0.0, 0.0},
             {0.0, 0.0, 0.0, 0.0, 0.0, 0.0, 0.5, 0.0, 0.5},
             {0.0, 0.5, 0.0, 0.0, 0.0, 0.0, 0.5, 0.0, 0.0}} ;
```

We can represent the probable location of a surfer either initially or after surfing for a while as a vector in which the ith number is the probability of being in the ith web page. This vector is technically referred to as a *probability distribution* and, for rather obvious reasons, the numbers in such a vector must sum to 1. We'll assume that initially the surfer can be in any one of the nine web pages, and so the probability distribution for the surfer's initial location is said to be *uniform* and is represented as:

```
In[2]:= u = {1/9, 1/9, 1/9, 1/9, 1/9, 1/9, 1/9, 1/9, 1/9} ;
```

A vector is represented in Mathematica as a list of numbers. In Chapter 13 we computed the dot product of two matrices, but we can also compute the dot product of a matrix and a vector. Here we define a 2 by 2 matrix and a vector of length 2 and then compute their dot product:

```
In[3]:= M = {{a,b},{c,d}} ;
In[4]:= v = {x,y} ;
In[5]:= M . v
Out[5]= {a x + b y, c x + d y}
```

The *transpose* of a matrix exchanges rows for columns and, again, is best understood by an example:

```
In[6]:= Transpose[M]
Out[6]= {{a, c}, {b, d}}
```

Now if we take the dot product of the transpose of the transition matrix and the vector corresponding to the surfer's initial location:

```
In[7]:= Transpose[A] . u
Out[7]= {0.222222, 0.0555556, 0.0555556,
         0.222222, 0.0555556, 0.0555556,
         0.222222, 0.0555556, 0.0555556}
```

the ith number in this vector is the probability that the surfer ends up in the ith location after one step of randomly choosing hyperlinks, given the initial uniform distribution. To convince yourself of this, go back to the definitions of transpose and dot product and work out how the first couple of numbers in the above vector are computed; if A[i,j] is the number in the ith row and jth column of the matrix A and u[i] is the ith entry in the vector u, then, symbolically, the first number in Transpose[A] . u looks like A[java,java] * u[java] + A[lobby, java] * u[lobby] + A[world,java] * u[world] + ... + A[edsoft, java] * u[edsoft]. The resulting vector is another probability distribution.

To confirm that the result is a distribution, the following exchange exploits Mathematica's functional programming notation: an expression of the form Apply[*fun*, *args*] applies the function *fun* to the arguments *args* and is equivalent to (apply *fun args*) in Scheme:

```
In[8]:= Apply[ Plus, Transpose[A] . u ]
Out[8]= 1
```

We've just simulated one step (or *iteration*) of an algorithm for determining the authoritativeness of web pages. After one step, the surfer is most likely to end up in one of the three pages, java, www or scheme, that we initially identified as the most authoritative from Figure 14.2. If we repeatedly execute the assignment u = Transpose[A] . u, the vector u will converge to a fixed vector called the *fixed point* of the equation u == Transpose[A] . u, where == represents equality. After only 10 iterations, the probability of ending up in any web page other than java, www or scheme is quite small:

```
In[9]:= Do[ u = Transpose[A] . u , {10} ] ; u
Out[9]= {0.333116, 0.000108507, 0.000108507,
         0.333116, 0.000108507, 0.000108507,
         0.333116, 0.000108507, 0.000108507}
```

And, after 100 iterations, our random surfer is extremely unlikely to end up in any page but these three. The good news is that our algorithm lets us quickly obtain stable estimates of authoritativeness. The bad news is that none of the pages in the outer ring seem to have inherited any of the authoritativeness of the pages they link to. Indeed, it's a fluke that the measure of authoritativeness for the pages in the inner ring is greater than that for the pages in the outer ring, however reasonable that may seem.

Some pages in the real web have no outgoing links, and so our simulated surfer would become stuck there. In our graph, all the pages have both incoming and outgoing links, but the three pages in the inner ring have no links that would let a random surfer jump outside the inner ring, and so when he eventually jumps to one of these three inner pages he will bounce around in the inner ring indefinitely.

We can fix our algorithm by modifying the transition matrix so that no matter what page the surfer is in he has some probability of ending up in any other page. Most of the time the surfer will jump more or less in accord with probabilities in the original matrix, but there is some small probability that the surfer will jump to some other page in the web graph. The fix is simple to arrange in Mathematica. First we add a small probability to every entry in the original transition matrix. The expression M + C, where M is a matrix and C is a constant, designates a new matrix whose entry in the ith row and jth column is the sum of C and the entry in the ith row and jth column of M:

```
In[10]:= B = A + 0.001 ;
```

Since each entry in the original transition matrix is meant to represent the probability of jumping from one page to another, the numbers in a given row should add up to 1. By adding 0.001 to each entry in A we've destroyed this property. The next computation restores the property by *normalizing* each row so that its entries sum to 1. The expression Map[Function[x, *body*]], *list*] is equivalent to (map (lambda (x) *body*) *list*) in Scheme.

```
In[11]:= B = Map[ Function[v, v / Apply[ Plus, v ]] , B] ;
```

And, in another demonstration of Mathematica's rather elegant functional programming notation, we check to make sure that the property is restored as desired:

```
In[12]:= Apply[ And, Table[1 == Apply[Plus, B[[i]]] , {i, Length[B]} ]]
Out[12]= True
```

Reinitializing the initial distribution, we run our new algorithm for a few iterations:

```
In[13]:= u = {1/9, 1/9, 1/9, 1/9, 1/9, 1/9, 1/9, 1/9, 1/9} ;
In[14]:= Do[ u = Transpose[B] . u , {10} ] ; u
```

```
Out[14]= {0.329209, 0.00206209, 0.00206209,
          0.329209, 0.00206209, 0.00206209,
          0.329209, 0.00206209, 0.00206209}
```

This turns out to be pretty close to the fixed point, as we see from a few more iterations:

```
In[15]:= Do[ u = Transpose[B] . u , {100} ] ; u
Out[15]= {0.329404, 0.00196464, 0.00196464,
          0.329404, 0.00196464, 0.00196464,
          0.329404, 0.00196464, 0.00196464}
In[16]:= Do[ u = Transpose[B] . u , {1000} ] ; u
Out[16]= {0.329404, 0.00196464, 0.00196464,
          0.329404, 0.00196464, 0.00196464,
          0.329404, 0.00196464, 0.00196464}
```

These numbers seem about right. The particular topology of our toy web graph is a little out of the ordinary in that the inner and outer rings are rather incestuous. If we include only the links that connect from the six pages in the outer ring to the three pages in the inner ring, we'd get a set of three isolated subgraphs, each one concerned with a distinct topic. Running our algorithm, we see that the pages in the inner ring now confer significantly more of their authoritativeness on the pages that cite them:

```
In[17]:= Z = {{0.0, 0.0, 0.0, 0.0, 0.0, 0.0, 0.0, 0.0, 0.0},
              {1.0, 0.0, 0.0, 0.0, 0.0, 0.0, 0.0, 0.0, 0.0},
              {1.0, 0.0, 0.0, 0.0, 0.0, 0.0, 0.0, 0.0, 0.0},
              {0.0, 0.0, 0.0, 0.0, 0.0, 0.0, 0.0, 0.0, 0.0},
              {0.0, 0.0, 0.0, 1.0, 0.0, 0.0, 0.0, 0.0, 0.0},
              {0.0, 0.0, 0.0, 1.0, 0.0, 0.0, 0.0, 0.0, 0.0},
              {0.0, 0.0, 0.0, 0.0, 0.0, 0.0, 0.0, 0.0, 0.0},
              {0.0, 0.0, 0.0, 0.0, 0.0, 0.0, 1.0, 0.0, 0.0},
              {0.0, 0.0, 0.0, 0.0, 0.0, 0.0, 1.0, 0.0, 0.0}} ;
In[18]:= Z = Z + 0.001 ;
In[19]:= Z = Map[ Function[v, v / Apply[ Plus, v ]], Z ] ;
In[20]:= u = {1/9, 1/9, 1/9, 1/9, 1/9, 1/9, 1/9, 1/9, 1/9} ;
In[21]:= Do[ u = Transpose[Z] . u , {100} ] ; u
Out[21]= {0.199523, 0.0669054, 0.0669054,
          0.199523, 0.0669054, 0.0669054,
          0.199523, 0.0669054, 0.0669054}
```

While total isolation is rare, groups of pages do seem to form topic subgraphs that rarely cite pages outside their group. Analysis of the subgraph structure of the web is a fascinating subject that uses more of the mathematics we've hinted at plus fundamental results in probability and statistics.

The basic idea behind this authoritativeness measure plays an important role in the algorithms used by the Google search engine. While I don't know exactly how Google works, a good guess is that it uses traditional sorts of information retrieval to obtain an initial set of pages, then ranks these pages using some combination of authoritativeness and various measures of document similarity such as the term-frequency methods we discussed. With this hint, it's interesting to submit queries to Google and then do various experiments analyzing the content and the links for the pages returned.

Link-based measures of authority are open to various schemes for artificially improving the authoritativeness of pages. For example, I could create pages with lots of links to my own pages (tantamount to citing your own work), pay lots of people to put links to my pages on their pages, or conspire with a bunch of other folks to cite one another. None of these tricks work particularly well on Google, but other, more complicated schemes that exploit both document similarity and link-based measures of authority require the folks at Google and every other search-engine company continually to improve their algorithms. To learn more about information retrieval techniques for searching the web, check out Soumen Chakrabarti's *Mining the Web: Discovering Knowledge from Hypertext Data*.

14.4 SEARCHING FOR EXOTIC FRUIT

Most search engines let you search for nontext sources of information such as images, music and movies. Such nontext sources present a whole new set of challenges for search algorithms. In an ideal world, images would be stored as structured data in relational databases. Databases store all sorts of information besides text and numbers, and we could use a variant of the music database in Chapter 3 to store textual information about songs and albums as well as the music itself, encoded in a digital format such as MP3.[5] Unfortunately, image and music data on the wild web is not so conveniently stored and catalogued.

---

[5] MP3 is the compression format used in a popular method of encoding digital audio files. The analog audio signal produced in recording an album is digitized by reading off and then storing values ("samples") of the signal at discrete time points (44,100 samples per second for audio CDs). The sampled data is stored as a sequence of integers in a file. To reduce the amount of storage required and speed downloading, this file is compressed by converting the data to a more compact format. A compression format might allow a compression algorithm to convert a sequence like 1742, 1742, 1742, 1742,

Most current techniques for searching the web for nontext-based information rely on using "nearby" text to index the nontext data. Image data is typically included in web pages using the IMG HTML tag, and so a statement such as <IMG src="images/adirondack.gif"> embedded in a web page would cause the specified image in "graphics interchange format" to be downloaded and then displayed in a browser window. If you're really lucky, the person who created the web page may have used the ALT attribute for IMG to give a textual description of the image, for example, <IMG src="images/adirondack.gif" ALT="adirondack chair">. The ALT attribute is useful as an alternative method of display in text-only browsers like lynx or even in a graphical browser if you're on a slow connection or have turned off graphics downloading for some other reason.

Hyperlinks in HTML are specified using the A (for "anchor") tag, and the "clickable" text that's displayed in your browser, usually underlined, emboldened or otherwise highlighted, is called the *anchor text*. For example, a web page for an online store featuring outdoor patio and garden furniture might contain this line of HTML code:

```
<A HREF="http://www.outdoors.com/adirondack.htm">adirondack chair</A>
```

When viewed with a browser, the anchor text adirondack chair is highlighted; if you click on this text, you'll jump to the indicated web page, which might feature images of chairs. You can also use images instead of text to anchor hyperlinks, in which case the pages they point to may yield clues about the image content. The online furniture store might display small product images called *thumbnails* that link to descriptions of the product, as in

```
<A HREF="adirondack.htm"><IMG SRC="images/adirondack.gif"></A>
```

Now when you click on the thumbnail image adirondack.gif you jump to the description of the chair, which may include more images.[6] There are all sorts of tricks for finding text that is associated with images and can be used for indexing; if suitable text can be found, then the problem of searching for images reduces to searching for text.

1742 into a specification like 1742 (5) or, in "lossy" compression, a sequence like 3241, 3242, 3241, 3241, 3239 3241 into the specification 3241 (6) which only approximately captures the original uncompressed data. The acronym MP3 derives from another acronym, MPEG ("motion picture experts group"), referring to a set of layered formats for compressing audio and video, and one format in particular, "Layer 3", which is the basis for MP3.

[6] The two examples using the HTML anchor tag demonstrate the two modes of specifying URLs allowed by the HTTP protocol, relative and absolute path names, which directly correspond to the two methods of specifying files and directories in most modern file systems.

There are also efforts afoot to use so-called *image understanding* and *pattern recognition* methods from the field of machine vision to extract clues directly from image data, but current techniques along these lines are at the bleeding edge of technology and not yet ready for prime time. In addition to searching still images, researchers are developing techniques for searching video images. Imagine a reporter for a cable news service wanting to search the studio's video archives for footage of Keanu Reeves getting out of a limousine for a news segment she's doing. A program to do this would have to identify the actor, distinguish a limousine from other objects, and somehow recognize a segment in which someone exits from a limo.

Whether extending traditional information-retrieval methods for searching text documents or developing new methods to search multimedia data, there's a lot of very interesting work to be done. Relevant techniques can be found in the study of linguistics, natural-language processing, speech recognition, image processing, machine vision and artificial intelligence. And, as fast as researchers figure out how to make sense of existing formats and media, artists and technologists will come up with new and richer ways of expressing themselves that will require even more sophisticated search methods.

CHAPTER FIFTEEN

Darwin's Dangerous Algorithm

In Daniel Dennett's *Darwin's Dangerous Idea: Evolution and the Meanings of Life*, the dangerous idea is *natural selection*, Charles Darwin's name for the mechanism governing the evolution of species that he codiscovered with Alfred Russel Wallace. Natural selection is the "process by which individual characteristics that are more favorable to reproductive success are 'chosen,' because they are passed on from one generation to the next, over characteristics that are less favorable".[1]

Natural selection explains how characteristics that promote reproductive success persist and under certain circumstances can come to dominate less favorable characteristics, but it doesn't explain how those characteristics are passed on or how new characteristics come into being. It was Gregor Mendel, living around Darwin's time, who suggested that heritable characteristics are packaged in the discrete units we now call genes and that offspring inherit a combination of their parents' genes.

When you combine Darwin's and Mendel's ideas, you have the basis for *genetic algorithms*, an interesting class of algorithms generally attributed to John Holland that take their inspiration from evolutionary biology. These algorithms simulate some aspects of biological evolution – while ignoring others – to tackle a wide range of problems from designing circuits to scheduling trains. Genetic algorithms allow the algorithm designer to specify the criterion for reproductive success by supplying a *fitness function*, alluding to the idea that in a competitive environment only the fittest survive to reproduce.

In biological evolution, the selection of favorable characteristics is determined by the environment, including the individuals living in that environment.

---

[1] Louis Menand, in this passage from *The Metaphysical Club* (p. 122), makes it clear that natural selection is blind to any particular design or plan, and that the choice or selection of characteristics is determined entirely by reproductive success.

Evolution does not move toward any grand design, nor is it likely to agree with our notions of progress except insofar as we can engineer our environment to select for those characteristics we deem valuable. In a genetic algorithm, however, the algorithm designer has complete control over reproduction. Genetic algorithms illustrate how computer programmers can simulate any natural process that they can articulate precisely and even modify their simulations to create processes not found in nature. Sound dangerous to you?

15.1 COMPETING HYPOTHESES

A few years back, six students asked me to be the faculty sponsor for a group independent study project (GISP) in the following semester. The proposed GISP's subject matter was all over the map: connections among such topics as evolution, natural selection, computational complexity, and combinatorial optimization. In particular, they wanted to explore genetic algorithms and genetic programming (basically, a methodology involving the use of genetic algorithms to automatically produce programs for particular purposes).

I was skeptical of both the material and the value of spending an entire semester studying it. From my perspective, genetic algorithms and the related genetic programming are simply methods for searching in a very large set of hypotheses, and not necessarily the best methods at that. This idea of searching among hypotheses is important in computer science and artificial intelligence in particular, and while the words "searching" and "hypotheses" are probably familiar to you, I wouldn't be surprised if you find their combination a bit puzzling.

Depending on the context, the term *hypothesis* might be to a possible answer to a question, a possible explanation for an observed event, or a possible solution to a problem. The set of all such possible (or *competing*) answers, explanations or solutions for a given question, event or problem is called a *hypothesis space*. In many computational problems, you proceed by looking at or *searching* such a space of hypotheses. If you're lucky, the hypothesis space has some inherent structure or regularity, so that, having examined one hypothesis and found it wanting, you can extract clues about how to transform it into one or more alternative hypotheses that might, just might, correspond to better answers.

This approach of searching in a large hypothesis space is often applied to computationally hard problems like the traveling salesman problem (TSP) in Chapter 12 in which we're looking for a minimal-length *tour* – a path in a graph that begins and ends with the same node and visits each node exactly once. In terms of searching among hypotheses, the hypothesis space for solving an instance of TSP is the set of all tours. There is an exponential number of such tours, and so for any reasonably large *n* the hypothesis space is very large indeed.[2]

In searching in the space of possible tours for a minimal (or at least relatively short) tour, imagine an algorithm examining its current hypothesis, the shortest tour it's come up with so far. Some portions of this tour may have the salesman ineffectively bouncing back and forth across the country. A clever algorithm might modify the current tour to have the salesman visit all the locations on the east coast before those on the west coast. Alternatively, it might take several of the tours it's encountered and combine the best parts of each to create a new tour that's better than any seen so far: for example, one tour might visit the west-coast locations efficiently and a second tour do a better job on the east-coast locations.

Search algorithms implement various strategies for systematically searching large hypothesis spaces by combining, transforming, and otherwise improving on the hypotheses they've seen so far. Genetic algorithms are search algorithms that exploit ideas from evolutionary biology to orchestrate their search. My skepticism about the subject matter of the GISP was simply that, however intriguing the mechanism of natural selection, I was reasonably confident that other search methods would be more effective for any given problem we might wish to solve. Nevertheless, I was interested to see if nature could teach us new computational tricks, and the very idea of simulated evolution seemed fascinating enough to occupy us for a semester, if not longer. I agreed to sponsor the GISP.

15.2   GENETIC ALGORITHMS

Genetic algorithms (GAs) are a general method (framework, really, as I'll explain shortly) for searching in very large hypothesis spaces. The "very large" qualifier is added because if the space is small enough, then we can search it exhaustively by simply enumerating every hypothesis and picking out the best one. Such general search methods can be used to solve so-called *combinatorial optimization* problems in which the component pieces of solutions can be combined in a large number of ways, or for learning problems like the spam-classification problem in Chapter 8 and automatic programming problems like synthesizing a robot program to guide a robot through a maze. It certainly would be nice to

---

[2] Actually, the number of tours depends on the structure of the underlying graph. If, however, we assume that a link connects each pair of nodes in the graph, then every ordering of these nodes constitutes a tour. You should be able to convince yourself that there are $n!$ (n factorial) possible orderings of n nodes and furthermore that $n! > 2^n$ for $n > 3$.

get a computer to write all your programs for you. Indeed, genetic algorithms are sometimes scathingly called the second-best method for solving just about any problem.

So I was skeptical, but I got caught up in my students' enthusiasm. GAs operate on whole collections or *populations* of hypotheses encoded as strings of *digital DNA*, that is, as data structures that programmers often think of in terms of genes, codons, and other terms familiar to molecular biologists. Hypotheses are subjected to simulated mutation and the "fittest" hypotheses are allowed to "reproduce", yielding offspring that combine features of the best hypotheses.

Once you get into the spirit, you can borrow just about anything you like from evolutionary biology. You could even incorporate ideas from currently unpopular theories such as that of Jean-Baptiste Lamarck (1744–1829), who proposed that evolution is directly influenced by the experiences of individual organisms over their lifetimes. Since you are writing the program that implements the simulation, you have a great deal of freedom. (It's a bit like playing God, which may explain some of its attraction.) More often than not, however, programmers tend to follow nature's suggestions, hoping, I suppose, that nature has stumbled upon some effective ways of searching in very large hypothesis spaces. Keep in mind, however, that nature isn't in any particular hurry, and also that natural selection isn't out to optimize anything.

They had me reading everything: Richard Dawkins's *The Selfish Gene*, James Watson's *The Double Helix: A Personal Account of the Discovery of the Structure of DNA*, Robert Axelrod's *The Evolution of Cooperation*, John Maynard Smith's *Evolution and the Theory of Games* and *Evolutionary Genetics*, to name just a few of the books on my night-time reading table. Genetic, molecular and evolutionary biology provide a wealth of ideas on which to base search heuristics. We were looking for anything to make our algorithms better or perhaps supply some missing piece, thereby letting us tap the power and mystery of natural selection. Why settle for some ho-hum low-fidelity version of simulated evolution when you can have a supercharged high-fidelity version with all the bells and whistles?

In addition to all the readings in biology and related fields, we also read Melanie Mitchell's *An Introduction to Genetic Algorithms*, a very readable introduction to the field. I had met Melanie two years earlier during a sabbatical stay at the Santa Fe Institute and she had managed to dispel some of my skepticism about the practical value of genetic algorithms. During my stay in Santa Fe, I had gained grudging respect for what a good programmer could do with GAs. It's important to point out, however, that they're not a ready-made solution to any particular problem; they offer a general framework for solving problems, but the programmer has to supply the most important pieces.

If we want to try to solve an instance of the traveling salesman problem using GAs, the first thing we need to think about is how to represent a hypothesis, that is, a tour. Once you have the basic ideas from biology, it's relatively easy to translate them into algorithms and data structures. For our purposes, a string of digital DNA corresponds to a list of simple tokens.[3] For the tokens in our TSP instance, we'll use the standard three-letter codes for the airports in six cities: BOS for Boston, BWI for Baltimore, DFW for Dallas–Fort Worth, ORD for Chicago, PVD for Providence and SFO for San Francisco.

A tour, then, is a list of six tokens. The final leg of a tour is a flight from the city corresponding to the last token in the list back to the city corresponding to the first. An example tour starting and ending in Boston would be (BOS PVD BWI SFO ORD DFW). We also need a matrix representing the distance between each pair of cities:

	BOS	BWI	DFW	ORD	PVD	SFO
BOS	0000	0371	1550	0867	0043	2704
BWI	0228	0000	1100	0621	0328	2400
DFW	1550	1100	0000	0802	1503	1464
ORD	0867	0621	0802	0000	0849	1846
PVD	0043	0328	1503	0848	0000	2654
SFO	2704	2400	1464	1846	2654	0000

Using this distance matrix, we can calculate that our example tour has length 6969. In terms of minimizing the distance traveled by our traveling salesman, the first part of the tour makes a certain amount of sense: we travel down the eastern seaboard from Boston (BOS) to Providence (PVD) to Baltimore (BWI). But then we shoot over to San Francisco (SFO), back across the country to Chicago (ORD), and down to Dallas–Fort Worth (DFW) before flying back to Boston. If we reverse the order of tokens corresponding to Chicago and San Francisco in the original tour, we get the tour (BOS PVD BWI ORD SFO DFW) of length 5852, a significant improvement.

You might imagine two tokens swapping positions as being a *mutation* of sorts. And you might implement this form of mutation by using a subroutine for generating random numbers. With such a subroutine, it's very easy to write a program

---

[3] If you know about genes you can think of them as tokens, but the analogy is a little rough. Genes are not atomic; rather, they can be broken down into sequences of *codons* that code for the twenty amino acids used to synthesize proteins. Codons can be further broken down into triples composed of the four chemical bases, adenine, cytosine, guanine and thymine, that comprise DNA. Most genetic algorithms make only superficial use of what is known about genetics and molecular biology.

that examines a list representing a tour and, with a given fixed probability, either reverses the order of two consecutive tokens or leaves them as they were. Such a program is called a *genetic operator* in the parlance of genetic algorithms. Is this form of mutation biologically plausible? Perhaps, but it doesn't really matter; we're calling the shots and we're free either to slavishly emulate natural selection as far as we understand it or to depart from reality as we see fit.

Other forms of mutation might not work out so well for our purposes. If our mutation routines were free to substitute any one token for any other token with some probability, a more plausible biological model, a tour might end up visiting the same city twice or, worse, inserting a city we didn't have to visit at all. Luckily we can tame natural selection to avoid genetic misfits, or, in our case, tours that lead us in circles or to destinations we'd rather not visit.

We can also arrange for programs to simulate sex and thereby enable hypotheses represented as strings of digital DNA to share their genetic heritage. Our current winner, (BOS PVD BWI ORD SFO DFW) (length 5852), has a good east-coast solution and a so-so finish. On the other hand, (BOS BWI PVD DFW SFO ORD) (length 6379) wanders up and down the east coast but takes a nice swing down through the south (DFW), over to the west coast (SFO) and then back across the country, stopping in Chicago (ORD) before returning to Boston (BOS). Suppose these two were to get together and swap their best characteristics.

We break (BOS PVD BWI ORD SFO DFW) into two equal parts, (BOS PVD BWI) and (ORD SFO DFW), and do the same for (BOS BWI PVD DFW SFO ORD), resulting in (BOS BWI PVD) and (DFW SFO ORD). Now we swap parts to form two new sequences: (BOS BWI PVD ORD SFO DFW) of length 6408, which ain't so great, and a second, golden child, (BOS PVD BWI DFW SFO ORD) of length 5648, the best we've seen so far. Does this have any analog in natural selection? Yes, during reproduction the strands of DNA from two parents are lined up and segments called *chromosomes* are swapped in a process known as *crossing over*. In the terminology of genetic algorithms, this exchange of genetic information is accomplished by a *crossover* genetic operator.[4] Unlike the simple mutation operator we discussed earlier, crossover operators require two strings of digital DNA to tango.

So, how do we simulate sex and reproduction in a genetic algorithm? First of all, we're quite clear about what it means for tours, corresponding to strings of digital DNA, to improve: shorter tours are more desirable and we're searching for the shortest possible tour. In natural selection, individuals are not necessarily getting

---

[4] This crossover example conveniently used two tours whose first and second halves contained the same cities, BOS, PVD and BWI in the first halves and DFW, ORD and SFO in the second. Clearly it's possible to choose a pair of tours that doesn't have this property. The crossover operator for TSP must be designed to avoid creating tours with multiple occurrences of the same city – an interesting design problem.

"better", even on average; natural selection simply selects for genes (which are basically programs for building individuals or pieces of individuals) that manage to do a good job at reproducing themselves. If such genes give rise to individuals that are stronger or smarter, that's interesting but it needn't happen. It's certainly possible for natural selection to stumble on a program for building small, fast, mindless individuals that are superior to us in reproducing so effectively that they wipe us off the planet. But, as designers of genetic algorithms, we are free to play fast and loose with what we know about natural selection. In particular, we get to define the criterion that governs who gets to reproduce and how much.

At any point in its operation, a GA has an existing population corresponding to the current generation, a set of tours in the case of TSP, that it analyzes to determine which entities will get an opportunity to reproduce. Using the results of its analysis, the GA then constructs the next generation by mutating and pairing selected entities from the current generation. The generation so produced becomes the current generation and the GA repeats this process. If an entity is found that meets some specified *termination criterion*, the GA halts; otherwise it continues until it has examined a specified number of generations. Exactly how entities are selected for reproduction is at the heart of designing a GA.

It shouldn't be hard to convince yourself that not all mutations and crossovers produce improvements; indeed, in our crossover example, only one of the two new tours was an improvement on its parents. We probably don't want to give all entities an equal opportunity to reproduce, nor can we expect that all entities resulting from reproduction will be equally desirable for future reproduction. We use the term *fitness* as our measure of how desirable or *fit* a string of digital DNA is for reproduction. The higher the fitness of a string, the more likely it will be selected for reproduction.

Since shorter tours are better than longer ones, we want a *fitness function* that's inversely related to tour length. Since we're interested in conferring a reproductive advantage within a given population, we focus on the entities within that population. Let's define the fitness function for a tour as the difference between that tour and the longest (worst) tour in the population. With this definition the longest tour is the least fit (it has a fitness of zero) and the shortest tour is the most fit. How can we use this measure of fitness to select tours for reproduction?

15.3 SURVIVAL OF THE FITTEST

Randomness seems to play a role in natural selection. Occasionally fit entities fail to reproduce and not-so-fit entities reproduce more than one would expect.

Randomness helps nature avoid heading down a reproductive dead end. In GAs, the process of selection is carried out like a lottery in which fit entities get more lottery tickets than less fit entities, but even a not-so-fit entity can hit the jackpot and reproduce a whole gaggle of offspring. Typically the probability that an entity will be allowed to reproduce is proportional to its fitness. A *probability distribution* assigns such a probability to each individual in a population. In Scheme, we might calculate the fitness and reproductive probability of the entities in a population using

```
(define (distribution population)
  (let* ((worst (apply max (map tour-length population)))
         (fitness (lambda (tour) (- worst (tour-length tour))))
         (total (apply + (map fitness population)))
         (probability (lambda (tour) (/ (fitness tour) total))))
    (map probability population)))
```

where (let* (*variable-value-pairs*) *body*) is like (let (*variable-value-pairs*) *body*) except that in the former variables defined earlier in the list of variable-value pairs can be referred to in defining variables appearing later in the list. We explored the map operator in Chapter 13.

This is a simplified version of what's done in practice. In practice, a distinction is typically made between individuals (referred to as *phenotypes*) and classes of individuals sharing the same genetic code (or *genotype*). For example, in a population of TSP tours, the same tour could appear multiple times. In designing a GA, you have to think not only about the fitness of a particular code but also about how often the code appears in the population. Having more than one individual with the same code gives some insurance that a particularly fit code won't be lost due to random selection.

But we won't worry about such fine points here. Let's consider the tiny population corresponding to the five tours we've mentioned so far. Here's the distribution corresponding to this population (technically, the distribution is the five numbers in the last column; these should sum to 1.0 but don't because they've been rounded for readability to the nearest 0.001):

```
> (display-distribution (distribution initial-population))
(BOS PVD BWI SFO ORD DFW) - Length: 6969, Fitness: 0000, Probability: 0.000
(BOS PVD BWI ORD SFO DFW) - Length: 5852, Fitness: 1117, Probability: 0.311
(BOS BWI PVD DFW SFO ORD) - Length: 6379, Fitness: 0590, Probability: 0.164
(BOS BWI PVD ORD SFO DFW) - Length: 6408, Fitness: 0561, Probability: 0.156
(BOS PVD BWI DFW SFO ORD) - Length: 5648, Fitness: 1321, Probability: 0.368
```

How do we go about picking the next generation? A typical GA might choose a set of entities in accord with the above distribution. This means that, on average, there would be 31.1% entities with (BOS PVD BWI ORD SFO DFW) for a code, 16.4% entities with (BOS BWI PVD DFW SFO ORD) for a code, and so on. Before we show exactly how to accomplish this in implementing a genetic algorithm, it's worth a short detour to explain how to simulate a process that makes selections in accord with a probability distribution.

Most programming languages support generating sequences of so-called *random numbers*. Roughly speaking, a sequence of numbers is said to be random if it's impossible to predict with certainty the next number in the sequence. Since computer procedures for generating random numbers are just implementations of algorithms, they can't, strictly speaking, generate random numbers – if you know the algorithm then, at least in principle, you can just run it to predict the next "random" number in the sequence. In recognition of this fact, the numbers generated by computer random-number generators are called *pseudo-random numbers*. With this caveat, the sequences of numbers generated by a well designed pseudo-random-number generator are about as random (that is to say, unpredictable) as you could want.

The Scheme invocation (random k) generates a (pseudo-) random number, an integer, in the range 0 to $k - 1$ according to a *uniform* distribution. This just means that any integer in the range is as likely to appear as any other. Here's a little Scheme program that generates a sequence of m random numbers in the range 0 to $k - 1$ and keeps track of the frequency with which each integer appears in the sequence. The histogram for such a sequence lists the frequencies for all the numbers. I won't explain the code in detail except to note that the function histogram-uniform uses the Scheme iteration construct (described in Chapter 5) to generate the random numbers and keeps track of frequencies using a vector of running counts.

```
(define (histogram-uniform m k)
  (do ((i 0 (+ i 1))
       (n (random k) (random k))
       (counts (make-vector k 0)))
      ((= i m) (display-histogram counts))
    (vector-set! counts n
               (+ 1 (vector-ref counts n)))))
```

For completeness, here's the procedure that displays the frequency information, also implemented using the Scheme iteration construct:

```
(define (display-histogram vec)
  (do ((i 0 (+ i 1)))
      ((= i (vector-length vec)))
    (fprintf (current-output-port)
             "~A occurs ~A times ~%"
             i (vector-ref vec i))))
```

Here we see how random works in generating random bits (0 or 1):

```
> (histogram-uniform 10 2)
0 occurs 4 times
1 occurs 6 times
> (histogram-uniform 100 2)
0 occurs 58 times
1 occurs 42 times
> (histogram-uniform 1000 2)
0 occurs 479 times
1 occurs 521 times
```

As expected, the number of 1s is not exactly equal to the number of 0s; however, as the lengths of the random sequences increase, the deviation from equal numbers of 1s and 0s drops precipitously, from 20% to 8% and then to 0.021%.

We can use random to make selections according to a distribution such as our GAs. First we use random to generate an approximation to a uniform distribution on the real numbers between 0.0 and 1.0. In this definition, we use $2147483647 = 2^{31} - 1$, the largest integer that random can handle:

```
(define (random-p)
  (/ (random 2147483647) 2147483647))
```

Now we're ready to define a function that takes a distribution, represented as a list of numbers that sum to 1.0, and returns an index into a list (a list of tours in our case):

```
(define (random-select dist)
  (do ((p (random-p))
       (i 0 (+ i 1))
       (q (car dist)))
      ((<= p q) i)
    (set! q (+ q (list-ref dist (+ i 1))))))
```

To understand how `random-select` works, think about how it modifies q.
Suppose that the single argument to `random-select` is (0.000 0.311 0.164
0.156 0.368), the distribution we produced from our initial population of tours
(again, with the numbers rounded off). Then suppose that p is initialized to 0.465.
In the first iteration, i is 0, q is 0.000 and the test (<= p q) evaluates to false.
In the second iteration, i is 1, q is 0.311 and the test evaluates to false. In the
third iteration, i is 2, q is 0.475 = 0.311 + 0.164, the test evaluates to true and
`random-select` returns the index 2. Let's test our selection function on our initial
population of tours:

```
> (define initial-distribution (distribution initial-population))
> (list-ref initial-population (random-select initial-distribution))
(BOS PVD BWI DFW SFO ORD)
```

Well, that's not very informative: a single randomly generated tour isn't going to tell us much of anything. So to test `random-select` I wrote a variant of
the `histogram-uniform` function that works with `random-select`. This function, called `histogram-nonuniform`, takes two arguments, an integer indicating the number of times to call `random-select` and a distribution, and then
prints out the number of times each index is selected. This run of `histogram-
nonuniform` shows how `random-select` approximates the distribution (0.000
0.311 0.164 0.156 0.368):

```
> (histogram-nonuniform 1000 initial-distribution)
0 occurs 0 times
1 occurs 312 times
2 occurs 162 times
3 occurs 165 times
4 occurs 361 times
```

So now we have the necessary machinery to select a population according to
a distribution weighted to take into account our measure of fitness, shortness of
tours. This is not the final population that will constitute the next generation;
it's simply the set of individuals that will be allowed to reproduce. In a GA these
individuals would be paired up, individually subjected to mutation, pair-wise subjected to crossover, and perhaps modified by other genetic operators as well. The
resulting mutations and sexual combinations would then comprise the next generation, perhaps with some culling (again with random variation) to produce a
generation of the same size as the previous generation. That's basically it: the GAs
produce generation after generation of entities until they stumble on one we're
satisfied with.

Often enough, lessons from biology can point the way to improved GAs. The above distribution assigned zero probability to the first tour we looked at. It could be, however, that an otherwise uninteresting (low-fitness) entity has a nice solution to some small part of the overall problem that isn't otherwise represented in the population. If that entity has no opportunity to reproduce, then that piece of the overall solution could be lost. There are lots of good reasons to maintain a diverse pool of individuals. Crossover operators can, at least occasionally, construct from two inferior entities an entity of high quality and high fitness.

A problem facing the designers of GAs as well as the designers of search algorithms concerns when to stop. We typically don't know what the best hypothesis looks like, and so we have to guess when to stop. For our little problem involving six cities we can check by performing an exhaustive search of all possible tours:

```
> (display-optimal-tour (exhaustive-search cities))
(PVD ORD SFO DFW BWI BOS) - Length: 5530
```

We aren't far off from an optimal solution, but, in general, there is no computationally tractable way for us to know this. Here there are only $6! = 6 * 5 * 4 * 3 * 2 * 1 = 720$ possible tours. But the factorial function increases faster than any exponential function – compare $10! = 3628800$ with $2^{10} = 1024$, or note that $100!$ has over 150 digits while 2^{100} has *only* 31.

You might think you could just keep track of statistics on how the entities in populations change over time. If the most fit entities in the last twenty populations have the same fitness within some small tolerance, then perhaps you can't get any better. Unfortunately, GAs, like other search algorithms, tend to get stuck on "fitness plateaus" where the entities in populations are all just about the same in terms of fitness and in terms of the availability of useful variations corresponding to pieces of the sought-after solution. The entities in these populations have neither an incentive nor a basis to evolve. Sometimes the GA designer can borrow from nature to create an incentive and thus inject variation into a moribund population. You can create complex simulated environments and determine fitness by having entities fight for survival in them. Some GAs use the digital analogs of parasites, symbiotes, competition, predators, and catastrophic events to spur evolution and encourage novel solutions.

The six students in the GISP studied the literature, invented new algorithms and reinvented old ones, struggled to apply the general GA framework to particular problems, and wrote code and performed lots of computational experiments. They were elated at times and frustrated at others. Sometimes the way seemed so clear, and sometimes the mountains of books and relevant papers were pretty daunting.

I think they certainly deepened their understanding of computer science. They discovered that genetic algorithms are not a panacea for hard computational problems. They learned that the metaphors and lessons from biology can be useful, but that other metaphors and mathematical approaches are just as useful. And they discovered that nothing replaces really understanding the computational problem that you're trying to solve.

I can certainly understand why they were attracted to the general area and to GAs in particular. Whether you buy into the metaphors and methodology of GAs or chose some other approach to searching very large hypothesis spaces, some way of simulating Darwin's dangerous idea is likely to prove useful in building intelligent machines. And keep in mind that simulated evolution is keeping pace with advances in computing hardware and accelerating exponentially. I'd be remiss not to point out that scientists studying natural evolution use computers to simulate their theories, thus providing interesting insights into biological systems. I especially like the accounts of such computer studies in Matt Ridley's *The Origins of Virtue* (on understanding the evolutionary basis for altruism and cooperation) and *The Red Queen* (on understanding the advantages of sex in reproduction). But studying naturally occurring evolution with computer simulations is only one possible avenue of inquiry. What about simulating alternative universes? What about tinkering with the mechanisms of life and even devising new life forms?

Scientists have long been fascinated with the connection between computation and life. In the late 1940s, John von Neumann devised a class of computations called *cellular automata* that were sufficiently powerful to support self replication. In 1970, the mathematician John Conway designed a class of cellular automata, now called "Conway's Game of Life", that has been the basis for numerous experiments and conjectures on the possibility of life forms that live entirely within the confines of computer memory.

The field of *artificial life* is based on the idea that programs can simulate various life forms; as computers become more powerful, experiments simulating artificial life have become more ambitious. An early pioneer in artificial life, Tom Ray, created a simulated world called Tierra in which to conduct experiments involving evolution and artificial life, and now experimenters the world over are tinkering with their own variations of Tierra as well as other simulated worlds. This may seem premature, since we don't yet understand natural life forms, but simulations allow us to explore the implications of our theories and weed out those that don't agree with experimental evidence.

So far, artificial life forms are largely confined to computers. However, there is nothing in principle stopping someone from using computers to accelerate the evolution of life forms and then producing bodies for the fittest individuals with

computer-aided design and manufacturing. It's already scary enough that programmers are tinkering with software life forms that can be set loose in the computer
networks our lives and livelihoods depend on. As often, with every use of advanced
technology that improves our lives come other uses that are threatening and
worrisome.

Biology may suggest a way to deal with rogue programs in our computer systems. Perhaps operating systems of the future will look more like biological systems,
with complex defenses and immune systems that adapt to such threats as computer
viruses. In the future a computer or a network may "feel under the weather" as its
immune system mounts a counterattack on a malicious virus or malevolent hackers. Perhaps operating systems will use a form of accelerated simulated evolution
to create effective antibodies against computer attacks and cooperating computer
systems will share antiviral vaccines to keep their networks healthy and running
smoothly. Indeed, all these suggestions already exist in prototype and will likely
become commonplace in the near future.

Darwin's dangerous algorithm is indeed a mixed blessing. But once you think
about the relationship between life and computation, the idea of simulating evolution is inevitable. And if nature is wondrous in its variation and fecundity, what
more might we expect of artificial variants of evolution boosted by human imagination and accelerated by an exponentially increasing computational ability?

CHAPTER SIXTEEN

Ain't Nobody Here But Us Machines

It's difficult to work with computers for long without thinking about the brain as a computer and the mind as a program. The very idea of explaining mental phenomena in computational terms is obvious and exciting to some and outrageous and disturbing to others. For those of us working in artificial intelligence, it's easy to get carried away and extrapolate from current technology to highly capable, intelligent and even emotional robots. These extrapolations may turn out to be fantasies and our robots may never exhibit more than rudimentary intelligence and sham emotions, but I think not.

Scientific knowledge about brains and cognition has expanded dramatically in recent years and scholars interested in the nature of mind are scrambling to make sense of mountains of data. Computer software is surpassing human ability in strategic planning, mathematical reasoning and medical diagnosis. Computer-controlled robots are cleaning offices, conducting guided tours in museums, and delivering meals in hospitals. However, a lot more is at stake here than solving engineering problems or unraveling scientific puzzles.

The various claims concerning the nature of mind are complicated and hotly contested. Many of them date back thousands of years. Some are believed to threaten the moral, religious and social fabric of society. It's feared by some that if individuals believe certain claims – whether or not they are true – they will no longer be bound by prevailing social and moral contracts. In this chapter, we'll examine a few of these claims and reflect on their implications for what it means to be human.

This chapter has more bibliographical references than any other in this book. It also has fewer answers. If you want to learn about computer architecture, I can point you to a book that will tell you most of what is known about that subject. If you want to learn about minds and machines, there are many claims and little agreement. In some cases, the exact framing of the question is not even agreed upon, and the meanings of the terms used in the debates are often difficult to pin down.

Here's some advice for reading the remainder of this chapter. Beware of acceding to a claim ("we are machines") before understanding what it really means. Scrutinize colloquial terms ("intelligence") used in technical arguments. Try to disentangle what you believe to be true (perhaps you side with Einstein in believing that the rules governing the universe are deterministic) from what you want to be true (you may choose act as though you are responsible for your actions even though this outlook is hard to reconcile with your belief in a deterministic universe). Remain skeptical and realize that these are hard questions without universally agreed-upon answers. The philosophical, psychological, ethical and sociological issues raised in this chapter are among the most interesting facing us as humans; if it's any consolation (or incentive), there is hope that some of them may be resolved in our lifetimes.

16.1 MACHINE INTELLIGENCE

Who am I? What am I? What is, could be, or should be my relationship to other beings? And, of course, what constitutes a "being" with which it makes sense for me to have a "meaningful" relationship in the first place? Such big questions. Such weighty issues. I used to think that I would eventually answer these questions and resolve the issues to my satisfaction. Now I'm reconciled to the fact that some of the questions are too imprecisely posed to admit succinct, precise answers and that others are beyond what science can answer and may remain forever so.

Part of the difficulty in pinning down the essential "me" is that I am changing, and so who and what I am are changing. This problem of the ephemeral, transient me is not a trivial one that I can resolve by just sitting down and seriously considering the question of my being for a day or a week or a year. I'm different for having thought about who I am, indeed I'm different for having recently thought about who I am and I'll be different again if for a while I don't think about who I am. I associate me with a process: the evanescent silvery thread of my thoughts and associations arising from but not satisfactorily explained by a sequence of chemical reactions in my brain.

By "not satisfactorily explained" I don't mean that additional insights in chemistry or physics will be needed to explain the machinery of the mind, though indeed they may. Rather, I mean that, like so many other complex phenomena arising from the interaction of simpler processes, the results of such interactions are hard to summarize more concisely than what's needed to describe the entire sequence of events, in the case of my thoughts a blow-by-blow account of molecules bouncing off one another. The very fact that I can contemplate such a process is remarkable; the fact that I can't fully comprehend it is unremarkable and fully to be expected.

There are, however, questions I think I can answer. I believe that I'm a machine, a biological robot equipped with a very practical array of sensors and effectors and controlled by a biological computer. In its ability to carry out the calculations governing my external behavior and determining my internal state, my biological computer is no more or less powerful than the computer I'm using to compose this paragraph. Like the computer in my laptop, my biological computer is a universal computer (in Turing's sense) except for the finiteness of its memory, a shortcoming that is inevitable but not particularly worrisome for many everyday calculations.

One argument that we're no more than machines has its origins in the atomism of Democritus and other ancient Greek philosophers and runs as follows. We're composed of atoms and molecules whose behavior is governed by the laws of physics. Nothing more than this mechanical description is required to account for our actions, including any observable manifestations of so-called intelligent behavior. One possible problem with this argument is that the governing laws of physics may rely on complex quantum-mechanical effects that brains somehow exploit. Even if we are machines in the sense of molecular machines, some aspects of our behavior may rely on components that can be realized only by the particular arrangements of molecules comprising our human bodies.

Getting from "we're molecular machines" to "we can be realized on conventional computing hardware" takes another leap of faith. Some arguments for the latter rely on the claim that a universal computer can simulate any process that can be described mathematically and, since conventional computing hardware can simulate a universal computer, it can simulate the biological processes of the brain. But even if, as many scientists believe, we can eventually describe biological processes mathematically, we don't know for sure that a universal computer can simulate, say, a quantum-mechanical process in finite time.

To avoid the possible pitfalls of simulating minds at the molecular level, some scientists claim that we'll soon be able to simulate the information-processing capabilities of individual neurons and map out the configuration of all neurons using brain-imaging techniques. Arguing that quantum-mechanical effects are irrelevant at this level of description, they believe that they'll be able to simulate the activity of whole brains using their techniques. So far, they've only been successful in simulating the neural circuitry of organisms equipped with just a dozen or so neurons. And, of course, even if they're successful, you may not find a wiring diagram of the brain any more satisfying than a blow-by-blow account at the molecular level.

From a purely computational standpoint, my laptop and my brain are most interestingly distinguished in terms of their software. I would love to have more memory and a faster, more reliable processor, but I don't lose any sleep over the limitations of my biological computing machinery. On the other hand, I've spent many a restless night pondering how we accomplish the simplest things and struggling to get a robot to perform similarly. From a roboticist's perspective, chess is easy compared with catching a ball or climbing a tree.

I'm not surprised that other biological robots (not just humans) roaming this planet have the machinery required to perform arbitrary computations within the constraints of their physical memory. But I believe that my software sets me apart from most other organisms in enabling me to exploit my computing machinery better. My genes equipped me with firmware that let me perform quite remarkable feats right out of the box. My parents, teachers and colleagues gave me some very useful software titles that run, with some adjustment, on my existing hardware. What is most remarkable about my software, however, is my ability to run software of my own design on my built-in computing machinery. What can I say? "Very cool!"

I'm also quite comfortable with – indeed view as inevitable – the prospect of future organisms, biological or otherwise, possessed of more powerful computing machinery, in the sense of more memory and faster processors, whose abilities to make sense of and manipulate their environment eclipse ours. After all, Intel has to watch out for Advanced Micro Devices, Motorola and IBM. Faster chips, better algorithms, new designs are fueled by joint efforts of humans and machines whose abilities are improving exponentially. Competition, innovation and selection are at work everywhere else we look. Why should the future be any more secure for the present self-proclaimed masters of the universe?

I claim that the exact way in which my internal calculations are carried out is largely irrelevant to our discussion. Certainly my brain can perform computations in parallel in a way that the computer on my desk cannot. But a single-processor computer can compute anything that a parallel computer can. Speed and memory capacity do matter; there are calculations that I could in principle carry out but will not attempt in my head, even with paper and pencil to supplement my internal memory. My brain performs some calculations faster than any currently known algorithm can, but the computer on my desk is faster at other calculations and its speed and memory are increasing at an exponential rate and will continue to do so for the foreseeable future. Soon computational power will be available in sufficient quantity and proximity to eclipse the computational capabilities of the human brain.[1]

---

[1] Ray Kurzweil, inventor, scientist, and author of *The Age of Intelligent Machines*, has predicted that a $1,000 personal computer will match the computing speed and capacity of the human brain by around the year 2020.

The last paragraph should have set off warning bells in your head. Perhaps the human brain has capabilities beyond those that can be accounted for computationally. But before we look at what possibly can't be accounted for computationally, let's consider what might be. It's clear that if the computer on my desk is ever to achieve a human level of autonomy and ability, it will require sophisticated software, like the firmware etched into my genes. I think it's only a matter of time before computers exhibit many human characteristics, including the ability to adapt to situations, pursue complex goals, plan for contingencies, and formulate models to predict the consequences of their own and others actions.

Some of the necessary software components already exist – at least in a primitive form – and others are currently under development. There exist algorithms for learning, planning, pattern recognition and problem solving that surpass those of humans in certain narrow domains. It will take some time to surpass humans in their natural environment – natural selection has had a long time to tinker with our physical bodies and the neural circuitry for animating them – but our vaunted logic is not likely to be a stumbling block. The first artificial beings to win our admiration in the intellectual arena may not have bodies at all; they may exist as disembodied robots, purely computational entities circulating in the World Wide Web.

However, I expect that the most interesting artificial intelligences will have bodies and sophisticated sensors and effectors to interact with the physical world. I admit we have a way to go in developing embodied intelligences that rival humans, but even so the current generation of robots can walk and roll about, avoid obstacles, recognize humans and perform useful work. But there's a difference between building a robot to perform a particular task and building a robot that is humanlike in its abilities.

Even if you're willing to believe that humans are nothing more than computing machinery, you're likely to protest that the software, broadly construed, governing *our* behavior is of a sort that can never run on traditional computing hardware. What of the ability to feel not only pain and pleasure but sadness, happiness and the full gamut of human emotional responses? How about the ability to be aware of your surroundings, to be conscious of your role in events, to remember the past, predict and plan for the future, and respond emotionally and practically to the present, the memory of the past and the anticipation of the future? I'm not interested in building an artificial intelligence to replace or even precisely mimic human behavior, but as an engineer I'm willing to concede that some of these characteristics are likely to prove useful in any sort of artificial intelligence.

In particular, I have trouble imagining a reasonably powerful autonomous robot that doesn't make use of some of the attributes associated with emotions.

There are good engineering reasons to build machines that continuously monitor and update their internal parameters summarizing, for instance, whether the machine has recently been subjected to damage, encountered something identified as a threat, suffered a loss or achieved a goal. In addition, any robot that successfully interacts with a complex environment is going to need a model of that environment and, if it interacts with humans or other robots, it will need models, both general and specific, enabling it to predict human or robot behavior. Augmenting a model of the environment to include a model of the robot itself (considered by some a prerequisite for consciousness) constitutes an interesting twist, but it's an obvious and relatively simple extension from a technical perspective. Using a model to explain the past, determine what to do in the present or predict and plan for the future is conceptually straightforward.

The words "consciousness" and "feeling" have aspects I've heard philosophers and cognitive scientists try to explain. I'll admit that these are fascinating and that I haven't a clue how to handle them computationally. I think of most of these aspects, say the mental states that follow upon a particular stimulus like pricking my finger with a pin, as manifestations arising from the complex interplay of relatively simple processes governing memory, sensation and the ability to formulate and use models. As a machine curious about my own functioning, I'm interested in reading about such epiphenomena and will continue to follow the relevant philosophical discussions. As an engineer trying to design a robot, I don't have any interest in explicitly writing software to ensure that such phenomena manifest themselves. I won't be surprised if they arise spontaneously out of the interaction of simpler capabilities, and I won't think it a serious deficit if they don't.

Let's pause for a moment and reflect on the claims made so far. Right off the bat, I gave up on a "complete" explanation of cognition – it's just too complicated to account for what, at least introspectively, happens in my head. I implied that eventually science will provide a blow-by-blow account of what happens at the molecular level, and admitted this might be the best explanation a self-reflecting being could hope for. I then shifted gears and focused on computational capabilities such as planning and modeling, arguing that eventually computers would surpass us in such capabilities. Admitting there are characteristics of human cognition that current computational theories cannot account for, I brushed these characteristics aside as epiphenomenal and irrelevant to engineers building robots.

You may feel that I'm brushing aside all the really interesting parts of cognition. What would satisfy you as an account of cognition? And would some accounts leave you feeling diminished, less special, less interesting? I've claimed that we'll eventually develop software capable of learning, planning, pursuing goals and other activities often associated with intelligent behavior. I've reduced emotion such as remorse, sadness and grief to mechanisms whose primary purpose is to encourage machines to anticipate and avoid the causes of such emotional states in the future.

This engineering perspective may seem largely irrelevant to an adequate account of human cognition and the prospect of highly intelligent machines may seem demoralizing. I happen to find the challenge of trying to build such machines and the prospect of succeeding enormously stimulating. The idea that we could even conceive of such an endeavor seems a testament to how special and interesting we are. And the prospect of someone or something smarter than I am seems both inevitable and desirable. Alas, I can't explain why I feel that way.

16.2 OTHER MINDS

One of my main interests in this chapter is to explore how we might, could, even *should* relate to alien intelligences and therefore, given my broad use of the words "alien" and "intelligence", to machines and one another. I'm interested in the moral and ethical issues that arise in our treatment of alien intelligences. I don't intend to be proscriptive or for that matter prescriptive; I simply want you to think seriously about the implications of the view that we are no more or less than machines.

I like order and complexity. I dislike inefficiency and the thoughtless squandering of energy or destruction of useful artifacts, whether made by humans or other natural processes. I appreciate diversity for its role in exploration and change. I love mechanical and social systems whose parts behave in accord with locally consistent and largely self-serving rules of behavior and the whole manifests a global coherence and purpose not evident in the parts. I especially appreciate mechanical and social systems in which the parts can look beyond their immediate needs to arrive at a consensus opinion, a truce, an equilibrium state in which, as long as all or most of the parts adhere to an agreed-upon pact, all of the parts gain and the whole functions more efficiently. These are more aesthetic judgments than ethical principles, but balance, order, symmetry, coherence, spontaneity, diversity and complexity all impact how I relate to other beings.

When it comes to making moral judgments, I'm not particularly interested in what something is made of, its physical appearance, or its history apart from what it does, what it has done and what I expect it to do in the future. I try not to be dismissive of those associations, fondnesses, memories or relationships that I don't understand but that one way or another are conducive to things I can otherwise appreciate. I may not be able see why people lavish affection on some inanimate objects but, if this affection provides sustenance for an otherwise productive life, then I respect both their right to bestow their affections where they choose and indeed the object itself as being part of what I appreciate.

I used the word "respect" in the previous paragraph to refer to things that I take into account in making moral judgments. My willingness to treat all machines, biological or otherwise, on an equal footing, all else equal, stems from a computational and informational view of what's important. For example, I respect human bodies in large part for their potential and for the connections, emotional and informational, that they're involved in. In this view, a newborn baby demands respect in large part for the investment required to create such a complex and potentially productive entity and for the emotional ties already established with the parents by the time of its birth. By a similar argument, a severely demented and infirm adult, unrecognizable from his or her younger self, deserves respect for the web of connections to surviving friends and family. In each case, arguments concerning the rights and responsibilities of the individuals hinge not on their physical bodies but on the processes in which those bodies are involved.

So the above explains why I respect other people, or at least those who work together cooperatively, engage in webs of interaction that provide sustenance to others in productive endeavors and generally contribute to order, efficiency, diversity and complexity. How do my aesthetic choices and my ideas about what to consider in making moral judgments imply that I should relate to other biological organisms and computing machinery? I can appreciate an ant colony for its role in a complex ecology that sustains me and because it pleases me aesthetically. I can appreciate an electromechanical robot for its complexity and beauty. But aside from the indirect sustenance that an ant colony provides, these are purely aesthetic reasons: I think ants are fascinating and I love to tinker with robots. Ethical questions arise when I have to *justify* making hard choices in doling out scarce resources.

What if it's a matter of destroying an ant colony or putting in a new driveway? Sacrificing the lives of thousands of experimental animals or finding a cure for cancer? Retaining the services of a faithful but outdated family robot or recycling its valuable parts to build a new, more efficient model? How do the ant colony, the experimental animals, the faithful robot measure up against a new driveway, a cure for cancer or a spiffy new robot?

In college I was for a time a believer in utilitarianism,[2] the philosophy or ethical doctrine that counsels the greatest good for the greatest number. I never advocated any particular variant of utilitarianism but I was intrigued with the notion of a calculus for determining what constitutes the greatest good. I used to believe that the most difficult part was grounding the calculus, establishing unassailable first principles. I read Kant's *Critique of Pure Reason* twice, thinking it held the key, before I concluded that Kant, being much smarter than I, was simply able to construct a compelling argument of sufficient complexity that I couldn't find its circularity.

At one point I despaired of establishing such unassailable principles and allowed a certain arbitrariness to creep in, which I called, somewhat derisively, the "I'm-wired-that-way" excuse. There are some reactions that I can't disassemble further but accept as expedients for getting on with life. Generally speaking, I prefer life to death, order to disorder, pleasure to pain. But these are almost cartoonish in their simplemindedness. The most difficult part of constructing a utility calculus or any other basis for dealing with people is maintaining consistency and designing a coherent policy to deal with the difficult cases. How does the doctor or family of a comatose patient determine how much pain is too much? How does the rescue worker in a burning office building choose between saving fourteen adults trapped in a conference room on the fourteenth floor and three children in a basement day-care center?

As I got older I came to believe that my "wired-that-way" excuse was no more than a pretext for avoiding difficult cases. My calculus evolved into a complex decision process combining internal deliberation and external probing and negotiation, my obligation to deliberate and investigate bounded only by time and my own computational limitations. The details of this decision process are complicated, personal and constantly in flux. I can imagine situations in which I would favor the death of a human being over the destruction of a toy if the psychological damage to the people linked to that toy was catastrophic enough. I can imagine cases in which thousands, even millions of people should be inconvenienced to preserve a colony of ants.

In most cases, the benefit to humans remains paramount despite my aesthetic raptures about complexity and order. But I hold cats, dogs, whales, and even ants and their respective webs of nonhuman interactions in high regard. Even from my humancentric perspective, in some cases the rights of animals should win out

---

[2] John Stuart Mill (1806–1873) is perhaps the best known exponent of the ethical theory of utilitarianism, which counsels us always to choose the act among those available that brings about the greatest good for or does the least harm to the greatest number.

over the rights of humans. Why? In part because of my aesthetic judgments about order and complexity, but also in part because what I see of animals' computational capabilities leads me to believe they have a mental life of some complexity and hence deserve my attention and efforts at engagement and negotiation.

And what about the rights of nonbiological machines? There are easy cases in which I can imagine siding with machines whose value accrues as a consequence of their relationship to humans. But philosophers love to pose difficult – twisted some would say – cases that make us feel uncomfortable even though they are merely hypothetical. Here's an example. Suppose there's a nice family of robots, little robots and big robots, complicated as you please, all caring for one another in a web of supportive relationships. Indeed, the social organization they've created is a model self-sustaining, peaceful, productive and successful society. As individuals, each one is significantly more intelligent than any human who ever lived.

Unfortunately, an asteroid is streaking toward earth and only two options are available. Either the asteroid will land on the family of robots, blowing them to oblivion, or the planetary defense system circling the earth can deploy the only laser capable of bearing on the incoming asteroid to deflect the asteroid so that it lands on a family of human ne'er-do-wells squatting listlessly and counterproductively a few miles away. Which is it going to be? Exemplary robots or no-account humans?

The asteroid example seems easy until you really put yourself in the role of the person in charge of the planetary defense system. What if you were merely doling out government farm subsidies or apportioning an education budget over robot and human school districts? Are these easier or harder to decide given that there are no "lives" at stake? I set up the asteroid example so that there was no benefit for humans in the robots' continued existence except perhaps an abstract appreciation of their more perfect social system. What if small advantages to robots could eventually lead to larger advantages for robots and ultimately to the relegation of humans to an intellectual and economic ghetto or, worse, extinction? It's easy to play these academic parlor games with hypothetical cases and nonexistent robots, but some of you may someday sit on a planning board or city council and pass laws that will allow or deny opportunities and rights for machines.

Some computer scientists sidestep the issues raised in these examples by claiming that we humans will evolve right alongside robots: biological and electromechanical prostheses will augment our abilities so that soon it may be hard to distinguish human from machine. Already, people calling themselves cyborgs walk around using powerful computers, tiny head-mounted displays, wireless data links and wide-spectrum cameras to enhance what they see and maintain a constant connection to the web and to one another. But despite the likelihood of some form of co-evolution, I expect the same basic ethical and moral issues will still arise, most likely with strange twists and turns that we can't anticipate now. The questions of what is right and wrong, what is just and fair and moral will be there waiting for us, whether or not we choose to prepare ourselves. In any case, thinking about how you relate to robots is an excellent exercise for thinking about how you relate to humans. Unless, of course, you think you're so special.

16.3 FREEDOM TO CHOOSE

Being free to choose ("having free will") seems a prerequisite for taking responsibility for your actions and a requirement for moral obligation. If you can't choose your actions, then you can't be held responsible for them. Without freedom, not only are you not accountable for your actions, you can't control your destiny. Then what's the point? A lot seems to hinge on your being free. Once again I'm going to sidestep the complex moral and ethical issues involved with responsibility and focus on the simpler issue of agency – who (or what) is in control of me.

It would seem from what the biologists and sociologists tell us that some aspects of how we think and act depend on our genes and others depend on what we picked up from our family, friends and acquaintances as we grew up. If that weren't enough outside intervention, any perceived shred of control remaining seems an illusion if one agrees with the findings of modern physics. If the universe is governed by physical laws and we're just scattered bits of the universe, then isn't my life and my future completely determined by these laws? (This view, closely related to the atomism of the ancient Greeks, is called *causal determinism* or simply *determinism* and is often associated with the French physicist and mathematician Pierre-Simon Laplace (1749–1827).) Where is there any wiggle room for me to choose?

In answering this question, it helps to be clear about what you really want. It's easy to get spooked by the image of physical laws tugging at your puppet strings and making you dance against your wishes. It also helps to be clear about this "me" whom we want to be in control. By "me" I mean the sum total of all my experiences, my flesh sensitized by a million touches and my brain etched by the traces of past thoughts and activated by my current thinking. All I really want is for this "me" to be the sole agent in charge of my actions.

But that's exactly what the laws of physics ensure. It's my thoughts, my feelings, my past that determine how I act – no more and no less. That the future is determined – the script already written – doesn't bother me. I have all the freedom I could possibly want. Indeed, it would upset me if it were otherwise.

If the universe is governed in part by random perturbations, say quantum effects, that is somewhat less desirable from a decision-making standpoint. But I can cope with uncertainty up to a point by identifying statistical patterns and acting so as to hedge my bets. I can deal with an uncooperative world. What I can't countenance is having my choices, my remaining room to maneuver, influenced by factors aside from who I am and how I came to be that way.

What about the parts of me that are determined by my genes, by my siblings and friends growing up, by where I went to school? These are factors I had little control over. Am I stuck with how they conspired to shape me? To some extent they mark me for life and determine at least in part how I will respond to the future. But they can be overcome to some extent by exploiting the fact that we're (self-) programmable machines.

I say this without total conviction just now, having recently experienced situations in which, despite extensive preparation on my part, I found myself deviating from my carefully planned behavior and reverting to primitive, deeply wired responses I did not resist: a failed New Year's resolution to exercise three days a week, a lapse in the plan to cut down on my daily caffeine intake. I suppose there are people who have no wish to change the way they are; however, for many, I expect it's important to believe that change, positive change, is possible. As a computer scientist aware of the power of programmable machines, it's natural for me to want to tinker with my own programming.

Why would programming your own responses be any different from programming a robot with a fixed set of sensors and manipulators and an existing software layer providing basic services and low-level drivers for all the robot's sensors and effectors? Well, aside from the fact that we don't have access to the source code for our brains, the biggest problem is that the low-level driver code for existing robots is fundamentally different from the subroutines and basic firmware governing behavior. For one thing, our firmware appears to be constantly adapting; every time you think about something, you change the way you think about it; every time you do something, you change how you do it and your motivations and predilections for doing it in the future.

Imagine writing code to get a robot to walk across the room, code that relies on a particular set of low-level driver routines. Suppose you finally get the robot to perform as you wanted, but when you try your code again the next morning, you find that the drivers have perversely rewritten themselves so that your code now makes the robot seek out the battery charger, plug itself in and go into sleep mode. We're always changing, but we don't always have complete control over those changes. People talk about being compelled to do things, about being wired to respond one way rather than another, about being unable to overcome their biases and predispositions.

Why would anyone design a system with basic components so resistant to change? Just posing the question suggests the answer: The components are resistant to change because they are too critical to the organism's health to let them be altered casually. You really don't want to start playing around with the systems that govern your breathing, heart rate, digestion and reactions to extreme temperatures or rapidly approaching projectiles.

In what sense are we free to act if we are constrained by our low-level hardware? The computer scientist Drew McDermott claims (2001, p. 98) that "a system has free will if and only if it makes decisions based on causal models in which the symbols denoting itself are marked as exempt from causality." McDermott's notion of causal model is similar to the sort of environmental model posited above for hypothesizing, evaluating and predicting the consequences of action. Being exempt from causality in this case simply means that the system is running a program using a causal model in which the actions performed by the system are determined by the program. Implicitly, the system believes (or acts as if it believes) that it is in control of itself.

But how can I be in control of myself if I can't even understand how I think and reason? What about those impulsive low-level drivers that "make me" miss my exercise class or sneak an extra afternoon espresso? The answer is that I can control myself without knowing everything there is to know about psychology and neurophysiology, much as I can control my car without knowing a lot about automotive engineering. Even when you're driving with the cruise control on, you feel that you're in control of the car. Your internal model distinguishes between those aspects over which you have absolute control (turning off at the next exit) and those over which you have only indirect or incomplete control (acceleration on the hills).

What possible mechanism might we employ to exert control over our biases and predispositions? We have the ability to process language, use logic to follow and critique arguments, construct models of our environment, hypothesize, evaluate and predict outcomes, absorb information, form plans, and formulate and perform experiments to test hypotheses. I admit that it's quite extraordinary of evolution to have contrived for us to have these capabilities, but have them we do and some of us exercise them every day.

So, it's simple, right? We just list and evaluate a set of possible outcomes, evaluate them to determine the ones we'd prefer, and then formulate and carry out plans to realize those outcomes. I have written code to make robots carry out a sequence of steps very much like this, and the fact that I can articulate the steps means that I could probably carry them out myself with one caveat: I may not feel like it! Does this mean I'm stuck, unable to "overcome" my programming and my hardwired biases and predilections? No. It just means that some of my programming is of a sort that requires a very different kind of reprogramming.

You've probably heard of B. F. Skinner's theory of *behaviorism* and his concept of *operant conditioning*. The idea is that by repeated exposure to a stimulus coupled with an appropriate (positive) reinforcing signal, an organism can be trained to respond to the stimulus even in the absence of the reinforcing signal. Complex responses (behaviors) can be "shaped" by reinforcing their component parts. Skinner has gotten a bad rap since, as often when a scientist single-mindedly pursues a theory, he tended see operant conditioning and behaviors determined by simple stimulus-response associations at work in every aspect of human behavior. But Skinner had one thing right – operant conditioning is an effective tool in the repertoire of a self-programmer.

Suppose I've had a bad experience in school and so I'm reluctant to attend class. But logic and a quick look around at people whose lifestyles I find appealing tell me that a good education is a ticket to realizing the outcomes I most want. Still, it's really tough to overcome my aversion to being in school. So I engineer situations such that the stimulus, being at school, is associated with a positive experience, such as taking a class I really like or working with a supportive teacher, and eventually my reluctance and aversion are extinguished and my interest and attraction become the dominant responses. Believe it or not, you can even do this in your head by simulating the stimuli and reinforcement signals, as it were: you simply imagine being at school and having a good time or learning amazingly useful stuff.

It sounds too good to be true but it works, and most of those "power of positive thinking" seminars you read about in the back of airline magazines are based on this simple idea. Robotics researchers use a similar technique called "reinforcement learning" in which a robot replays its past experiences, both pleasant and unpleasant, over and over in order to modify its behavior. In some cases, the robot formulates a particularly undesirable experience, like falling down a flight of stairs, as part of an effort to ensure it never has that experience.

So I can use self-inflicted operant conditioning to rewire parts of my firmware if I can recognize what I want to change and devise a conditioning method to instill the target stimulus-response behavior. You need to know what makes you tick and hence there are probably limits on how much you can change your behavior, but it's possible to make significant alterations. With a little insight, you could probably condition those perverse adaptive motor drivers I mentioned earlier to get your robot to walk across the room reliably.

So, for me, self-programming is the combination of searching for and recognizing desirable outcomes, using conditioning when appropriate to get my desires in line with whatever seems reasonable and then means-ends analysis to figure out how to bring about the desirable outcomes. Sounds so simple, doesn't it? Well, it isn't, but then neither is programming a silicon-based machine to do anything halfway interesting.

All this talk about self-programming is leading to a point about self-reliance and freedom. However difficult it is to program ourselves (and it's clearly nothing like writing code for a web server), we can change our behavior just by thinking it. You'll have to wrestle with your sense of right and wrong but you can't claim to lack control over your actions. If anything, understanding what we are capable of accomplishing as subtle and adaptable computing machines should make us expect more of ourselves. The power inherent in computing machinery should convince us that our limitations are few, our potential is extraordinary and our responsibilities are open-ended.

16.4 CARRYING ON

Think it odd for an engineer, scientist, or specifically a computer scientist to talk about themes usually the province of philosophy or theology? Not so. Scientists, mathematicians and academics of all stripes tend not to be shy of tackling big questions. In the fall of 1999, Don Knuth gave six public lectures at MIT about the interactions of faith and computer science (see *Things a Computer Scientist Rarely Talks About* for an edited transcription). The final lecture concerned computer programmers as creators of new universes and computational complexity as an approach to thinking about free will.

Over a hundred years earlier, William James (1842–1910) gave an address to Harvard Divinity School students entitled "The Dilemma of Determinism" (included in his *Essays on Faith and Morals*) and emphasizing similar issues. It is clear that we make decisions every day in an attempt to order our lives and thus, according to James, we must believe (or at least act as though we believe) in free will; the alternative is unacceptable.

In addition to being a noted philosopher, James was a scientist and, in particular, a very influential psychologist (see Louis Menand's *The Metaphysical Club: A Story of Ideas in America* for an absorbing account of his life and times and those of his contemporaries including Charles Sanders Peirce, whose writings on the foundations of probability, statistics and the scientific method helped shape how we think today). The philosophically inclined will find it very instructive to read Knuth's account of determinism and free will and then James's account.

I'm very interested in the questions raised in this chapter and I read whatever I can find on them. For insights into the connections among genetics, evolution, psychology, sociology, I recommend Steven Pinker's *How the Mind Works* and Matt Ridley's *Genome: The Autobiography of a Species in 23 Chapters*. For predictions about simulating human minds and creating robotic intelligence, check out Hans Moravec's *Mind Children: The Future of Robot and Human Intelligence* and *Robot: Mere Machine to Transcendent Mind*, Ray Kurzweil's *The Age of Intelligent Machines* and *The Age of Spiritual Machines*, Neil Gershenfeld's *When Things Start to Think* and Rod Brooks' *Flesh and Machines*.

If you're unsure whether or not you're conscious or indeed what that might mean, I recommend Daniel Dennett's *Consciousness Explained* and *Brainchildren: Essays on Designing Minds* and Drew McDermott's *Mind and Mechanism*. If you found my account of emotions and machine cognition unsatisfying, take a look at David Gelernter's *The Muse in the Machine* for a computer scientist's theories about how emotions influence memory and creative thought and Antonio Damasio's *Looking for Spinoza* for a neuroscientist's speculations on the role of emotions and feelings in cognition.

The issues of how we're wired and whether and to what extent our attitudes and behavior are determined by our genes are very much in the popular press these days. For interesting accounts of what it means to have free will, whether we are free in any sense of the word, and the implications of various attitudes toward freedom, read Daniel Dennett's *Elbow Room: The Varieties of Free Will Worth Wanting* and *Freedom Evolves*. The issues concerning free will and various forms of determinism are highly controversial, so proceed with caution. You would be well advised to track down dissenting views for the ideas that appeal to you most strongly and not to depend entirely on my suggestions for relevant reading. There are good reasons that many of these questions have remained unresolved for millennia.

I'm somewhat embarrassed to say that I have no particular favorites among modern texts on ethics and morals. In college, I read John Stuart Mill (*Utilitarianism*) and William James (*Pragmatism* and *Essays on Faith and Morals*) along with a host of other moralists and ethicists, from Aristotle to Hume. Recently, I reread James and the work of some of his contemporaries, including Oliver Wendell Holmes, Jr., and I particularly enjoyed James's "The Moral Philosopher and the Moral Life" (in *Essays on Faith and Morals*) and various of Holmes' writings that translate his particular brand of moral philosophy into political and legal policy.

I remain intrigued by Nietzsche's statement "God is dead" and his prediction that, without God as a basis for guilt, a "total eclipse of all values" would lead in the twentieth century to conflicts of unprecedented brutality and scope. World War I and II were certainly conflicts of terrible violence and broad scope, but it's not clear that these events were caused by any changes in our values. I avoided talking about values and morality here in part because I'm not satisfied with existing biological and computational accounts of morality, for example, in Steven Pinker's *The Blank Slate*. You might want to look at some of the earlier work on morality and ethics before sampling the latest offerings. I find it heartening that the writings of Aristotle, James, Holmes, Hume, Mill, Nietzsche, and other long-departed philosophers are still so relevant today.

Of late I've been particularly interested in approaches to moral philosophy influenced by evolutionary biology and the theory of strategic games as they apply to cooperation and altruism. Daniel Dennett, a philosopher familiar with such influences, lists (2003, p. 218) the key components of human morality as "an interest in discovering conditions in which cooperation will flourish, sensitivity to punishment and threats, concern for reputation, high-level dispositions of self-manipulation that are designed to improve self control in the face of temptation, and an ability to make commitments that are appreciable by others." All these components involve interaction of one sort or another in discovering, experimenting with, and negotiating the terms of our shared moral pact. It's not hard to see computation lurking in each of these key components.

Many of the issues raised in this chapter are currently beyond what science can answer and some of them may remain forever so. Not everything admits or warrants a scientific explanation. Our attitudes concerning who we are and how we relate to one another and to the universe tend to be very personal. At the same time there may very well be moral absolutes whose truth we can convince ourselves of. Grappling with the difficult issues raised in this chapter is an important way to come to terms with ourselves and learn to understand and appreciate the perspectives of others.

As far as I know, there are no definitive answers to the big questions about "life, the universe and everything" (borrowing the title of Douglas Adams' third volume in *Hitchhiker's Guide to the Galaxy*). These questions require (and merit) a lifetime investment, and one of the best ways of seeking the answers is to listen to others, particularly others who don't hold the same opinions as you. I defer to Don Knuth on a wide range of questions concerning computer science and mathematics, but I disagree with (or perhaps misunderstand) his views on determinism and free will. Still, I get a lot out of listening to what he has to say. In reading William James and Charles Sanders Peirce, I find some of what they had to say embarrassing (James was the president of a society for psychical research from 1894–1895 and told his brother, Henry, to watch for evidence of James's continued presence after his death) but much of their work is as relevant today as it was over one hundred years ago. I suppose that in some very real sense James is with us today as much as he was in his lifetime (as is the American Society for Psychical Research, so who am I to scoff and snicker?).

Some of you may feel that the idea of being "merely" machines somehow diminishes us. The fact is that we are truly remarkable machines and by understanding ourselves better we demonstrate yet another aspect of what makes us so remarkable. By thinking of ourselves as computational machines, we gain greater insight into how we work and what we are capable of achieving. By thinking of others as machines, we learn to appreciate what's important in our relationships with them. And by acknowledging our self-programmability, we admit to a level of self-determination and responsibility that distinguishes us, at least for the time being, from any other machine. Just as I'm different for having thought about who I am, so we are all different for having thought about what sort of machines we are and imagining what sort of machines we might become.

Alan Kay, who dreamed up the idea of the laptop computer, once said, "The best way to predict the future is to create it." Kay was one of the inventors of the Smalltalk programming language, a pioneer in object-oriented programming, and the architect of the modern graphical user interface. He, along with a host of other computer scientists, helped invent our future by imagining what computers might do and then realizing their ideas in hardware and software. With advances in computer science, molecular biology and neuroscience, the canvas prepared for the next generation of scientists and engineers is rich in possibilities. We've only just begun to tap the power of computing and hence the power to transform ourselves and humanity. It's a fascinating time to be an intelligent machine.

Bibliography

Abelson, Harold and Gerald Jay Sussman (1996). *Structure and Interpretation of Computer Programs*. Second edition, MIT Press, Cambridge, MA.

Adams, Douglas (1995). *Hitchhiker's Guide to the Galaxy*. Ballantine Books, New York, NY.

Arnold, Ken and James Gosling (1998). *The Java Programming Language*. Second edition, Addison-Wesley, Reading, MA.

Axelrod, Robert (1984). *The Evolution of Cooperation*. Basic Books, New York, NY.

Baum, D., M. Gasperi, R. Hempel, and L. Villa (2000). *Extreme Mindstorms: An Advanced Guide to Lego Mindstorms*. Apress, Berkeley, CA.

Braitenberg, Valentino (1986). *Vehicles: Experiments in Synthetic Psychology*. MIT Press, Cambridge, MA.

Broder, A. Z., S. R. Kumar, F. Maghoul, P. Raghavan, S. Rajagopalan, R. Stata, A. Tomkins, and J. Wiener (1999). Graph structure of the Web: experiments and models. In *Proceedings of the Ninth International World Wide Web Conference*.

Brooks, Rodney (2002). *Flesh and Machines: How Robots Will Change Us*. Pantheon Books, New York, NY.

Budd, Timothy (2000). *Understanding Object-Oriented Programming with Java*. Addison-Wesley, Reading, MA.

Bush, Vannevar (1945). As we may think. *Atlantic Monthly* 176(1): 101–108.

Chakrabarti, Soumen (2002). *Mining the Web: Discovering Knowledge from Hypertext Data*. Morgan Kaufmann, San Francisco, CA.

Cormen, Thomas H., Charles E. Leiserson, Ronald L. Rivest, and Clifford Stein (2001). *Introduction to Algorithms*. Second edition, MIT Press, Cambridge, MA.

Damasio, Antonio (2003). *Looking for Spinoza: Joy, Sorrow, and the Feeling Brain*. Harcourt, New York, NY.

Darwin, Charles (1859). *The Origin of Species by Means of Natural Selection, or the Preservation of Favoured Races in the Struggle for Life*. John Murray, London.

Davis, Martin (2000). *The Universal Computer: The Road from Leibniz to Turing*. W. W. Norton, New York, NY.

Dawkins, Richard (1989). *The Selfish Gene*. Oxford University Press, Oxford.

Dean, Thomas, James Allen, and Yiannis Aloimonos (1995). *Artificial Intelligence: Theory and Practice*. Addison Wesley, Reading, MA.

DeGroot, Morris H. (1986). *Probability and Statistics*. Second edition, Addison-Wesley, Reading, MA.

DeGroot, Morris H. and Mark J. Schervish (2002). *Probability and Statistics*. Third edition, Addison-Wesley, Reading, MA.

Dennett, Daniel (1984). *Elbow Room: The Varieties of Free Will Worth Wanting*. MIT Press, Cambridge, MA.

Dennett, Daniel (1991). *Consciousness Explained*. Penguin, London.

Dennett, Daniel (1995). *Darwin's Dangerous Idea: Evolution and the Meanings of Life*. Simon & Schuster, New York, NY.

Dennett, Daniel (1998). *Brainchildren: Essays on Designing Minds*. MIT Press, Cambridge, MA.

Dennett, Daniel (2003). *Freedom Evolves*. Viking, New York, NY.

Duda, R. O., P. E. Hart, and David G. Stork (2001). *Pattern Classification*. Second edition, John Wiley & Sons, New York, NY.

Edelson, Edward (1999). *Gregor Mendel and the Roots of Genetics*. Oxford University Press, Oxford.

Engelbart, Douglas C. (1962). *Augmenting the Human Intellect: A Conceptual Framework*. Technical report No. 3578, Stanford Research Institute, Menlo Park, CA.

Even, Shimon (1979). *Graph Algorithms*. W. H. Freeman, New York, NY.

Felleisen, Matthias, Robert Bruce Findler, Matthew Flatt, and Shriram Krishnamurthi (2001). *How to Design Programs: An Introduction to Programming and Computing*. MIT Press, Cambridge, MA.

Fodor, Jerry (1975). *The Language of Thought*. Harvard University Press, Cambridge, MA.

Gardner, Martin (1970). The fantastic combinations of John Conway's new solitaire game of 'Life'. *Scientific American* 223: 120–123.

Gardner, Martin (1989). *Gardner's Whys and Wherefores*. University of Chicago Press, Chicago, IL.

Garey, Michael and David Johnson (1979). *Computers and Intractability: A Guide to the Theory of NP-Completeness*. W. H. Freeman, New York, NY.

Gerlernter, David (1994). *The Muse in the Machine: Computerizing the Poetry of Human Thought*. The Free Press, New York, NY.

Gershenfeld, Neil A. (1999). *When Things Start to Think*. Henry Holt, New York, NY.

Gleick, James (1999). *Faster: The Acceleration of Just About Everything*. Pantheon Books, New York, NY.

Harel, David (1987). *Algorithmics: The Spirit of Computing*. Addison-Wesley, Reading, MA.

Harel, David (2000). *Computers Ltd: What They Really Can't Do*. Oxford University Press, Oxford.

Hennessy, John L. and David A. Patterson (1997). *Computer Organization and Design: The Hardware/Software Interface*. Second edition, Morgan Kaufmann, San Francisco, CA.

Hiltzik, Michael (1999). *Dealers of Lightning: Xerox PARC and the Dawn of the Computer Age*. Harper-Collins, New York, NY.

Hodges, Andrew (1983). *Alan Turing: The Enigma*. Simon & Schuster, New York, NY.

Hofstadter, Douglas (1979). *Gödel, Escher, Bach: An Eternal Golden Braid*. Basic Books, New York, NY.

Holland, John (1975). *Adaptation in Natural and Artificial Systems*. MIT Press, Cambridge, MA.

James, William (1962). *Essays on Faith and Morals.* Selected from *The Will to Believe and Other Essays*, 1898; *Talks to Teachers on Psychology*, 1899; *Memories and Studies*, 1911. Meridian Books, New York, NY.

James, William (1963). *Pragmatism and Other Essays.* Selected from *The Will to Believe and Other Essays*, 1896; *Pragmatism*, 1907; *The Meaning of Truth*, 1909. Washington Square Press, New York, NY.

Kant, Immanuel (1781). *Critique of Pure Reason.* Reprinted 1965, St. Martin's Press, New York, NY.

Knudsen, J. B. (1999). *The Unofficial Guide to Lego Mindstorms Robots.* O'Reilly, Sebastopol, CA.

Knuth, Donald (1997a). *Fundamental Algorithms.* Third edition, Addison-Wesley, Reading, MA.

Knuth, Donald (1997b). *Seminumerical Algorithms.* Third edition, Addison-Wesley, Reading, MA.

Knuth, Donald (1998). *Sorting and Searching.* Third edition, Addison-Wesley, Reading, MA.

Knuth, Donald (2001). *Things a Computer Scientist Rarely Talks About.* University of Chicago Press, Chicago, IL.

Kochan, Stephen G. and Patrick H. Wood (1989). *Unix Shell Programming.* Second edition, Sams, Indianapolis, IN.

Kurzweil, Ray (1992). *The Age of Intelligent Machines.* MIT Press, Cambridge, MA.

Kurzweil, Ray (1999). *The Age of Spiritual Machines: When Computers Exceed Human Intelligence.* Viking, New York, NY.

Langton, C. G. (1989). Artificial life. In Langton, C. G., editor, *Artificial Life I, Santa Fe Institute Studies in the Sciences of Complexity*, pp. 1–44. Addison-Wesley, Reading, MA.

Licklider, J. C. R. (1960). Man-computer symbiosis. *IRE Transactions on Human Factors in Electronics* 1: 4–11.

Licklider, J. C. R. and Robert W. Taylor (1968). The computer as a communications device. *Science and Technology 76.*

Lodge, David (2001). *Thinks.* Penguin, London.

Lozano-Pérez, Tomás (1983). Spatial planning: A configuration space approach. *IEEE Transactions on Computers* 32: 108–120.

Macrae, Norman (1992). *John von Neumann.* Pantheon Books, New York, NY.

Martin, Fred (2001). *Robotic Explorations: A Hands-On Introduction to Engineering.* Prentice Hall, Upper Saddle River, NJ.

McDermott, Drew (2001). *Mind and Mechanism.* MIT Press, Cambridge, MA.

Menand, Louis (2001). *The Metaphysical Club: A Story of Ideas in America.* Farrar, Straus & Giroux, New York, NY.

Mill, John Stuart (1863). *Utilitarianism.* Reprinted 1979, Hackett Publishing, Indianapolis, IN.

Minsky, Marvin (1987). *The Society of Mind.* Simon & Schuster, New York, NY.

Mitchell, Melanie (1996). *An Introduction to Genetic Algorithms.* MIT Press, Cambridge, MA.

Mitchell, Tom (1997). *Machine Learning.* McGraw-Hill, New York.

Moravec, Hans P. (1988). *Mind Children: The Future of Robot and Human Intelligence.* Harvard University Press, Cambridge, MA.

Moravec, Hans P. (1999). *Robot: Mere Machine to Transcendent Mind*. Oxford University Press, Oxford.

Newell, Allen (1990). *Unified Theories of Cognition*. Harvard University Press, Cambridge, MA.

Nietzsche, Friedrich (1886). *Beyond Good and Evil: Prelude to a Philosophy of the Future*. Reprinted 1966, Vintage Books, New York, NY.

Oram, Andrew and Steve Talbott (1991). *Managing Projects with make*. Second edition, O'Reilly, Sebastopol, CA.

Papadimitriou, Christos (1994). *Computational Complexity*. Addison-Wesley, Reading, MA.

Perlis, Alan J. (1982). Epigrams on programming. *ACM SIGPLAN Notices* 17(19): 7–13.

Pinker, Stephen (1997). *How the Mind Works*. W. W. Norton, New York, NY.

Pinker, Stephen (2002). *The Blank Slate: The Modern Denial of Human Nature*. Viking, New York, NY.

Powers, Richard (1995). *Galatea 2.2*. Farrar, Straus & Giroux, New York, NY.

Quigley, Ellie (2001). *Unix Shells by Example*. Third edition, Prentice Hall, Upper Saddle River, NJ.

Ray, Tom (1991). An approach to the synthesis of life. In Langton, C. G., C. Taylor, J. D. Farmer, and S. Rasmussen, editors, *Artificial Life II, Santa Fe Institute Studies in the Sciences of Complexity, Volume XI*, pp. 371–408. Addison-Wesley, Reading, MA.

Rheingold, Howard (2002). *Tools for Thought: The History and Future of Mind-Expanding Technology*. MIT Press, Cambridge, MA.

Ridley, Matt (1993). *The Red Queen: Sex and the Evolution of Human Nature*. Viking, London.

Ridley, Matt (1996). *The Origins of Virtue: Human Instincts and the Evolution of Cooperation*. Viking, London.

Ridley, Matt (1999). *Genome: The Autobiography of a Species in 23 Chapters*. HarperCollins, New York, NY.

Russell, Stuart and Peter Norvig (2003). *Artificial Intelligence: A Modern Approach*. Second edition, Prentice Hall, Upper Saddle River, NJ.

Segaller, Stephen (1998). *Nerds 2.0.1: A Brief History of the Internet*. TV Books, New York, NY.

Shasha, Dennis Elliot and Cathy A. Lazere (1995). *Out of Their Minds: The Lives and Discoveries of 15 Great Computer Scientists*. Copernicus Books, New York, NY.

Silberschatz, Abraham, Peter Baer Galvin, and Greg Gagne (2001). *Operating System Concepts*. Sixth edition, John Wiley & Sons, New York, NY.

Silberschatz, Abraham, Henry F. Korth, and S. Sudarshan (2001). *Database System Concepts*. Fourth edition, McGraw-Hill, New York, NY.

Skinner, B. F. (1971). *Beyond Freedom and Dignity*. Knopf, New York, NY.

Smith, John Maynard (1982). *Evolution and the Theory of Games*. Cambridge University Press, Cambridge.

Smith, John Maynard (1989). *Evolutionary Genetics*. Oxford University Press, Oxford.

Tanenbaum, Andrew S. (1996). *Computer Networks*. Third edition, Prentice Hall, Upper Saddle River, NJ.

Ullman, Jeffrey D. (1988). *Principles of Database and Knowledge-Base Systems*. W. H. Freeman, New York, NY.

von Neumann, John (1966). *Theory of Self-Reproducing Automata*. University of Illinois Press, Urbana, IL.

Waldrop, M. Mitchell (2001). *The Dream Machine: J. C. R. Licklider and the Revolution That Made Computing Personal*. Viking, New York, NY.

Wall, Larry, Tom Christiansen, and Jon Orwant (2000). *Programming Perl*. Third edition, O'Reilly, Sebastopol, CA.

Watson, James D. (1980). *The Double Helix: A Personal Account of the Discovery of the Structure of DNA*. W. W. Norton, New York, NY.

Wolfe, Tom (1979). *The Right Stuff*. Farrar, Straus & Giroux, New York, NY.

Index

Abelson, Harold, 97
abs, 19
absolute path name, 6
acyclic graph, 216
adjacency list, 217
adjacency matrix, 224
agent, 123
AI, *see* artificial intelligence
ALGOL, 198
algorithm, 58, 197
alias, 46
ALU, 147
anchor text, 255
AND gate, 141
API, 86
append, 219
applet, 193
application layer, 189
application programming interface, 86
arithmetic and logic unit, 147
array, 182, 214
artificial intelligence, 85, 123, 210, 271
artificial life, 269
ASCII, 194
assembly language, 157
assert, 14
assoc, 107, 218
association list, 214, 218
atomism, 273
awk, 9

backward chaining, 16
bag, 213

bash, 24
Bayes, Thomas, 135
bc, 179
behaviorism, 284
big-endian, 148
bison, 127
bit, 146
Boole, George, 141
Boolean function, 141
Borning, Alan, 97
bot, 123
Bourne, Steven, 24
branch instruction, 154
breadth-first search, 221
brickOS, 172
Bush, Vannevar, 13
byte, 148, 153
bytecode, 116, 193

C, 65, 82, 159, 172, 199
C++, 94, 110
cadr, 219
car, 218
cat, 10
cd, 228
cdr, 19, 218
cellular automata, 269
central processing unit, *see* CPU
CGI, 192
chdir, 228
class, 108, 110
classification, 131
client-server model, 186

clock cycle, 170
collaborative filtering, 125
combinatorial optimization, 259
combinatorics, 204
command language, 23
comments, 173
   Java and C, 173
   machine code, 157
Common Lisp, 18
compiler, 159
composite data type, 213
computational complexity, 206
computational geometry, 233
computational model, 71
cond, 111
conditional probability, 134
configuration space, 233
connected graph, 216
cons, 107
consciousness, 276
constraint programming, 95
context switch, 171
convergence, 249
Conway, John, 269
Cook, Stephen, 209
CPU, 153, 163
   cycle, 169
cross section, 223
crossover operator, 262
csh, 24
curl, 238
cyborgs, 280

DAG, 216
Darwin, Charles, 257
data mining, 55
data structure, 58, 197, 213
data-link layer, 190
database, 48
   attribute, 49
   join, 53
   query, 51
   record, 49
   table, 49
debugging, 81
decidability, 206
decision tree, 133
define, 64, 74

degree of freedom, 233
Democritus, 273
Dennett, Daniel, 287
depth-first search, 217
determinism, 281
diagnostic characteristic, 124
digital abstraction, 144, 170
Dijkstra, Edsger, 216
directed graph, 214
directory
   home, 6
   root, 6
   working, 26, 228
distribution, 250
   uniform, 250, 265
do, 83
documentation, *see* comments
dot product, 225
dynamic content, 192

echo, 28
edge, 214
egrep, 45
email, 122
environment variable, 29
escape character, 45
eval, 30
exceptions, 171
execi, 172
exponential scaling, 202
expressiveness, 86
expt, 200

factorial, 63
Fibonacci sequence, 199
field, 110
firewall, 2
fitness function, 257, 263
fixed point, 251
flex, 127
flip-flop, 149
flow of control, 25
for loop, 82
formal parameter, 75
Fortran, 17
free will, 281
frequency, 265
FTP, 187, 237

ftp, 187
full adder, 147
function, 75
    argument, 75
    definition, 75
functional programming, 222

gene, 257
genetic algorithm, 257
genetic operator, 262
GIF, 192
gigahertz, 170
GISP, 258
Gödel, Kurt, 206
golden mean, 200
graph, 214
    algorithm, 217
    directed, 215
    search, 217
    topology, 214, 253
    undirected, 215
grep, 43, 239

hacker, 103
half adder, 146
halting problem, 206
ham, 124
hash table, 218
histogram, 265
    word, 240
Holland, John, 257
hosting web pages, 187
HTML, 7, 192
HTTP, 187, 237
hyperlinks, 192
hypothesis, 258
    space, 258

implementation, 58
INBOX, 125
incompleteness, 206
infinite loop, 160, 239
info, ii
information retrieval, 240
inner product, 225
instance, 110
instantiate, 112
instruction address register, 154

interface, 58, 108
interrupt, 171
intractability, 206
inverse document frequency, 245
inverter, 142
IP, 190
ISO 8601, 110, 194

James, William, 285
Java, 65, 93, 110, 239
Java virtual machine, 116, 193
jobs, 39
Joy, Bill, 24
JPEG, 192
JSR, 165
jump instruction, 154

Kant, Immanuel, 279
Karp, Richard, 209
Kay, Alan, 210, 288
kernel, 23
kill, 168
kilobyte, 153
Knuth, Donald, 119, 285
Korn, David, 24
ksh, 24
Kurzweil, Ray, 274

Lamarck, Jean-Baptiste, 260
lambda, 88, 223
LAN, 191, 215
Laplace, Pierre-Simon, 281
latch, 149
Lego Mindstorms, 156, 172
length, 18
let, 88
Levin, Leonid, 209
lex, 127
lexer, 126
library, 86, 107
Licklider, J. C. R., 13
linear algebra, 225
linear scaling, 202
link, 214
Lisp, 18
list, 105
list-ref, 105
list-tail, 105

little-endian, 148
ln, 229
loader, 157
local variable, 88
logarithm, 202
logic diagram, 142
logic gate, 141
ls, 7, 25, 228

machine language, 152
machine learning, 123
main, 66, 115, 172
make, 16
makefile, 16
man, ii
map, 19, 222, 264
Maple, 13
Mathematica, 12
Matlab, 13
matrix, 224, 250
McCarthy, John, 123, 210
McDermott, Drew, 283
megabyte, 153
megahertz, 177
memoization, 90
Mendel, Gregor, 257
method, 110
Mill, John Stuart, 286
mkdir, 228
multitasking, 162, 171
mutation, 261
mv, 9

NAND gate, 142
natural selection, 257
network layer, 190
Newcomen, Thomas, 61
Nietzsche, Friedrich, 286
node, 214
NOR gate, 150
normalization, 252
NOT gate, 142
NP-complete problem, 206
numerical analysis, 202

object-oriented programming, 92, 104
Occam's razor, 131
opcode, 148

operant conditioning, 284
operating system, 5
option, 26
OR gate, 141

parameter, 75, 167
parser, 127
path, 215
Perl, 10, 241
perl, 11
Perlis, Alan, 95
physical layer, 191
piano-movers problem, 233
PID, 39, 170
pipes in Unix, 8, 37
PLT Scheme, 111
Polish notation, 63, 75
polynomial scaling, 203
POP, 164
port, 186
primary key, 49
probability distribution, see distribution
process, 38
    asynchronous, 37, 174
    heavyweight, 168
    identifier, 39, 170
    parent, 38
    thread, 168, 172
processor, see CPU
processor clock, 170
program counter, 154
programming environment, 12
Prolog, 13, 48
    database, 14
    variables, 14
prompt, 5
protocol, 185
ps, 38, 178
pseudo-random number, 265
PUSH, 164
pwd, 26

quasi quote, 132
queue, 164

raisin bread, 125
RAM, 153, 181
random number, 265

random-access memory, 153
RCX, 172
recursive definition, 16, 59, 248
redirection, 34
   input (<), 36
   output (>), 34
register, 150
register machine, 153
regular expression, 43
relational database, *see* database
relative path name, 6
relay, 144
reverse, 19
rmdir, 228
robot, 155, 172
   arm, 232
   mobile, 155, 233
   program, 157, 172
root, 216
RTS, 165

Scheme, 18, 160, 198, 239
search engine, 239
sed, 8
semantics, 76
semaphore, 177
server, 186
server farm, 239
server process, 186
set!, 89
set-car!, 105
set-vector!, 107
sh, 9, 24
shell, 2, 23
   script, 7, 24
   secure, 2
   variable, 29, 228
sign bit, 148
sink, 231
Sketchpad, 97
Skinner, B. F., 284
sleep, 38
Smalltalk, 94, 95
SMTP, 187
sockets, 40
software engineering, 92
sort, 241
sort, 36

spam, 124
spam filter, 124
specification, 58
SQL, 49, 193
ssh, 2
stack, 164
standard input, 35
standard output, 34
stemming algorithm, 244
stepper, 80
stop word, 242
string, 26
strongly connected graph, 231
structured data, 48
structured query language, 49
subgraph, 216
subroutine, 163
substitution model, 77, 86
subtree, 216
supervised learning, 124
Sussman, Gerald, 97
Sutherland, Ivan, 97
symbolic link, 6, 229
syntactic
   saccharin, 115
   salt, 115
   sugar, 114
syntax, 57

task management, 169
TCP, 189
tcsh, 24
TELNET, 187
term frequency, 245
thread, *see* process
thumbnail image, 255
time sharing, 121
token, 126
topology, *see* graph
tour, 208, 258
training examples, 124
training set, 130
transition matrix, 249
transport layer, 189
transpose, 250
traveling salesman problem, 208, 258
tree, 214
truth table, 141

Turing, Alan, 206
typed variable, 64

UDP, 189
unicode, 194
uniq, 36
universal computer, 207, 273
URL, 192, 237
utilitarianism, 279

vector, 225, 244, 250
vector, 107
vector-ref, 107
vertex, 214
virtual memory, 181
VLSI, 145

von Neumann architecture,
    153
von Neumann, John, 269

WAN, 215
wc, 4
whitespace, 26
wildcard, 6, 51

XHTML, 192
XOR gate, 143

yacc, 127
Yeager, Chuck, 205

Zeta Lisp, 104